THE MYSTICISM OF
SAINT AUGUSTINE

Augustine's vision at Ostia is one of the most influential accounts of mystical experience in the Western tradition, and a subject of persistent interest to Christians, philosophers and historians. This book explores Augustine's account of his experience as set down in the *Confessions*, and explores his mysticism in relation to ancient Platonism. John Peter Kenney argues that while the Christian mysticism created by Augustine is in many ways founded on Platonic thought, Platonism ultimately fails Augustine in his efforts to arrive at an enduring contemplation of the divine. The *Confessions* offer a response to this impasse by generating two critical ideas in medieval and modern religious thought: firstly, the conception that contemplation provides only knowledge of God, in contrast to Neo-Platonism; secondly, the distinction between salvation and enlightenment.

John Peter Kenney is Dean and Professor of Religious Studies at St Michael's College in Vermont. He is the author of *Mystical Monotheism: A Study in Ancient Platonic Theology* (1991).

D1518243

THE MYSTICISM OF SAINT AUGUSTINE

Rereading the *Confessions*

John Peter Kenney

Routledge
Taylor & Francis Group

NEW YORK AND LONDON

First published 2005
by Routledge
270 Madison Ave, New York, NY 10016

Simultaneously published in Great Britain
by Routledge
2 Park Square, Milton Park, Abingdon, Oxon OX14 4RN

Routledge is an imprint of the Taylor & Francis Group

© 2005 John Peter Kenney

Typeset in Bembo by Keystroke, Jacaranda Lodge, Wolverhampton
Printed and bound in Great Britain by MPG Books Ltd, Bodmin, Cornwall

Library of Congress Cataloging in Publication Data
Kenney, John Peter.
The mysticism of Saint Augustine : re-reading The confessions /
John Peter Kenney. – 1st ed.
p. cm.
Includes bibliographical references and index.
ISBN 0–415–28832–0 (hardcover : alk. paper) –
ISBN 0–415–28833–9 (pbk. : alk. paper)
1. Augustine, Saint, Bishop of Hippo. Confessiones. 2. Mysticism–History–
Early church, ca. 30–600. I. Title.
BR65 .A62K46 2005
270.2′092–dc22
                                    2004021211

British Library Cataloguing in Publication Data
A catalogue record for this book is available from the British Library

ISBN 0–415–28832–0 (hbk)
ISBN 0–415–28833–9 (pbk)

FOR MY PARENTS
JOHN P. KENNEY
CATHERINE M. KENNEY
IN GRATEFUL REMEMBRANCE

CONTENTS

CONTENTS

PREFACE

In his poem "Aubade" Philip Larkin captured the modernist attitude toward religious belief (Larkin 2003: 190):

> Religion . . .
> That vast moth-eaten musical brocade
> Created to pretend we never die.

This book is written against that common sentiment of our age. It is an inquiry into the theology of Augustine, for whom transcendence – both human and divine – was a verity. Indeed, the profound discontinuity between the leveled, modernist portrait of reality and the visionary architecture of classical Christianity occasioned it. It is an essay on the weaving of that vast musical brocade and on the vocation of its weavers. Contemplation of things unseen was central to Augustinian theology and so it is the main theme of this monograph.

For ancient Christians like Augustine knew – as many today do not – that the interior life of the self discloses more than a complex bundling of mental impressions, but instead betokens a deeper reality – beyond body, mind, and time – a self grounded in the eternal and the divine. This fissure of sensibility has profoundly affected the way that ancient contemplative texts are now read. The popular psychology of the twentieth century has provided a culturally established prism through which to interpret these ancient documents. We read, and we discover mystical experiences; we examine, and we find spiritual feelings. Throughout we discern ourselves.

This essay is intended as a gesture of partial restoration, a compensatory endeavor to recover Augustine's depiction of contemplation in the *Confessions*. It is an effort to read Augustine's text in a conceptual idiom closer to his own. Its goal is not so much accuracy as authenticity – to free our representation of contemplation from a cluster of modern assumptions so that this ancient notion can be more fully grasped. Reconstruction is thus not an end in itself, but a foundation for understanding Augustine's confession of the ineluctability of transcendence. As my title suggests, this book is an effort to capture Augustine's invention of the Latin Christian conception of mysticism.

To study Augustine is to risk becoming an Augustinian, for in his thought the ancient brocade is finely wrought and especially beguiling. Among that austere company of patristic authors, Augustine stands out for the sheer charm of his prose and the personal force of his intellect. The intensity of his religious questioning and the probity of his classical solutions still weigh upon us, defining options both continuous with, yet fractionally removed, from our own. As such the Augustinian risk seems worth taking, promising to disclose the ancient brocade's persuasive patterning. And thereby we might come to grasp his settled conviction: that we never die, but we will have instead a resurrected self.

A vast number of books have been written on Augustine. Adding to them requires some excuse. Several plausible ones come to mind. I have been writing for some time on the conceptual and historical foundations of philosophical monotheism. My concerns are those of a philosopher of religion interested in the initial iteration of classical theism, in the hope that we might better understand its conceptual shape. This volume follows upon an earlier study of Platonic theology, *Mystical Monotheism*, which concentrated on the pagan monotheism of Plotinus. The present volume is intended to advance this general line of inquiry in order to comprehend more fully early Christian monotheism. But classical theism was never an abstract theory, and my work on these ancient thinkers is an effort to avoid separating the metaphysics of theism from theology. For that reason, this book is focused on Augustine's depiction of Christian contemplation in an effort to come to terms with it. In order to do so, we will need to get around the assumption that the *Confessions* is simply an autobiographical record of mystical experiences. The modern notion of "mysticism" is useful in reading the *Confessions* only when we recognize that the idea of mystical experience had its remote origins in Augustine's efforts to make sense of his own experiences. And that understanding then helped to separate his new Christian theology from pagan Platonism. So this book is an effort to capture Augustine's articulation of Christian contemplation in the *Confessions*, a conception that he adhered to throughout his later writings and that became so influential in medieval and modern Christianity.

One further excuse for this study follows from this point. Interpreters of Augustine's account of contemplation have had to face the uneasy and sometimes neuralgic issue of its relation to the pagan Platonism of Plotinus and his school. I propose to describe the salience of Augustine's Christian theology of contemplation over against that of Plotinus, while recognizing Augustine's indebtedness to him and to other Platonists. When freed from a psychological model of mystical experience, Augustine's efforts to frame his experiences theologically in contrast to Plotinian Platonism can be brought into new relief. So we will begin with a sustained examination of Plotinian accounts of contemplation before turning to Augustine. The goal will be to represent Augustine's thought in a fashion that makes "the books of the Platonists" a point of theological departure rather than merely a source.

No book is written without a community of assent. My greatest debt is to my family, especially to my beloved wife Ann, who has been unfailingly encouraging and has given me much guidance with the project itself. It has been a particular delight to me that our children, Madeline and Ted, have taken an interest in this book, and have been supportive of my efforts to compose it in the interstices of my decanal duties and our family life.

This project has gone through two distinct phases. It began in my years as Professor of Religion and Humanities at Reed College. Reed offered substantial institutional support for this recusant endeavor and I remain grateful. I also derived invaluable support from many former colleagues during those days in Oregon, including Gail Kelly, Raymond Kierstead, Roger Miles, Mark Franklin, Edwin Gerow, and Steven Wasserstrom. In addition the National Endowment for the Humanities awarded me a research fellowship in 1991–1992. Thus I owe the citizens of this great republic my thanks for public support of this research into the history of Western religious thought. A second Vermont phase followed, during my years as Dean of the College at Saint Michael's College. I am particularly grateful to President Marc A. vanderHeyden for granting me a research leave to help complete an initial draft and to my administrative colleagues who filled in during my temporary emancipation, including Janet Sheeran, Edward Mahoney, and Robert Letovsky. Both Julie Eldred and Tara Arcury, Executive Assistants to the Dean, have been most helpful throughout this enterprise. I am grateful in particular to Tara Arcury for facilitating the final production of the manuscript. I have profited from discussions with faculty colleagues at Saint Michael's, especially Ronald Begley and John Izzi. And John Reiss has been a valued scholarly friend and advisor.

Scholars have an obligation to express gratitude to the libraries and librarians that have been significant to their research. This is especially true for those who work in somewhat out-of-the-way locations such as Oregon and Vermont. I want to thank the Benedictine community of Mount Angel Abbey and in particular Fr. Hugh Feiss, OSB, their former librarian, for access to that excellent patristic library, without which this research would have been very difficult to pursue from the remoteness of Oregon. Thanks also to the staff of the Durick library at Saint Michael's College, to the Andover Newton library at the Harvard Divinity School, and to the Bailey/Howe Library of the University of Vermont.

Several scholarly colleagues have been essential to the development of this project. The late A. H. Armstrong, whose loss is much lamented, was a teacher and interlocutor over many years until his death in October 1997. I am grateful to James O'Donnell of Georgetown University, Robert Wilken of the University of Virginia, and Bernard McGinn of the University of Chicago for their responses to earlier papers that laid the foundation for this book. Portions of this study have been revealed at various academic institutions and conferences, including the International Conference on Patristic Studies in Oxford University, the American Academy of Religion, the North American

Patristic Society, the University of Chicago Divinity School, the University of Tennessee, and Brown University. I have found these scholarly exchanges to be beneficial and I appreciate the interventions of various interlocutors on those occasions.

A few remarks regarding scholarly procedures and some official acknowledgments are in order. Augustine might have called a book like this a *libellus*, a short volume of collected ideas. It is modeled in part on a renowned little study on the same topic, *La Vision D'Ostie*, by that great student of Plotinus and Augustine, Paul Henry, SJ. Like Henry, I have written the book as an essay, concentrating primarily on analysis of the ancient texts and the ideas that emerge from them. Because I hope that this book will be accessible to more than just scholars, I have kept notes to an absolute minimum. Professional Augustinians may wish to consult my earlier works listed in the bibliography for matters of detail. In accordance with the policy of the press, the "Harvard" method of citation within the text has been employed, so that the reader can see the reference immediately. A selected bibliography of books directly related to the topic has been included. I have used the excellent and widely available Oxford translation of the *Confessions* by Henry Chadwick so that readers can more readily consult the full text. The Loeb editions and translations of the *Enneads* by A. H. Armstrong have been used for the same reason. For the text itself I have used the Latin edition of James O'Donnell, along with his superb commentary. Other translations from Latin or Greek are my own.

Permission to reprint from *Saint Augustine: Confessions*, translated by Henry Chadwick, Oxford, 1991 has been granted by Oxford University Press. Quotations from Plotinus are reprinted by permission of the publishers and the Trustees of the Loeb Classical Library from *Plotinus I–VII*, Loeb Classical Library Vols. 440–445, and 468, translated by A. H. Armstrong, Cambridge, Mass.: Harvard University Press, 1966–1988. The Loeb Classical Library ® is a registered trademark of the President and Fellows of Harvard College. Permission to incorporate material from my earlier articles has been granted by the editors of *Studia Patristica* and *The American Catholic Philosophical Quarterly*. These include: "The Presence of Truth in the Confessions," *Studia Patristica*, XXVII, Leuven: Peeters Press, 1993; "Mysticism and Contemplation in the Enneads," *American Catholic Philosophical Quarterly*, Vol. LXXI, No. 3, 1997; "St. Augustine and the Invention of Mysticism," *Studia Patristica*, XXXIII, Leuven: Peeters Press, 1997; "St. Augustine and the Limits of Contemplation," *Studia Patristica*, XXXVIII, Leuven: Peeters Press, 2001.

I have been both fascinated and puzzled by the *Confessions* since I first read it in the late 1960s at Austin Preparatory School under the direction of teachers from the Order of Saint Augustine. I grew up "north of Boston" in Massachusetts, to use the phrase of our native poet Robert Frost, where the Augustinian Friars were then a strong presence. Saint Augustine loomed large in that place and in those days as a preeminent source of Christian wisdom. I am grateful to those members of the Order who encouraged me to pursue the study of philosophy and religion, a project that eventuated many years later in this book.

In the light of Saint Augustine's emphasis on the spiritual value of recollection, this book is dedicated to the memory of two Augustinians, my beloved parents, John P. and Catherine M. Kenney. I would offer the same invocation and exhortation that Augustine did for his own parents at the close of his autobiographical narrative (IX.xiii (37): *Meminerint cum affectu pio parentum meorum in hac luce transitoria, et fratrum meorum sub te patre in matre catholica, et civium meorum in aeterna Hierusalem.*

Saint Michael's College, Vermont
August, 2004

ACKNOWLEDGMENTS

Extracts from Plotinus reprinted by permission of the publishers and the Trustees of the Loeb Classical Library from "Plotinus: Volumes I–VII," translated by A.H. Armstrong, Cambridge, Mass.: Harvard University Press, 1966, 1967, 1984, 1988. The Loeb Classical Library ® is a registered trademark of the President and Fellows of Harvard College.

Extracts from "Saint Augustine: Confessions" (1991), translated by Henry Chadwick reprinted by permission of Oxford University Press.

INTRODUCTION

In the history of scholarship, Saint Augustine seems at times like the city of Jerusalem, layered with the framework of past and present occupiers, yet symbolic still of some higher, heavenly prize. For his readers today that prize is an understanding of the contour of classical Christianity as it appeared to its greatest expositor. This volume seeks to remove some of the interpretive scaffolding that modern scholars have erected over the last century in their studies of the contemplative texts of the *Confessions*. Its purpose is the recovery of the theological salience of contemplation in the *Confessions*. It is an effort to look beneath the long-standing parapets of scholarly interpretation and indeed behind the sophisticated ingenuousness of Augustine's spiritual autobiography.

Central among the interpretive constructs that modern scholars have brought to the study of the *Confessions* is the concept of "mysticism." As a flame held over silver makes its random scratches seem concentric, so has the modern notion of mysticism in the antique silver of the *Confessions* lent a semblance of interpretive structure. This has been a productive strategy, allowing an ancient text to remain a stimulating presence. But interpretive categories can also become lazy-minded, conferring finality to a chosen reading and veiling anachronism in an aura of certainty. Contemporaneity can have its costs. In the case of mysticism, we need to weigh its impact in the study of the *Confessions*.

"Mysticism" is a neologism born both of convenience and intention. Its provenance has been considerable over the past century, having now become part of the religious vernacular. While its contemporary use goes back to the early modern period, it was the employment of the term "mysticism" by Romantics in the nineteenth century that first led to its wider popularity. This was part of a larger conceptual shift in the meaning of religion in Western culture, a change in emphasis from social and cultural aspects of spiritual life to personal experience. As collective rituals and institutions came to be seen by many as suspect, the experiences of the private self became more significant. It has become characteristic of modern thought that religion is understood primarily as a matter of personal experience, and only secondarily as a civic, social, or institutional phenomenon. And within the sphere of personal religious experience, mystical experiences are those that are seen as the most intense, most complete, and most spiritual. Mysticism might be defined as the apex of personal religious experience, in which the self experiences spiritual reality immediately. As such mysticism is understood as the culmination of true religion. It represents the apogee of the modern Western cultural trend toward the personal in religion (Taylor 2002).

It is also notoriously vague in meaning. The famous study of William James, *The Varieties of Religious Experience*, first published in 1902, might be helpful in this regard. James brilliantly captures – and promotes – this great cultural shift to the personal and experiential in religion. Mysticism was for James a subjective or psychological state of an individual, an especially intense religious experience. James characterized this experience as being ineffable, transient, passive, and noetic (James 1985: Lectures XVI and XVII). A mystical experience would be a mental state that provided an immediate sense of access to deeper spiritual truth, and would thus offer a feeling of the noetic, in the parlance of James. It would be one whose content would defy description in categories of ordinary language, and so would be ineffable. Moreover it would be neither a sustainable mental state, nor one induced by active means. Mysticism refers then to an unusual experience: intense, psychologically distinct from ordinary consciousness, resistant to linguistic description, non-habitual and highly unusual, episodic, transitory. Above all mysticism is a mental state, a psychological event, something that a person experiences.

There is little evidence in ancient Christian literature of mysticism when so defined. But if there is any text that appears to conform to this model of personal experience, it is the *Confessions*. Its autobiographical depictions of intense religious episodes lend themselves to this reading. So it should not be surprising that the interpretation of the *Confessions* as a preeminent instance of early Christian mysticism emerged in the mid-nineteenth century, in 1863 to be exact. There has been a scholarly debate since that time regarding the number and nature of Augustine's mystical experiences as recorded in the *Confessions*. Any scholarly debate that has continued for so long has much to tell us, offering valuable if conflicting insights into the texts themselves. But it also calls attention to the common commitments and methodological assumptions that have engendered such profound disagreement and impasse (McGinn 1991: 228–232).

Finding personal mysticism in the *Confessions* had much to recommend it. It offered to focus attention on the lived experience of a founder of Western Christianity at the time of his painful conversion. And, by concentrating on the autobiographical, it might even offer some irenic relief from the theological combat that rival denominations have brought to the theological reading of the *Confessions*. Here was the promise of an approach that moved past theological abstractions to real life experiences. This respite from theology in the reading of the *Confessions* might thus be seen as mirroring the initial appeal of the concept of mysticism itself. For its framers, like James, were keen to step away from ecclesiastical categories to more compelling psychological ones, to move from the theoretical to the experiential. So the study of mysticism became the study of the personal, and the study of mysticism in the *Confessions* emerged as the quest for the historical Augustine.

That quest centered on a small set of dramatic passages from the central books of the *Confessions*. These texts recount Augustine's experiences from 386–387, but were composed more than a decade later when Augustine had become a Catholic bishop. They contain what might be called "ascension narratives," that is, accounts that describe – in varying degrees of autobiographical specificity – the pilgrim soul's journey into the transcendent world. Two are found in Book Seven, which describes a period when Augustine had become disillusioned with Manicheism, the sort of esoteric Christianity that he had adopted in late adolescence. At VII.x (16) Augustine tells us that he had read "the books of the Platonists" and been admonished by them to turn his search for truth toward his inner self. There he encountered a level of reality beyond his soul, so that by entering into himself, he could also go up to a higher plane of reality. And this true Being that he entered was God. "Eternal truth and true love and beloved eternity: you are my God." Shortly thereafter at VII.xvii (23), the text describes the pilgrim's interior association with God, which came upon him suddenly in the midst of his meditations on the basis for aesthetic judgments. Having recognized the unchangeable realm upon which such decisions are based, his soul encountered God: "So in the flash of a trembling glance it attained to that which is." Both texts depict Augustine's spiritual state before his decision to become an orthodox Christian through baptism, and to adopt a life of asceticism.

The final ascension narrative, found at *Confessions* IX.x (23–25), is the most famous. The "Vision at Ostia" from Book Nine is set in a garden in that Roman seaport, where Augustine and his party had come in the midst of civil war to await passage back to North Africa. It is the final days of his mother Monica's life, who would not live to make the journey. While looking down into a quiet garden, the minds of the newly baptized Augustine and his mother "were lifted up by an ardent affection toward being itself." Together they "touched it in some small degree by a moment of total concentration of the heart." At that moment, "in a flash of mental energy," they both "attained the eternal wisdom which abides beyond all things." This remarkable description, together with those of Book Seven, make up the primary texts that depict the immediate presence of the soul to the divine. These are the passages that modern interpreters have commonly identified as mystical experiences. To come to terms with this line of interpretation, we need to look at some works by its leading proponents.

The emergence of mysticism as an interpretive category in the study of the *Confessions* is quite evident in the early part of the twentieth century. A good example is the 1922 study by the British Benedictine, Dom Cuthbert Butler, *Western Mysticism* (Butler 1922). It nests in a larger burst of English studies of mysticism, including Dean W. R. Inge's *Christian Mysticism* (Inge

3

1899), and Evelyn Underhill's *Mysticism* (Underhill 1930). Butler regarded Augustine as the "Prince of Mystics." He placed considerable emphasis on experiential characteristics which he discerned in Augustine's texts. These are broadly Jamesian, especially transience, ineffability, passivity, and "rapturous joy." He also emphasized the "ecstatic quality" of these mental events and their removal from ordinary consciousness. Butler was keen to advance the thesis that mysticism is a universal human phenomenon and that the characteristics of the experiences described in the *Confessions* are commonly found in all cultures. This so-called "common-core hypothesis," which holds that all mystical experiences are the same, was itself a common feature of writing on religion in the first part of the century (Katz 1978: 22–74). It not only provided a compelling category of analysis, it also suggested, by the apparent scope of the phenomenon, that mysticism was a true disclosure of reality. Butler's reading thus cast Augustine as a theological interpreter of his own mystical experiences, whose roots lay buried in a universal human phenomenon.

The most influential readings of mysticism and the *Confessions* have been those of Paul Henry, SJ, a co-editor of the critical edition of the works of Plotinus, and Pierre Courcelle, the leading authority on late antique Latin literature. They emerged at mid-century, as the influence of more theological analyses of the *Confessions* began to wane. Both Henry (1938; trans. 1981) and Courcelle (1950; 1963) offered a fresh perspective derived in part from their attention to the Neoplatonic background of Augustine's text and their measured grasp of that pagan tradition. Henry sketched an Augustine who was powerfully influenced by Plotinus. On his account, the mystical experiences of Milan and Ostia follow the pattern for the contemplative ascent of the soul in the *Enneads*. Henry attributed this fact to several factors. The Platonic reading that Augustine did in 386 initiated and framed the experiences themselves, giving them a Plotinian character. As Henry explained (Henry 1981: 27):

> Having just read the *Enneads*, it was only natural that Augustine should have turned to their vocabulary and should have been influenced by their style in his expression of the thoughts and inspirations which they aroused in him.

Moreover, Augustine's subsequent efforts at autobiography were themselves informed by the continued influence of the *Enneads*. So, for Henry, Augustine enjoyed a series of mystical experiences that were catalyzed by reading Plotinus, immediately understood in those terms, and subsequently interpreted in the light of Neo-Platonism.

At the same time Henry insisted that the Ostian episode was additionally formed by Augustine's reading of scripture, especially St Paul, the Prophets, and the Psalms, so that Christian ideas were incorporated into the event itself. The vision at Ostia was thus a complex alloy of Plotinian and Biblical language both for the young Augustine and for the episcopal autobiographer. The scriptural allusions or quotations that saturate the *Confessions* expand upon the Christian ideas that were part of Augustine's initial reflections on his experiences. Henry drew the following important conclusion:

> If Augustine turned to the Bible in order to express his sentiments during the vision at Ostia, it was no mere rhetorical device. Such a technique is used frequently throughout the Confessions, which are decidedly biblical in tone, but here it is employed because Augustine recognized Plotinian concepts in scriptural terms. In other words, we must reject the easy and deceptive pleasure of cutting the account of the vision into "successive drafts" that we might ascribe certain elements to the period of the actual event and others to the period during which the *Confessions* were written.
>
> (Henry 1981: 39–40)

Henry's regnant idea was that Augustine's experiences represent a synthesis of Platonism and Christianity. This was true both of the mystical experiences of Milan and the vision at Ostia (Henry 1981: 82). For Henry the contemplative experience of Milan was more philosophical in nature, yet still Christian, whereas that of Ostia was re-balanced toward a greater emphasis on the Christian element of this synthesis, largely through the influence of Monica. It must be said that Henry's analysis has much to recommend it. It avoided overstating the divergence of Platonic and Christian thought as they appeared to Augustine. And Henry acutely underscored some of the difficulties associated with efforts to offer redactional analyses of the texts themselves, in the interest of recovering an historical or experiential account. To this matter we will return shortly.

In contrast to Henry, Pierre Courcelle constructed a reading of the *Confessions* that claimed to uncover the efforts of the historical Augustine to achieve Plotinian mystical experiences. On this reading, Book Seven recounts a series of unsuccessful attempts at Plotinian ecstasy – "vaines tentatives d'extases Plotiniennes" (Courcelle 1950: 157–167; 1963: 17–88). But Augustine failed in these efforts because he had not yet adopted an ascetical life. Having done so, and having become an orthodox Christian, he achieved this mystical goal at Ostia. Unlike Henry, Courcelle held that Augustine's text can be analyzed to disclose its underlying historical strata, by removing the scriptural references added by the episcopal redactor and by triangulating the text with extant early works written at Cassiciacum in 386 before Augustine's baptism, and with those treatises of Plotinus that Augustine read. The result is an autobiographical record of initially abortive efforts at mystical experience, followed by the achievement of "Plotinian ecstasy" at Ostia.

In the half century since Courcelle's study, his position has come to define the parameters of scholarly discussion. James O'Donnell, in his magisterial commentary – the most important piece of scholarship on the *Confessions* during that period – follows Courcelle's approach, although in a modified and critical fashion (O'Donnell 1992). He agrees with Courcelle that the first attempt at Plotinian ecstasy recorded at VII.x (16) fails. But for O'Donnell the second attempt, described at VII.xvii (23), succeeds: ". . . the second 'tentative' of Book 7 is, *on Plotinian terms as Augustine understood them*, a complete success" (O'Donnell 1992: xxxiii). So unlike Courcelle, O'Donnell wants to qualify this achievement with the recognition that Augustine was proceeding with a limited and mediated understanding of Plotinus. Two points are critical to this revision of Courcelle. First, O'Donnell recognizes that Augustine's transition from Manicheism requires something beyond mere conviction. So one of Augustine's attempts at contemplating transcendent being must succeed in Book Seven, otherwise the theological plot would be frustrated. Second, O'Donnell also recognizes that the vision at Ostia cannot plausibly be viewed as a successful Plotinian experience, despite the textual parallels adduced by Courcelle. For its Christian components cannot be easily relegated to a secondary status as merely interpretive commentary. O'Donnell is well aware just how murky such exegetical efforts are which proport to know what was, or was not, part of the original experiences of Milan or Ostia, or how much Christian conceptualization and imagery was inherent, or how much was subsequently adduced. These worries lead O'Donnell to a critical insight regarding the entire project of Courcelle and his successors (O'Donnell 1992: 124): "The underlying error is the assumption that the 'experiences' of Milan and Ostia are recoverable and that the text is only a transparent instrument to be used in that exercise."

This point is exactly right and serves as the starting point of the present inquiry. It might be amplified by reflecting on the vagueness of the conceptual currency involved in this discussion. Exactly what is "Plotinian ecstasy?" What are the criteria to be used in determining success or failure in an effort to achieve such an experience? And how are we, as readers, to peer through the nuanced and studied rhetoric of Augustine's text in order to discern his actual experiences. These are questions not readily answered. To them may be added an additional difficulty. There seems to have developed a tacit assumption that the contemplative texts of the *Confessions* could be shorn of their Christian elements, especially their scriptural references, and that this would then reveal an underlying Platonic stratum. This redaction is assumed by Courcelle and his successors to be more authentic or original, as if this construct were some-how closer to Augustine's experiences. But the books of the Platonists also provided a theological language that informed Augustine's experiences and established a basis for their interpretation, just as Christian texts did. Platonic discourse must also be sifted out from the texts by those who seek to recover the original experiences, just as Christian language was removed. But too often it has been assumed that the Platonic aspects of the text are somehow more authentic and closer to the record of the actual experience. Yet Platonism is as much an interpretive language as is Christianity. So any effort to discover the true experiential record behind the texts must go deeper, if it is to be pursued at all.

That effort has indeed been attempted, most notably by the eminent Augustinian scholar Gerald Bonner. While Bonner had expressed doubt about the "personal mysticism" of Augustine, in a recent volume devoted to the subject of Augustine's mysticism and its influence, Bonner has developed his position further, based on modern studies in comparative religion (Bonner in Van Fleteren 1994: 113–157). Alert to the sort of questions we have raised regarding the approach of Courcelle, Bonner places his analysis into a larger frame of reference. He concludes as follows:

> It may be said that such an understanding of the vision of Ostia is a Christian theological interpretation of a Neoplatonic ecstasy. However . . . there is no reason to call the ecstasy as such specifically and peculiarly Neoplatonic. Rather, it appears to be an example of what studies like *Mysticism and Philosophy* and *The Spiritual Nature of Man* suggest to be something widely experienced, without any essential philosophical or religious preparation. The three experiences of Milan and Ostia have in common a sudden and instantaneous apprehension of reality, accompanied by joy and happiness, such as have been recorded by all believers of all religions and none, by the devout, by the unbelieving, and by the indifferent. It may be objected that such an understanding deprecates the value of the Christian experience; but against this it may be argued that it is not the experience, in itself.
>
> (Bonner in Van Fleteren 1994: 135)

This analysis moves beyond Courcelle's, scrubbing the Christian and Neoplatonic elements from the text and reading the *Confessions* as an instance of a universal human phenomenon. It endorses a "common core" theory: that mystical experiences have certain core characteristics that recur independently of religions or cultures. Moreover, Bonner is clear about the need to remove theology, and indeed any religion, in order to get at that core of the experiences of Milan and Ostia. Neither Christianity nor Platonism was really part of those experiences themselves.

Much of the scholarship of the last half of the twentieth century on the mysticism of the *Confessions* can be characterized as an effort to move away from denominationally based analyses. One can understand the intent of that project, one that has tracked the development of the modern academy itself. Yet earlier theological analyses had the merit of appraising the texts of the *Confessions* from the vantage point of a live spiritual tradition, and thus had the advantage of taking seriously what Augustine himself actually believed on the basis of his experiences. As the trajectory just explored indicates, the recent project of recovering the mysticism of the *Confessions* requires increasingly strenuous efforts to remove the theological meaning of these texts in the interest of recovering their experiential content. But there are costs to this endeavor and methodological problems as well. Chief among these issues of interpretation is the apparently neutral exactness that the use of "mysticism" conveys. But the concept itself has, as we have seen, its own developmental history and cultural purposes, embedded in a larger project of re-conceiving religion as fundamentally a matter of personal experience. Nor is its meaning a settled matter, for the identification of a widely accepted set of common characteristics has evaded phenomenologists. Indeed the whole "common-core theory" has been the subject of intense criticism and controversy in recent years (Katz 1978; 1983; 1992). The result of its employment in the study of the *Confessions* is not the discovery of a settled foundation for the interpretation of the texts, but rather a misplaced certainty, a failure to recognize the provisional and culturally freighted nature of the very concept itself.

Besides this problem of misplaced concreteness, there is the matter of textual transparency to which James O'Donnell drew attention. All attempts to identify the experiential core of the ascension narratives of the *Confessions* must offer a principle of disclosure that allows the reader to get behind the opacity of the texts themselves and to uncover a deeper truth beyond the religious meaning assigned by the author. Yet the line between what constitutes the underlying characteristics of the core experience and what constitutes interpretation is itself open to interpretation. Indeed the demarcation between culturally bound interpretation and the "pure" data of experience is itself highly suspect. It rests upon a sharp dichotomy between experience and interpretation, between data and theory. Is there such a thing as the un-interpreted or pre-conceptual core of experience? Perhaps, but that is a matter of controversy among epistemologists of religion. Thus the imperative to remove theology from a reading of the ascension texts of the *Confessions* – on the grounds that it is an interpretive distraction – is based on a string of methodological assumptions that are at best questionable. Hence the application of this line of analysis to the ascension texts of the *Confessions* is open to fundamental criticism regarding its foundations, its adequacy, and the degree of closure it provides.

The point might be put in a somewhat more practical way by considering the scheme that Peter Moore developed for the study of mystical texts (Moore in Katz 1978: 101–131). Moore argued that the experience–interpretation dichotomy was too simplistic and offered four distinct categories as a replacement. These are:

1   Retrospective interpretation, which refers to doctrinal interpretations formulated after the experience is over.
2   Reflexive interpretation, which are spontaneously formulated during or immediately after the experience.
3   Incorporated interpretation, that stem from the prior beliefs of the mystic.
4   Raw experience, that is, the features unaffected by prior beliefs.

Even in this refined model it is a problem to discern pure observation statements, which would constitute the raw data of experience. But, laying that theoretical issue aside, one can see the pragmatic difficulty in applying this more nuanced typology to the ascension texts of the *Confessions*. The disputed issue of scriptural references is a case in point. Courcelle considered them to be obvious instances of retrospective interpretation. Yet, following Henry's argument, they might also be plausibly regarded as incorporated interpretations, the result of Augustine's memory of his earlier, initial readings in the Christian scriptures. These ideas and phrases, introduced into the prodigious memory of the young rhetorician, might have helped to mold the character of the experiences themselves, and then become the subsequent basis for more exact, retrospective quotation much later. This is a possible, indeed plausible, scenario. We have, in fact, no way to settle the matter, to determine the exact stage at which this scriptural language emerged in Augustine's consciousness or at what level of explicitness. This underscores once again the frustrations which surround the project of identifying the "personal mysticism" of the historical Augustine. Even with a sophisticated typology such as Moore's, the project remains a fertile source of methodological dispute and seems predestined to controversy almost by design.

The costs of this quest for the personal mysticism of the historical Augustine have been considerable. The principal loss has been theological. By displacing the spiritual content of these ascension texts, we are left with vague, putatively universal characteristics like joy, peace and a feeling of disclosure. But these same feelings may also accompany the experience of a fine dry Riesling, and do not pertain uniquely to this type of religious experience alone. Nor do they disclose anything special about the nature of reality, a fact of which James was acutely aware in propounding his own phenomenological analysis. Such an analysis generates a set of characteristics about the experience itself, not about the reality to which the experience pertains. In the case of Augustine, we might well wonder – on such a reading – what all the fuss was about, and why he drew from these experiences such profound personal conclusions. The ascension texts of the *Confessions* do not readily lend themselves to this sort of phenomenological analysis. For Augustine was never simply the observer of his own experiences from which he drew conclusions through interpretation. The experiences that he described were, above all, foundationalist in nature, that is, he believed that they provided cognitive access to reality directly and immediately. And they were apodictic in character, and not subject, as he repeatedly tells us, to any doubt or lack of certainty. They were moments of the soul's grasp of the source and author of reality. Whatever feelings accompanied them were epiphenomenal and incidental, and so not an adequate basis for their analysis.

The search for the mystical experiences of the historical Augustine has had, paradoxically, an impoverishing effect on our ability to understand what really mattered about these episodes to Augustine himself. Yet he tells us very clearly what he brought to those events, how he interpreted them, what he came to perceive because of them, and what their fruits were in his life. It is this larger context that should be the basis for reading the ascension texts of the *Confessions*. Put differently, it is the conceptual content of these texts – their theology – that should be the center of our own attempts to grasp the meaning of these passages. In saying this I must admit that I view phenomenological analyses of contemplative texts in general to be thin and uninformative. This is particularly true of the *Confessions*. In this respect I share the approach of historians of contemplative literature who have emphasized the need to recover the context of these texts and to restore the religious concepts and symbols that are the real keys to their intelligibility (Kenney 1991: xix–xxii). In the contemporary study of Christian mysticism that approach is best exemplified by Bernard McGinn's authoritative history of that tradition (McGinn 1991). Given the work of McGinn and some other recent interpreters of Augustine on this topic, such as Van Fleteren (in Van Fleteren 1994: 309–336) and Teske (in Van Fleteren 1994: 287–308), it would be an overstatement to suggest that the purpose of my inquiry is the restoration of theology to the reading of the contemplative texts of the *Confessions*. But that is nonetheless the cause to which this study is meant to contribute.

The depreciation of theology has indeed been the result of the search for personal mysticism in the *Confessions*. Simply put, it has diverted attention from Augustine's central themes and disturbed the intellectual rhythm of his narrative. What might be called the "consensus reading" – following Courcelle – holds that the pre-baptismal events recorded in Book Seven are failures, instances of abortive mysticism. But the post-baptismal vision of Ostia in Book Nine is a success, the crowning episode in the autobiographical narrative. This pattern has considerable appeal, privileging a specific mystical experience as the central event in the text as a whole and assigning the sequence on the death of Monica to the role of a quiet coda. Moreover this reading has found further support because of its apparently Christian scheme, which exhibits successful mysticism as the aftermath of baptism and conversion. The convergence of these satisfying hermeneutical trajectories has ensured the widespread acceptance of this reading.

Yet there is cause for caution. As will be subsequently argued, there is little significant difference between the contemplative ascents of Book Seven and Book Nine. The Christian vision at Ostia is no more a success than the episodes of Book Seven. All share the same theological evaluation in Augustine's eyes. They are moments that offer certification of human transcendence and intimations of the soul's post-mortem life. They are acts of contemplation that disclose much about a higher level of reality, although they all share in a failure to insure the soul's sustained existence in that higher realm. And that is because the soul is fallen and powerless to effect its own salvific destiny. On this alternative reading, the contrast between contemplation and confession, iterated at the end of Book Seven applies consistently throughout the *Confessions*. It is the work's title theme. All experiences of transcendence must give way to the supreme Christian act of confession, the recognition of the soul's need for the mediation of Christ. It is this admission of the human condition that opens the soul's way to the home of bliss. Contemplation, far from being an end in itself, serves to open the Christian soul to confession.

That is just how Augustine's narrative proceeds, by the syncopated rhythm of contemplation and confession. The pilgrim Augustine is prepared for conversion through contemplation in Book Seven, by real instances of transcendence that dispel his earlier materialism and skepticism. His confession of the need for Christ as a salvific mediator follows from his simultaneous recognition of the limitations of contemplation. Thus he seeks instruction in the practices of Christianity, in its mysteries and sacraments, and is baptized. The joint contemplative ascent with his mother at Ostia then follows. It underscores his new Christian understanding of the soul and of the transcendence of God. And it designates the place of hope for both their souls. From this episode he derives the certain knowledge of the heavenly life of the saints and the Wisdom to which these souls are eternally joined. From it he discovers the spiritual strength to face what is – in fact – the culminating event of the autobiographical narrative, the death of Monica.

This alternative reading proceeds without the need to "freeze-frame" certain episodes and identify them as instances of an independently defined type of mystical experience. It also re-valorizes these events in Augustine's narrative. These contemplative ascents can be seen as part of a larger Christian assertion of the transcendence of God and of the soul's ability to grasp that higher realm directly through contemplation. Moreover, they are coherent parts of a larger conversion narrative, interweaving theology with autobiography, which runs from Book Seven through to Book Nine. Indeed, in that light, these ascension texts emerge with a very different meaning and significance than in the "consensus reading." On that account, baptism improved the pilgrim's ability to achieve a successful mystical experience at Ostia, after the failures described in Book Seven. But on the alternative interpretation, the significance is reversed. Augustine can be seen principally as sketching a consistent Christian portrait of his soul's discovered limitations and his need for a divine mediator. Contemplation laid the groundwork for baptism, painfully disclosing a new estimation of his soul's spiritual capacity. Salvation, not successful mysticism, is the product of baptism. And it is contemplation that should be seen in Augustine's narrative as its necessary catalyst.

In his volume on modern medievalists, Norman Cantor makes the following observation:

> We cannot interpret medieval culture or any other historical culture except through the prism of the dominant concepts of our thought worlds. When we look back, some of these interpretive concepts have become stale and out of date, and we're embarrassed then by our own

reflexive trendiness; but there was a time when these concepts were productive and stimulating and were appropriately relished in their application.

(Cantor 1991: 37)

It might well be asked whether the concept of mysticism had outlived its usefulness in the study of the *Confessions* and should be retired. But, as the title of this book indicates, I believe that it does have continued utility in reference to Augustine for one paramount reason. It is Augustine, more that any other ancient author, who served as the originator of what became the Western conception of mysticism, first in its medieval Christian form, and later in a secular guise. He molded in the *Confessions* an account of contemplation in which the soul discovers its transcendence of the lower world and comes to know directly the existence of God. But that is only a moment of recognition, not an instance of salvation. Through it the soul achieves certain knowledge, a personal wisdom that must serve as a harbinger of its final state of beatitude. But the soul does not discover, in these moments of ascension, its own latent divinity, nor does it restore its fundamental connection to the divine world. It cannot achieve a moment of enlightenment that is at once a complete act of deification. Nor can it succeed in its flight from this dreary world of time through the profound dignity and power of a deeper self, nor assert its native claim on a higher world through an inner act of self-transcendence. Contemplation is only momentary vision, and the unity that the soul enjoys with the divine is fleeting, and partial, and never an enduring one. That is what contemplation came to mean in the Christian West under the auspices of Augustine. The ascension texts of the *Confessions* contributed powerfully to this orthodox Christian understanding of the scope of the self and the place of the divine. They were uniquely formative, and became, in fact, dispositive for the Western Christian tradition of contemplation. In some measure this circumscribed idea of mysticism, of only momentary access to the presence of God, was Augustine's invention, for it is to these texts in the *Confessions* that we can point when we seek the origins of this trajectory in Western religious thought. Mysticism in the modern sense has its roots in Augustine's account of a specific form of Christian contemplation. When we grasp this point, we are longer bound in our reading of the *Confessions* by this modern conception of mystical experience and by our natural tendency to read Augustine's experiences through that prism. We can instead recognize how Augustine perceived the episodes of his life according to his own narrative prism, derived from his acculturation in Platonic and Christian thought. And we can recognize therein his invention of a novel account of contemplation.

Invention is itself a trope of post-modern times. No doubt this intellectual disposition will itself be studied in the future for what it reveals about the assumptions or suspicions of those who employed it so. We should be circumspect in employing any term that comes so readily to the fore in the conceptual lexicography of our times. Nonetheless it seems fair to say that Augustine's audacious act of spiritual autobiographical created more than just his own retrospective self. He also framed his theology in light of his experiences and in doing so articulated with persuasive clarity a sharply delineated account of personal transcendence. And it was this Christian rendering of self-transcendence that laid the groundwork to what would become mysticism in the West. It was invention with a clear purpose: to assert a Catholic understanding of transcendence and chart the depth of the human self in relation to a personal Creator. In that sense the invention of mysticism in the *Confessions* was an apologetic act.

Surely that cannot surprise us. Augustine was a supreme polemist whose works are often arguments – whether tacit or overt – against the views of others. In the *Confessions* he constructed a reading of his life and through that account a new understanding of the scope of the inner self and the power of the human soul to realize immediately the presence of transcendent Wisdom. As a result, the *Confessions* may well be the finest and most subtle ancient Christian apology, and its arresting depictions of its author's inner spiritual life are surely the reasons for its persuasiveness. While a personal portrayal of theology, it is nonetheless a polemical work, etching into the story of a life the main lines of – what might be called – orthodox Christian transcendentalism. Its principal targets are made quite explicit, though in varying degrees. They include Manichaeism, pagan Platonism, and finally the literalist and unsophisticated Christianity of Augustine's youth. All are superseded in the narrative by his new theology – the philosophically informed orthodoxy of Ambrose and the Catholic intellectual circles of Italy. The crux of Augustine's argument in the *Confessions* is his advocacy of transcendentalist Christianity and his espousal of a Christian form of contemplation. Both moves involve a rejection of positions common in antiquity and still prevalent in modern thought, including dualism and the idea of a limited God, materialism and the rejection of a transcendental level of existence, and finally the view that human beings can achieve salvation through their native powers alone. For this reason a reader of the *Confessions* needs to be alert to the wider valence of its tacit advocacy, since the text is a subtly crafted polemic given habitation in the person of its author and his story.

It is just this wider theological significance and the force of Augustine's novel account of contemplation that are lost in the historical search for Augustine's mystical experiences. The personal mysticism of Augustine has too often stood in the way of the mystical theology of Augustine so that his invention of mysticism, as a specific form of contemplation, has been lost from modern view. This essay is an effort to shift the focus of analysis back to the theological reading that Augustine offers us, to his interpretations of his experiences – whether incorporated, reflexive, or retrospective. But to do so is not simply to return to a theological reading of the *Confessions* as such. While theological appropriation of the text is a worthy task, that is not the purpose of the present study. Its more modest goal is the recovery of Augustine's own theology of contemplation in the *Confessions*.

The plan of the volume follows that intention. We shall begin with the Platonists whose importance Augustine made explicit in the central books of the *Confessions*. Here the point is to understand that complex and arcane theology as best we can. For little is accomplished in the history of religious thought when ideas are only inventoried, like epigraphic recordings of "kings and battles." Grasping the religious philosophy of the Plotinian school will set the stage for coming to grips with Augustine's depiction of contemplation. We cannot be sure, in the end, exactly what Augustine took from his reading of the "books of the Platonists," but we can consider them anew and reflect on what might be found there. Chapter 1 is devoted to that project. Chapter 2 offers an initial review of the three great ascension narratives from the *Confessions*. Here the main lines of Augustine's account of contemplation emerge, set into relief by that of the Platonism of Plotinus. Chapter 3 is a series of reflections on issues made salient by the autobiographical texts of the *Confessions*. Following Augustine's own practice in the later books of the *Confessions*, this chapter considers the questions that emerge there regarding Christian contemplation. The volume concludes with an epilogue that considers some texts pertaining to contemplation from Augustine's other works. With some luck, we may emerge with a coherent account of the mysticism of Augustine, although as has been said, luck is but the residue of design.

Part I

FLIGHT TO THE ALONE

"Through a man puffed up with monstrous pride, you brought under my eye some books of the Platonists, translated from Greek into Latin." Thus in Book Seven of the *Confessions*, Augustine recounts his discovery of several Platonic works that helped advance his philosophical reflections and catalyze his rejection of Manichaeism. We will never be certain what Augustine read. But it is almost certain that Augustine studied sections from the *Enneads* of Plotinus and perhaps some works by Plotinus's student (Brown 1967) . When he wrote the *Confessions* more than a decade after the events, it was the distinctive theories of the Plotinian school that became central to his representation of Platonism. Regrettably we do not possess the Latin translation by the Christian convert and rhetorician Marius Victorinus that Augustine used, so we cannot be sure exactly what Augustine had before him as he investigated those complicated treatises. These Platonic texts were initially mediated through the influence of Ambrose and his Christian intellectual circle in Milan. In the decade or more after his first reading of the Platonists in June or July of 386 until his writing the *Confessions*, Augustine may well have continued his Platonic studies on his own in North Africa. Indeed his Christian associate Nebridius, in a letter written in early 389, approves of the fact that Augustine's epistles to him are "full of Christ, and Plato, and Plotinus" (*Epistle* 6). Yet we can only guess at how systematic and sustained Augustine's engagement with Platonism actually was.

Uncertainty regarding Augustine's Platonic syllabus is only a minor concern. The *Confessions* make abundantly clear that Augustine was profoundly influenced by the *libri Platonicorum* and he presents that debt both as an endorsement of the intellectual sophistication of his new Christian theology and as a point of departure against which to develop his Christian theology. The *Confessions* explicitly claim Platonism as an ally of Christianity, especially in reference to contemplation of the transcendent. But Platonism is also chastised as deficient in its claims about the powers of the soul and the salvific efficacy of contemplation. It is this ambivalent appropriation of Platonism that warrants our independent analysis of the thought of the Plotinian school. On that basis we will then be able to consider the full significance of Augustine's nuanced theological critique, and come to some judgment about the larger significance of this crucial exchange at a defining moment in the development of Western theology.

1

THE ROOT OF THE SOUL

"The world is full of gods" (Kirk and Raven 1957: 94). Such was the view of Thales of Miletus from the sixth century BC. Eight centuries later, in the Rome of Plotinus, little would seem to have changed. The spiritual world of late antiquity remained suffused with divinities, indeed, the vocabulary of gods, powers, and spirits had been enriched by the cosmopolitan reach of the Roman imperium. New spiritual faces appeared in old roles, novel names answered to ancient pleas, yet the discourse of petition and propitiation had remained much the same. The surface logic of cultic polytheism had endured. Both civic polytheism and the more personal cults of salvation were central to the religious life of the empire. The former had been much transformed to meet the needs of the great imperium, while the latter had become central to the religious lives of men and women throughout the vast Roman world.

But the old gods of classical antiquity, however august their power and intimate their presence, were not transcendental beings. Never did they break free from the dome of the physical cosmos, independent of the constraints of time and space. They inhabited the same universe as humans, although their status within that sphere was highly exalted and their power greatly to be feared. They were the invisible ones, the immortal ones, whose life was a continuous and everlasting prolongation of time. They were readily to be envied, for the human imagination could grasp quite immediately the joys of their unending existence. Their cult often required physical proximity, while claims of their occasional association with mortals demanded that their presence be made ascertainable in human lives. Yet they too were bound in their immortality by time, defined by the logic of their everlasting existence. They were free only from the exigencies of temporality, not time itself. Nor were they independent of space, however remote the locus of their dwellings. Their invisibility itself betokened spatiality, attenuating this dimension by redrafting its defining visual field. Indeed the gods were so worthy of human fear, respect, and tender gratitude, because they were common members of our cosmos. (Burkert 1985; 1987)

There was more, however, to the story of Greco-Roman religion than the gods of polytheistic cult. Beside the tapestried pantheon, there was another, less anthropomorphic spiritual tradition, one whose distinctive representation of divinity would grow increasingly persuasive in late antiquity. This alternative trajectory was given definition by a tangled cluster of self-described philosophers who claimed the mantle of Plato. While the origins of this separate current in ancient theology are various and its history replete with differing accounts of the character of sacred reality, it was the Platonist school that emerged by the second century AD as the dominant strain. The Platonists of late antiquity understood themselves to be the inheritors of a spiritual tradition of great antiquity. Even by the standards of contemporary scholarship, this claim is credible. The Platonism of Plotinus and his school has demonstrable foundations in archaic Pythagoreanism and more directly in the Old Academy of Plato and his successors (Dillon 1977: chapters 1, 5–7).

This lineage defined a spiritual understanding that did not so much reject the pantheon as decline to privilege it. Indeed the gods featured prominently in the apologetic literature of the Platonist school, beginning with Plato's *Apology*. Socrates is there depicted as enjoying Delphic support for his theological questioning and as being under the tutelage of a personal *daimōn*. Again, in late antiquity, the trope of divine aegis was invoked by Porphyry in support of the authority of his master, Plotinus. In the tenth chapter of his *Vita Plotini*, he portrays the "philosopher of our time" as having as his tutelary spirit no mere *daimōn*, but an actual god (Armstrong 1966: 33–36). Not surprisingly, the life of the sage was replete with portentous events. When he died, Amelius, his pious philosophical associate, inquired of the Delphic oracle where the soul of Plotinus had gone. Porphyry reverently recorded Apollo's lengthy reply. Apollo exhibits his long-standing preference for the Platonist school, dating back to his recognition of Socrates as the "wisest of men," and eulogizes Plotinus. This oracular encomium from "Phoebus of the thick hair" tells us much about the religious sensibilities of learned pagans of the third century. It presents the gods as active supporters of Plotinus's spiritual quest to be free of the incarnate world, from "the bitter wave of this blood-drinking life." It was they who had sent to him "a solid shaft of light so that your eyes could see out of the mournful darkness." As a result, the philosopher was able to see "many fair sights which are hard for human seekers after wisdom to see." Thus represented, the gods had become, as it were, accessories to a deeper spiritual process, one whose logic was independent of them. The oracle thereby discloses a fundamental understanding of the nature of things to which the gods conform and which they serve. The gods were thus enlisted to support a spiritual tradition that would conserve their presence while also superseding them.

The center of gravity in pagan theology now plainly lay elsewhere, beyond the gods. To be sure, these divine beings would continue to receive respectful interest in philosophical circles; they remained the foundation of Hellenic cultic piety and as such were never religiously displaced. But for later Platonists, the cosmos had deeper spiritual strata. The archaic Pythagoreans had discovered this, with their devotion to numbers. Such powers were unlike the gods of the pantheon, not only because of their remote, numerical natures, but above all because they seemed to dwell in a different domain. The implication of such thinking was made abundantly clear by Plato, whose two world theory – of being and becoming, of forms and particulars – articulated, with remarkable force and some measure of clarity, the notion of a transcendental realm. The forms or ideas in Plato's dialogues initiated prolonged reflection on a level of reality outside the spatial confines of the physical cosmos and independent of time. These conceptions did not emerge with complete exactness in the Platonic dialogues, although a general outline of the idea of transcendence did.

It was to this transcendent realm of being that theological interest among Platonists was focused throughout late antiquity. What was the scope of this world outside time and space? What were the powers of its constituents? Were they sufficient for the production of the lower world of becoming, or were other forces required as well? These were questions upon which the closely associated Pythagorean and Platonist schools exercised their training in dialectic and to which they gave differing answers. Yet they were unified in their commitment to this transcendent and divine realm, and clear in their belief that it could be made accessible in some measure to the highest capacity within the human soul. This program of access to the transcendent was termed *theōria*, contemplation. If religious initiates in the mysteries of cultic polytheism could mix easily with the unseen, so too could philosophers become spectators of the eternal world of being itself, once purified by the practice of virtue and directed by the mental exertion of dialectic. The project of intellectual and moral ascension outlined by the mantic priestess Diotima in the *Symposium* and reiterated in the *Republic* became for later Platonists an immediate and persuasive ideal. For Platonic theology in late antiquity, *theōria* became the central religious ideal, for it constituted the practice of transcendence.

The force of this ancient transcendentalism was intense in the *Enneads* of Plotinus, a collection of treatises on philosophical themes written in Rome between about 254 and 270, and published by Porphyry, Plotinus's student, in 301. Plotinus described human life to be an unsteady spiritual state, not only in a psychological or moral sense, but ontologically. For on his account, our inner self can shift between different levels of reality. Our soul is a spiritual rover, awakening to its subsistence in the interstices of temporal flux and immutable being. Our inchoate goal is to transcend the exigencies of life in the world. Indeed our end is divinization, becoming "like unto the divine," in the famous phrase of *Theaetaetus* 176b, now read as assimilation to being and to the divine forms. Of this Plotinus was certain. He contrasted the Olympians gods, understood by him as contemplatives of a superior station, with the higher divine objects of intellectual gaze:

> For all the gods are majestic and beautiful and their beauty is overwhelming: but what is it which makes them like this? It is Intellect, and it is because Intellect is more intensely active in them, so as to be

visible . . . They are surely beautiful just because they are gods. For they certainly do not sometimes think rightly and sometimes perversely: their thinking is always right in the calm and stability and purity of Intellect, and they know all things and are acquainted, not with mortal matters, but with their own divine ones, with all which Intellect sees. The gods which are in heaven, since they are free for contemplation, continually contemplate, but as if at a distance, the things in that higher heaven into which they raise their heads: but the gods in that higher heaven, all those who dwell upon it and in it, contemplate through their abiding in the whole of that heaven.

(V.8.3: 18–31)

This contemplation is characteristic of both mortals and immortals alike, although human embodiment weakens our contemplation, making it a pro-treptical hope rather than a natural state.

But the intelligible forms were not, in Yeats's phrase, "the ghostly paradigms of things." They are more vital, more vivid, more real. Everything that emerges into temporal instantiation in the material world is present there, original and perfect. Nor do these principles separately exist in some heavenly inventory. They are interrelated, following complex patterns of intelligible connections which human dialectic can only begin to describe. Thus the transcendent realm was for Plotinus a composite unity. This unity-in-diversity can be seen in the following description of the vitality of the intelligible world:

If one enquires, therefore, where the living beings come from, one is enquiring where the sky there comes from; and this is to enquire where the [universal] living being comes from, and this is the same as where life comes from, and universal life and universal Soul and universal Intellect, when there is no poverty of lack of resource there, but all things are filled full of life, and we say, boiling with life. They all flow, in a way, from a single spring, not like one particular breath or one warmth, but as if there was one quality which held and kept intact all the qualities in itself, of sweetness along with fragrance, and was at once the quality of wine and the characters of all tastes, the sights of colours and all the awarenesses of touch, and all that hearings hear, all tunes and every rhythm.

(VI.7.12, 20–30)

Plotinus understood the Platonic forms to be both the intelligible objects of knowledge and themselves intelligences. The contemplative soul encounters not merely an interstitial collection of paradigms, but a host of entities each engaged in the process of self-reflection. By thinking themselves, these self-thinking minds reflect not only upon their own natures, but, in the process, come to grasp the nature of other forms. The cold logic of conceptual entailment now

20

crackles with synaptic life as these intelligible minds contemplate their inter-relationships. This Plotinian doctrine is one of his most striking innovations and seems to be a concept drawn from several sources, including: the Aristotelian notion of a self-thinking divine mind, the plurality of divine minds intimated at *Metaphysics*, Lambda 8, Plato's account of the weaving together of the forms at *Sophist* 248c ff., and the Middle Platonic conception of the forms as divine thoughts (Kenney 1991: 15–32). What emerges in the *Enneads* is a living net-work of transcendental and eternal divine minds, intellects that have a capacity for mutual perception. They are, in Leibnizian terms, monads with windows. In a passage that follows the one just quoted from V.8, Plotinus explains this divine life; he begins with the Homeric notion of the easy life of the gods:

> For it is "the easy life" there, and truth is their mother and nurse and being and food – and they see all things, not those to which coming to be, but those to which real being belongs, and they see themselves in other things; for all things there are transparent, and there is nothing dark or opaque; everything and all things are clear to the inmost part to everything; for light is transparent to light. Each there has everything in itself and sees all things in every other, so that all are everywhere and each and every one is all and the glory is unbounded; for each of them is great, because even the small is great; the sun there is all the stars, and each star is the sun and all others. A different kind of being stands out in each, but in each all are manifest.
>
> (V.8.4, 1–11)

The transcendental world is thus a unity of distinct entities that are bound together by the very process of contemplating their own natures. Unlike the lower world, where the constituents of becoming must struggle against the constraints of time and space to discover their foundational selves and their true connectivity with others, each intelligible asserts its connection to all others as an outgrowth of own life.

One of the most striking aspects of Plotinus's account of being was his commitment to the existence of ideas of individuals (V.7 and IV.3.5). It was not unprecedented, having been debated, as far as we can tell through the dim historical record, by some Middle Platonists such as Alcinous (*Didaskalikos*, 9). Plotinus's regnant intuition seems to have been personalist in character, that is, that there is a fundamental significance that attaches to human individuals and this must be written into the structure of the transcendental world. Thus there is an idea of Socrates, an "Autosocrates," that endures throughout eternity and is the subject of periodic reincarnations. This thesis was critically important, since it is this higher self that allows both for our immediate knowledge of the forms and for our contemplative access to transcendental being. What is at stake is made evident at the very beginning of Plotinus's treatise devoted to ideas of particulars:

Is there an idea of each particular thing? Yes, if I and each one of us have a way of ascent and return to the intelligible, the principle of each of us is there. If Socrates, that is the soul of Socrates, always exists, there will be an absolute Socrates in the sense that, in so far as they are soul, individuals are also said to exist in this way in the intelligible world.

(V.7.1, 1–5)

The doctrine was thus grounded in the idea of "soul," and so applied to all animate entities and perhaps beyond them even to apparently inanimate entities where there is still some vestigial presence of "soul." The doctrine seems to have originated in Plotinus's reflections on the ultimat significance of human individuality. He rejected the notion that there could merely be a single form of humanity, which would serve as the universal, abstract principle of all humans. Human individuals must be more than just the fleeting instances of a single transcendental form. The significance of their individual natures seemed to him to be sufficient to warrant inclusion in the intelligible world:

No, there cannot be the same forming principle for different indi-viduals, and one man will not serve as a model for several men differing from each other not only by reason of their matter but with a vast number of special differences of form. Men are not related to their form as portraits of Socrates are to their original, but their different structures must result from different forming principles.

(V.7.1, 18–23)

This thesis was novel and striking, presenting a personalist aspect to Platonic formalism, and giving yet more force to the Plotinian insight that the intelligible world was full of vitality. For our real self can be numbered among the forms, among the ultimate constituents of reality. The foundation of human persons is to be found there, even if the lower self may not be easily recognized in its absolute paradigm. The true self is an intelligible one, at a level more real than that displayed in empirical consciousness. The fractured, temporal sense of the human person found in empirical consciousness betrays a deeper source of human life, one that can be discovered beneath the flux of our mental states. That is where our real life is lived.

This was the poignant dichotomy of human existence for Plotinus: that our true self is transcendent, while our soul finds itself awakening amidst the disorder of time and the confusion of materiality. Nor is that true self merely a theoretical abstraction. It is what we truly are, and it is, even in our present earthly state, something to which we are somehow connected. Plotinus is resolute about this, so much so that he innovated in his Platonism, developing his own unique doctrine that the soul does not entirely descend into the lower world. This was a controversial position in ancient Platonism. Its logic, given the notion of forms of individuals, seems clear enough. We should not be conceived as cut off from our real selves in the intelligible realm. Rather, we are, as it were, merely attenuated across different levels of reality. The story of our shifting spiritual self-recognition is played out against a stable ontological background. Our focus shifts up and down, now highly temporal and fractured, now informed by the intelligible, the stable, and the authentic. But this spiritual movement does not change the foundation of the self there among the eternals. The deepest part of soul is always in the intelligible realm, and so continues to exercise the characteristic contemplative activity of intellect, even if this often goes unrecognized by the incarnated soul, occluded as its vision usually is in its present condition. This point is made quite explicitly:

> And, if one ought to dare to express one's own view more clearly, contradicting the opinion of others, even our soul does not altogether come down, but there is always something of it in the intelligible; but if the part which is in the world of sense-perception gets control, or rather if it is itself brought under control, and thrown into confusion [by the body], it prevents us from perceiving the things which the upper part of the soul contemplates.
>
> (IV.8.8, 1–6)

This thesis is of the utmost significance for any assessment of Plotinus's theology, since it means that human beings are never entirely members of the temporal and spatial world around us. We have, as it were, a secret self, a tacit presence in the eternal realm. We are not, in the final analysis, constituents of this lower world. Ours is a richer spiritual patrimony, a deeper transcendental destiny. This was the metaphysical foundation for the pronounced religious optimism of the *Enneads*. We have an undescended aspect of the self. The burden of Plotinian theology is to bring us to this recognition. This "ontic hook" is what prevents our complete descent into time and space, anchoring us among the forms. Thus Plotinus chose a distinctive approach to the classical Platonic problem of psychic immortality, conceiving of the soul as in part actually eternal. It is not just akin to the forms; rather, it is at base an intelligible in its own right. Hence the soul can aspire to more than reincarnation, to more even than a temporally enduring life among the gods, free at last from the wearying round of reincarnation. It can rediscover its hold upon the eternal, beyond the reach of time, finding there what it had lost in its declension into becoming. For Plotinus, eternity was the only sort of immortality truly worth having.

The implications of this notion of personal transcendence will remain with us throughout our inquiry. It had a profound effect on Augustine and his estimation of human interiority. We will return to consider its significance more fully when we assess Plotinus's contemplative theology in the next chapter. But one further point bears immediate mention. It would be a mistake to suppose that this idea of a transcendental self was a mere scholastic innovation for Plotinus. Quite to the contrary, since recognition of the transcendent was a matter of personal immediacy. In one of the rare autobiographical passages in the *Enneads*, Plotinus recounts both his recognition of transcendence and his pained puzzlement at its loss:

> Often I have woken up out of the body to my self and have entered into my self, going out from all other things; I have seen a beauty wonderfully great and felt assurance that then most of all I belonged to the better part; I have actually lived the best life and come to identify with the divine; and set firm in it. I have come to that supreme actuality, setting myself above all else in the realm of Intellect. Then after that rest in the divine, when I have come down from Intellect to discursive reasoning, I am puzzled how I ever came down, and how my soul has come to be in the body when it is what it has shown itself to be by itself, even when it is in the body.
>
> (IV.8.1, 1–10)

Exiled from "the country of the gods" (IV.8.1, 19) amidst the raving strife of the world, the soul discovers its loss. Yet it can also recognize its sameness or identity with the divine. This sense of transcendental identity is emblematic of Plotinian theology; it is the fulcrum for the soul, the basis for its yet deeper understanding and association with higher things. In a beautiful image, Plotinus describes the soul as submerged in the body, but capable nonetheless of drawing itself up by its salient portion (VI.9.8, 16). And this is the "ancient nature of the soul" (VI.9.8, 14–15).

It is discursive, philosophic activity, conducted in time, which prepares the soul for its restoration. The soul needs to purge itself morally and to conduct certain dialectical exercises that allow for its elevation. Plotinus understands this ascension to be a dramatic spiritual breakthrough back into the transcendent level of the soul. These themes are mixed together in a passage that vividly describes the transcendence of Intellect, the divine unity-in-diversity of the intelligible gods:

> Let there be, then in the soul a shining imagination of a sphere, having everything within it, either moving or standing still, or some things moving and others standing still. Keep this, and apprehend in your mind another, taking away the mass: take away also the places, and the mental picture of matter in yourself, and do not try to apprehend another sphere smaller in mass than the original one, but calling on the god who made that of which you have the mental picture, pray him to come. And may he come, bringing his own universe with him, with all the gods within him, he who is one and all, and each god is all the gods coming together into one; they are different in their powers, but

24

by that one manifold power they are all one; or rather, the one god is all; for he does not fail if all become what he is.

(V.8.9, 7–19)

While this use of religious language helps to underscore the spiritual character of Intellect, we must be wary of discovering here a formal theory of divine intervention. The soul's contemplative turning toward the transcendental world is primarily a matter of its own initiative. Plotinus's use of the language of prayer and of the gods in reference to Intellect should not be surprising, for this juncture between the embodied soul and the intelligibles is the initial fault line in his Platonic theology. It is the gap the spiritual self must cross in order to achieve its eternal heritage and restore its true nature. It is, moreover, a neuralgic point, resonant of classical Hellenic religious anxiety and piety. It is also the moment when the soul achieves transcendence of the lower world and dares to consort with the gods. For this moment of self-restoration is what the god, Intellect, promises – not salvation offered from without. In Plotinus, it is not a new self that is discovered, but an ancient one.

The transcendentalism of Plotinus was thus far more than a theory of universals, indeed, more than a hypothesis about degrees of reality. It was a theology of human eternality, articulating a personal eschatology for the soul. Indeed, it is the strongest statement within Greco-Roman metaphysics of the ultimate significance of the individual human soul. The intelligible self bears little resemblance to the empirical self, and its real nature is defined in communitarian terms, established by its complex interrelationships with all other intelligibles within the Intellect. This contrast between the apparent and the real self is a common enough religious trope, as is the shock of recognition attending the discovery of our deeper nature. But the admission of this personalistic component into the Platonic doctrine of the forms had the effect of closing the gap between the abstraction of being and the concreteness of becoming. No longer is there a sense of hypostatization associated with the divine ideas, no hint of airy reduplication of this world in some other. For the transcendentals are now vividly displayed and immediately accessible. We have an immediate share in them, not just an approximate association to the degree that we seek to imitate them in their august stability. We share in their nature directly because we are, in the last analysis, eternal forms ourselves. Our share in the transcendent is inalienable; it is an option we can exercise whenever we wish.

We do so through contemplation. Of this, Plotinus had – for once – little that is novel to say. He was a traditional Platonist in his understanding of the proper means for perception of the intelligibles. *Theōria* is the true way. It consists primarily in ethical rigorism, moderate asceticism, and the practice of philosophical dialectic. The latter comprised Socratic discussion, or *diaresis*, as well as mental exercises, such as the process of conceptual abstraction iterated above at V.8.9. We become our true selves through the practice of the virtues, which are purgative – removing the deleterious effects of bodily instantiation. Practical

25

wisdom, justice, temperance, and fortitude train the soul to control its association with becoming and to fix its errant attention onto the real. Plotinus was also committed to the view that the virtues are cognitive in import, that they are more than just corrective or propaedeutic to contemplation. Through moral training the soul not only sloughs off the accretions of its embodiment, but also reverses its vector of descent. Moreover, it achieves visionary assimilation to its transcendental nature. This is the final purpose of *theōria*. In this reorientation there are neither shortcuts nor palliatives. As noted already, Plotinus uses the language of divine intervention, but he never suggests that our renewed association with our transcendental self comes about through divine activity, power, or initiative. Nor is petitionary prayer an effective catalyst of divine aid. When he employs that sort of language, he does so as a traditional form of religious discourse parallel, but subordinate, to the discourse of philosophy. Above all, he eschewed any specific ritual practices. Theurgy, the "sacramental magic" of Greco-Roman religion, was not a means to transcendence; it neither supplanted nor supported philosophical *theōria* (Armstrong 1967: 277–287; Shaw 1995: 1–17).

The transcendentalism of Plotinus was thus grounded in the rich tradition of Greco-Roman pagan practice and thought. It liberated the soul from otherworldly journeys across the cosmos and the search for heavenly guides through those distant regions, since the soul's true path was to go within itself, and thence into a level of being wholly distinct from the physical cosmos. What the soul could discover there was, however, more than transcendence. The perfection of being does not exhaust what the self might disclose through the practice of contemplation. It might even find the source of all reality, the "root of the soul" (VI.9.9, 2), buried deep beyond even the perfection of the intelligibles. It is to that ultimate power that our inquiry must now turn.

2

A LONG LIFE STRETCHED
OUT

The novelty of Plotinus's view on transcendence is exhausted neither by the doctrine of the undescended soul, nor his commitment to forms of individuals. For there is a further notion of transcendence to be found in the *Enneads*, one that pertains to the foundation of the intelligibles. Plotinus was convinced that the process of contemplation disclosed to the ascendant soul more than its home amidst myriad intellects, more than its station among the transcendentals. *Theōria*, contemplation, intimates a source deeper than the eternal forms, the hidden and previously unrecognized root of all multiplicity. This is the One, the ultimate divine principle in Plotinus. It is the One, the Good, that the soul desires, its nature drawn to contemplation because of an obscure craving for ultimacy. As a result, even the beauty, the orderliness, the stability of Intellect, does not suffice. However rich its content and immutable its nature, Intellect betrays its penultimacy to the contemplative soul. The soul desires a final and total unity, beyond the complexity of Intellect. Intellect for Plotinus is inherently multiple, since it is comprised of a vast number of forms, each a conscious mind engaged in reflection. Thus Intellect is always complex, something that Plotinus takes as a token of its secondary and derivative character. For beyond it there must be a principle free from collectivity, an absolute unity.

Plotinus's theology of a final divine One helped to establish this type of pagan monotheism more firmly in the theological imagination of late antiquity, although it had a long history in classical religious thought. The One is the "root of the soul," the "spring of intellect," the "principle of being," the "cause of good" (VI.9.9, 1–2). In its interior contemplation, the soul is able to recover the continual presence of the Good, something it had come to neglect in its exterior diversions in space and time. It restores its contact, and discovers the basis for its previously inchoate longing:

> And we must consider that men have forgotten that which from the beginning until now they want and long for. For all things reach out to that and long for it by necessity of nature, as if divining by instinct that they cannot exist without it. The grasp of the beautiful and the wonder and the waking of love for it come to those who, in a way, already know it and are awake to it. But the Good, since it was there

long before to arouse an innate desire, is present even to those asleep and does not astonish those who at any time see it, because it is always there and there is never recollection of it: but people do not see it, because it is present to them in their sleep.

(V.5.12, 4–15)

The Good is present to all, as the ontological source of all reality. This presence can be discerned in the vague sense of disquiet which afflicts the soul in its fractured and embodied state. But *theōria* allows the soul initially to recover its transcendental nature, although even then its longing is not satiated, for its final "root" is in the One. The true lure of the soul is not the eternal self, resplendent among the intelligibles, but the Good, whose impacted presence, deep within the core of the soul, draws the soul back to its source. The Good arouses innate desire within us; even throughout our unconscious life it is present. Nor are we shocked when we do discover the Good, for it has been tacitly available within the soul and within the obscurity of the soul's longings. This ancient, unperceived desire for the Good motivates the soul (V.5.12, 17). And this One is always accessible, for it exercises no volition in its presence to the soul. As in Aristotle, the theological vector is unidirectional: the One draws the soul to itself as an omnipresent goal. It does not intervene directly or take notice of the soul, for to do so would, according to Plotinus, violate its nature. It merely is what it is, the perfect Good, and this suffices to initiate the movement of the imperfect soul toward it. In an attenuated sense, the One is understood by Plotinus to be beneficent: it is always available to the soul. Its very lack of volition or selective intention toward entities outside itself insures its universal beneficence. As Plotinus remarks: "The Good is gentle and kindly and gracious, and present to anyone when he wishes" (V.5.12, 33–34).

It is this Good that the soul discovers through interior contemplation. To those acculturated to the cadences of a different theology, the One might seem foreign, indifferent, or remote. But this is to mistake the grammar of Plotinian theism. The soul in its contemplative breakthrough into the deeper transcendence of the One discovers, not another entity, however exalted, but the foundation of itself and all else. As the foundation of reality, the One eludes assimilation to the class of things that can be defined or classified. Thus the One, the source of being, cannot be identified with any form nor described by any predicate or property. To see it as an agent, however benign, would be to mistake it for an entity, something that engages in outward activity. Neither beneficence nor malevolence nor indifference is apposite to the One. Each is a category mistake, displaying a false theological grammar; all are indicative of confusion regarding the One. When Plotinus uses such discourse, he means to reorder Hellenic religious sensibilities, directing attention away from the One as the supreme God of the pantheon, a god responsive to petitionary prayer and cultic offering, and toward a different conception of the divine. It is precisely because the One cannot be construed as exercising – or withholding –

beneficence that the language of graciousness is strangely apposite. As the foundation of all value and the root of the spiritual self, the One cannot be understood except as the persistent source of goodness. The soul's recognition of the recessive presence of the One is thus a critical advance, one that occasions, or perhaps clarifies, the true nature of the divine. Older religious concepts such as beneficence or moral goodness are revalorized, construed to comport with the One's position as an absolute foundation for reality and value.

The soul's breakthrough to the One is understood by Plotinus to follow upon its cognitive grasp of the intelligibles through dialectic and the practice of the virtues. This grasp is – as we have seen – also ontological in import, since it involves the recovery of an abandoned higher self. In coming to know the intelligible and divine archetypes, the contemplative soul has affixed itself again to that blessed company. Its further discovery of a more fundamental divine level beyond eternal being is swift and, it seems, conclusive. But what exactly is involved in this breakthrough to the One? Does Plotinus understand this re-association with the "root of the soul" to be an instance of transformation or a resolution of the soul back into the Good? Does the soul merge into the One through contemplation? In order to address these questions, we need to reflect further on the import of Plotinian transcendentalism.

That access to the One is sudden is quite explicit in the *Enneads*. Grasp of the One emerges from the practice of philosophy, but it is, nevertheless, not a studied, gradual accession. This is made especially clear in a striking description of contemplative ascent to the One at VI.7. Plotinus is discussing knowledge or touching of the Good, which, he notes, Plato considered to be the "greatest study." But this study applies to our philosophical preparation, not to our actual looking at the Good. He explains as follows:

> We are taught about it by comparisons and negations and knowledge of the things which come from it and certain methods of ascent by degrees, but we are put on the way to it by purifications and virtues and adornings and by gaining footholds in the intelligible and settling ourselves firmly there and feasting on its contents. But whoever has become at once contemplator of himself and all the rest and object of his contemplation, and, since he has become substance and intellect and "the complete living being," no longer looks at it from outside – when he has become this he is near, and that Good is next above him, and already close by, shining upon all the intelligible world. It is there that one lets all study go; up to a point one has been led along and settled firmly in beauty and as far as this one thinks that in which one is, but is carried out of it by the surge of the wave of Intellect itself and lifted on high by a kind of swell and sees suddenly, not seeing how, but the vision fills his eyes with light and does not make him see something else by it, but the light itself is what he sees.
>
> (VI.7.36, 6–21)

Once the contemplative soul has immediate knowledge of the intelligibles and has become a contemplator of itself and of all other intelligibles, it has established itself within the "living being" of Timaeus 31b, the fully real world of the forms. Then it must let go of its own studied initiative; passively, it is lifted up by the wave of Intellect and suddenly its vision is filled with light. It is important to notice the importunate character of this event and the soul's passivity in relation to it. Initiative ends – as it were – at the trough of the Intellect. The soul is carried aloft from there by the surge of the Intellect, and in a sudden moment its vision is filled with light. Of course, temporality is, strictly speaking, inappropriate at the level of Intellect, since the conditions necessary for time only emerge at the level of soul. Thus Plotinus's use – indeed emphasis – on the suddenness of the breaking wave is both suggestive and perplexing. Plotinus is often quite explicit in the *Enneads* about the difficulty of using spatial or temporal language, whose proper location is the sensible world, in reference to the intelligibles (e.g. V.1.6, 19 ff.). Yet, when he does use such temporal language, it is usually in order to get at some aspect of that higher world which has emerged into a temporal frame of reference, but whose original character can only be approximated by this level of description. On this reading, the momentary character of this enlightened vision would betoken a relation that obtains between Intellect and the One, indicating that Intellect's grasp of the One is always partial and incomplete. For Intellect is not the One, but distinct from it, and its connection to the One, however intimate, is never total. Any contact that occurs, as in the case of an individual soul or intellect, is not applicable to Intellect as a whole. Intellect is not the One; its relation with the One is that of the next level in reality looking upon its ontological source.

Yet we cannot ignore the more personal aspect of the wave image. What it conveys, among other things, is the individual soul's description of its state when removed from the constraints of time and the body, when restored to its eternal self, when further exalted beyond even that transcendent life. To express this recognition, the contemplative soul is forced to employ the tenebrist palette of earthly description, and so it resorts to temporality in its portrayal. That may be a condition of its present vantage point, inured by time and matter. But it may also suggest the limited grasp on the One which the soul has as an intelligible self, even when freed from the opacity of incarnation. Thus the incipience of the One in Plotinus's theology is dramatic and its impact profound.

A sense of momentousness, even danger, is associated by Plotinus with the soul's approach to the One. Because the One is not an entity but the source of all things, its lack of finitude or limitation may unnerve the soul, producing a kind of contemplative panic:

> But in proportion as the soul goes toward the formless, since it is utterly unable to comprehend it because it is not delimited and, so to speak, stamped by a richly varied stamp, it slides away and is afraid that it may

have nothing at all. Therefore, it gets tired of this sort of thing, and often gladly comes down and falls away from all this, till it comes to the perceptible and rests there as if on solid ground.

(VI.9.3, 4–10)

There is, then, a certain disquietude that can afflict the contemplative soul, a state of fright followed by weariness. Delimitation or finitude is the soul's natural frame of reference. So the soul may be alarmed by the non-finite character of the One. Its natural tendencies draw it away from the One, and *theōria* is foreshortened.

Despite this disquietude, the soul may also persist, having within itself the capacity to pursue its inner journey. This interior turning is critical in Plotinus; by going within itself, the soul can discover both the way and the means to begin its journey to its source. Interiority is the primary spiritual vector for the contemplative soul. Yet this interior focus is no self-affirmation. For the soul has become what it now is – a painfully distinct entity cut off from its true life above and embodied in a physical frame – precisely because of its initial desire for individuality. Plotinus calls this irrational desire for distinctiveness *tolma* – the audacity that caused the soul's initial spiritual fall. He understands the soul's precipitation into becoming as the result of a mistaken, indeed tragic, choice in favor of individuality in space and time. This theme is especially clear in the jolting introduction to the early treatise *On the Three Primary Hypostases*:

> What is it, then, which has made the souls forget their father, God, and being ignorant of themselves and him, even though they are parts which come from his higher world and altogether belong to it? The beginning of evil for them was audacity and coming to birth and the first otherness and the wishing to belong to themselves. Since they were clearly delighted with their own independence, and made great use of self-movement, running the opposite course and getting as far as possible, they were ignorant even that they themselves came from that world.
>
> (V.1.1, 1–9)

Souls are thus engaged in an ambiguous activity when they practice the interiority of contemplation. They must now attempt to set aside their "first otherness." They have chosen to distinguish themselves by a false individuality, a sort of individuation made extreme by a misplaced desire to be more distinctive. This has occasioned their declension into the sensible world, where they can revel in separation, and pay its price, which is continued reincarnation. But by turning within itself, the soul can – as we have seen – begin to reverse this psychic precipitation. Individuality is thus an ambivalent notion in Plotinian theology; it can be construed either as the fruit of an audacious act of self-constitution, or it can be seen as the soul's eternal birthright within the

31

community of intelligibles, far from the fractured individuation it evinces in time and the body. True and false senses of individuality vie for supremacy.

By turning within itself, the soul must take care not to augment its otherness, its willed distinctiveness. To do so would be to plunge more deeply into instantiated life and to invite continued exile within the succession of time. It must instead concentrate upon the deeper, eternal elements within interior reflection. As such the soul is not salvifically transformed in any dramatic way, nor is it rescued by a power other than itself. Rather, it turns – admittedly with great moral and intellectual effort – to its undescended core. Its embodied adventures and its experiences within time are vain in this endeavor. Only an interior focus on its inner core avails the soul of transcendence, which, when complete, might include its visionary association with the Good:

> Since, then, that which we seek is one and we are considering the principle of all things, the Good and the First, one must not go far away from the things around the primary by falling down to the last things of all, but as one goes to the primary one must lift oneself up from the things of sense which are the last and lowest, and become freed from all evil since one is hastening to the Good, and ascend to the principle in oneself and become one from many, when one is going to behold the Principle and the One. Therefore one must become Intellect and entrust one's soul to and set it firmly under Intellect, that it may awake to receive what that sees, and may by this Intellect behold the One, without adding any sense-perception or receiving anything from sense-perception into the Intellect, but beholding the most pure with the pure Intellect, and the primary part of Intellect.
>
> (VI.9.3, 14–27)

Interior contemplation thus discloses to the soul a multi-layered transcendence: first of its embodied self, and then – paradoxically – of its true and eternal self. Both are superseded by a unitive vision of the final principle, the Good. The language of purity and simplicity is instructive in this regard. The soul becomes aware initially, in its inner ascension, that it exists at two levels, that it has been living a transcendental life, while distracted by sensory consciousness. By turning within, it recovers the higher life of its intellective self. Plotinus compares this to concentrating our hearing on an unexpected voice. Transcendence requires that one keep "the soul's power of apprehension pure and ready to hear voices from on high" (V.1.12, 20–21).

Yet this blessed recovery of the eternal self is not the final destiny to which the soul might aspire, for a more complete interiority is possible, by surrendering even this higher self:

> But if this is so, the soul must let go of all outward things and turn altogether to what is within, and not be inclined to any outward thing,

but ignoring all things (as it did formerly in sense-perception, but then in the realm of forms), and even ignoring itself, come to be in its company and had, so to put it, sufficient converse with it, come and announce, if it could, to another that transcendent unity.

(VI.9.7, 16–23)

This higher unity, this presence superior to knowledge, completes the self's interior transcendence in Plotinus. For within the soul the tacit presence of the One can be uncovered. Only by an interior pilgrimage through and beyond the self, both empirical and eternal, can the Good be recovered. The soul can thus ascend out of the scumbled darkness of its incarnate life – something it had once chosen by an act of insolent audacity. *Theōria* is the soul's necessary and sufficient means for salvation; it is the practice of transcendence that secures its deliverance. This is the principal desideratum of Plotinian spirituality.

Yet this conception of interior contemplation of the One is not an easy one for us to understand fully. In some measure this is because we are culturally conditioned by a different sort of monotheism, derived from the Biblical tradition. Plotinian theology is best understood as a special form of monotheism, one which emerged from a long line of antecedents in Greco-Roman theology. This pagan monotheism was distinct from the Biblical variety in that it continued to countenance the existence of a plurality of derivative divine manifestations or modes of the ultimate first principle (Kenney 1986, 1991; Athanassiadi and Frede 1999). In appearance, it was polytheistic, for the practices and pieties of Greco-Roman religious life were retained. But ancient paganism was a complex religious phenomenon that admitted not just many gods, but many strategies for understanding and associating with the divine. One important dimension of its development was the growth of a philosophical religion within it, one that provided both an integrated theology and a soteriology. Central to this philosophical religion was its capacity to provide a systematic representation of reality. It did so, in part, by drawing out longstanding Greco-Roman ideas about the divine force behind the pantheon, a deep unity of which the many divine powers were but manifestations.

This pagan monotheism was the theological background of Plotinus's conception of contemplation of the One. The One of Plotinus is neither the "One with no other" of monism nor the exclusive God of Biblical monotheism. Rather, it is the inclusive God of late pagan spirituality. The One, based on a long tradition of reflection on the pantheon, was the final divine unity, the ultimate source of all reality – of all gods, all powers, all souls. Yet, while the One is the unique basis of all things, the mode of its distinctness is different from that of Biblical monotheism. The One is not an active agent or demiurge. Moreover, Plotinus is at great pains to avoid presenting the One as another entity, albeit ultimate and supreme. For this reason, he can disconcertingly maintain the radical immanence of the One to all things, and insist as well that all things are distinct from the One without complete separation. The operative notion here is ontological dependence. But by denying that the One stands as a distinct being in relation to its consequents, Plotinus was not endorsing monism. He did not believe, in the end, that all things are simply the One. Rather, he presented a specific sort of a theistic principle, understood as the ultimate but present source of all realities. This is succinctly put by Plotinus in the following passages:

> The One is all things and not a single one of them: it is the principle of all things, not all things, but all things have that other kind of transcendent existence; for in a way they do occur in the One; or rather they are not there yet, but they will be.
>
> (V.2.1, 1–3)

> All these things are the One and not the One: they are he because they come from him; they are not he, because it is in abiding by himself that he gives them. It is then like a long life stretched out at length; each part is different from that which comes next in order, but the whole is continuous with itself, but with one part differentiated from another, and the earlier does not perish in the later.
>
> (V2.2, 24–29)

These passages underscore the character of Plotinian monotheism. Because the One is the ultimate "ground of being," it is separate from all things derived from it. These entities aspire, however inchoately, to return to it. And Plotinus is committed to the existence of levels of reality distinct from the One. Thus the central insight of monotheism is secured: the primary separation of the first principle from its ontological derivatives. Yet Plotinus is not willing to make that separation abrupt or especially sharp. The fact that lower levels of reality continue in existence indicates that a subtle ontological link remains between them and the Good. On this point Plotinus grounds his notion of the omnipresence of the One, the thesis that the One is present wherever there are existent things. Hence all levels of the great chain of being demonstrate the presence of the One, whose power manifests itself as a vast theophany.

As these citations also indicate, the One is distinct from all things, not because it is different in its nature, but because it cannot be characterized as a thing. Central to the logic of divine transcendence in Plotinian monotheism is *apophasis*, "negation," or *aphairesis*, "abstraction." These are procedures for denying or removing most, if not all, predicates of the One. This paradoxical approach served to establish both the distinctiveness and the ultimacy of the One. As V.3.14, 6–7 indicates in regard to the One: "we say what it is not, but we do not say what it is." Plotinus's portrait of deity is sketched through the claim of ontological ultimacy and by assertion that the One uniquely exceeds any capacity for finite conceptual representation. The unknowability of the One becomes for Plotinus a technique for revealing the soul's fundamental relation to this ultimate principle.

34

The One is thus a "long life stretched out" and we remain connected to it and in its presence. Our very existence gives witness to this ontological relation. And there are very few levels of reality that separate the contemplative soul from the Good. "Since the soul is so honorable and divine a thing, be sure already that you can attain God by reason of its being of this kind, and with this as your motive ascend to him: in all certainty you will not look far; and the stages between are not many" (V.1.3, 1–5). Contemplation is the only means necessary to the recovery of the presence of the One within our souls.

3

A KIND OF REST

Distilled in the alembic of the *Enneads* are many strands of Greco-Roman philosophy and theology. But the quintessence of Plotinian thought is the doctrine of the divine One and its interior presence to the contemplative soul. In the *Enneads* Plotinus describes how the soul achieves an inner realization of its intimacy with the One. There is a vatic vastness to the classical cosmos, with its ranks of daemons, gods, and powers in the foreground, and its remote but hidden source behind. Contemplation in the *Enneads* serves as a counter-balance to this sense of religious remoteness. It is as an act of spiritual magnification, disclosing the soul's underlying relation to the One. Contemplation is not a transformation of the self, merely its sudden grasp at how deep – as it were – the self goes. In contemplation the Plotinian soul discovers that it is rooted in the One, and that it has never really departed from it.

Contemplation is an act of spiritual recognition. It is the supreme spiritual value for Plotinus. While lower divine manifestations of the One may become accessible through sacrifice and propitiation, the Good cannot be. It is a theological category mistake to think it so. Since the Good is not an entity of any finite sort, the dualistic logic of cultic activity, of worship or of propitiation, is not applicable to it. Hence it is not surprising that Plotinus had so little interest in such activities; his real spiritual focus lay elsewhere, in contemplation of the divine One.

It is critical that the contemplative texts of the *Enneads* be read with this theological dimension in view. Indeed, one important aspect to the *Enneads* is its rich modulation of religious and philosophical discourse. The *Enneads* display a complex combination of these distinctive sorts of discourse, both of which have been interwoven in the Platonic school since Plato. This mixture of voices helps to define the special character of the *Enneads*. The language of the Greek mystery cults is frequently employed by Plotinus in discussing contemplation: the ascension and descent of souls, purification, sanctuary imagery, etc. This language is dynamic, centering on notions of psychic release from embodiment and salvation. The famous final phrase of the *Enneads* (VI.9.11, 51), "flight of the alone to the alone," is an excellent example. It suggests the drama of psychic flight and the exigencies of spiritual escape.

At the same time, this religious language is counterbalanced in the *Enneads* by the austerity of classical ontology. What might be called "Eleatic" discourse harks back through Plato's *Parmenides* to Parmenides of Elea himself. It is a static mode of reflection, with an emphasis on articulating relations that obtain within the structure of reality. It is aprioristic in tone, proceeding without immediate reference to the soul and its adventures. What Plotinus does repeatedly in the *Enneads* is answer the vexing questions of the embodied soul with Eleatic solutions. What makes the *Enneads* both powerful, and at times confusing, is this combination.

It should not be surprising that Plotinus would do so. He is, from his perspective, addressing souls who are journeying through a plane of existence consistent with their spiritual level, a medium temporally extended and also spatially elongated. The outer movement of incarnate souls, to a temple to offer sacrifice for example, is a token of their inner development. And even their spiritual development is inherently temporal, for it takes time for embodied souls to learn. The spiritual movement of souls, their manifestation of moral change, is marked out by time. The urgency of this spiritual struggle is never far from the surface in the contemplative texts in the *Enneads*. In the end, however, it is not a struggle that changes the nature of reality. The One is what it is without alteration or cessation, and the soul is what it has always been, an eternal product of that One. In contemplation, the soul comes, with great effort, to recognize that compelling truth.

A passage from V.1 exhibits both modes of discourse, and indicates how Plotinus employs both religious language to make vivid the soul's contemplative development and ontological language to resolve its predicament. Here Plotinus executes a subtle transposition from the soul's spatial and temporal existence to a higher plane:

> Let us speak of it in this way, first invoking God himself, not in spoken words, but stretching ourselves out with our soul into prayer to him, able in this way to pray alone to him alone. The contemplator, then, since God exists by himself as if inside the temple, remaining quiet beyond all things, must contemplate what correspond to the images already standing outside the temple, or rather that one image which appeared first; and this is the way in which it appeared: everything which is moved must have some end to which it moves. The One has no such end, so we must not consider that it moves. If anything comes into being after it, we must think that it necessarily does so while the One remains continually turned towards itself. When we are discussing eternal realities we must not let coming into being in time be an obstacle to our thought; in the discussion we apply the word "becoming" to them in attributing to them causal connection and order, and must therefore state that what comes into being from the One does so without the One being moved.
>
> (V.1.6, 9–15)

What Plotinus recognizes here is the inadequacy of the temporal framework in which the soul is situated, for its language will distort eternal verities. Yet this discourse is also necessary, and must be used as a concession to the soul's current condition, while effort must be made to overcome its deficiencies. The language of ontology, apodictic and unchanging, is commensurate with its subject, and so provides a means for the soul to advance to a higher plane of understanding, to the level of intellect. This strategy is common in the *Enneads*, offering solutions to the problems of psychic embodiment by turning to the discourse of the intellect. This is the beginning of contemplation.

Plotinus frequently employs images whose efficacy is calibrated to our state of soul and whose truth is but a quotient of eternal reality. But our souls should not be misled by this language, attributing to these images of contemplative movement and change a misplaced concreteness. The real drama of contemplation is unobservable; it is the silent emergence of ontological understanding within the soul. At its most acute, contemplation is the recognition by the embodied soul of its true nature, rooted eternally in the One. It is, in the language of the mysteries, a salvific moment for the soul, but no real salvation is involved, no act of return, no cathartic transformation of what the soul is. It is "a kind of rest" (VI.9.11, 15–16), a securing of truth about one's nature, a discovery of eternity within the self and of its inalienable association with the One. For Plotinus, contemplation is salvation, when both are properly understood. The Eleatic ontology of the One answers the spiritual questions posed by the pagan religious mysteries.

The *Enneads* describe several instances of ontological recognition by the soul. In order to gain a better understanding of Plotinus's notion of contemplation, we might consider several passages from the great ascension text, *Ennead* VI.9. It was probably written at Rome, where Plotinus had settled after the death of his mysterious teacher in Alexandria, Ammonius Saccas, and after the failure of his efforts to reach India by joining the expedition of Gordian III to Persia. According to his biographer Porphyry, Plotinus had "converted" to philosophy at the age of about 28, in 232, and studied with Ammonius for eleven years. After many years in Rome he began to set down his views for the immediate members of his school. It was early in the troubled reign of Gallienus, around 253–255; Plotinus was around fifty.

The texts as we find them do not record "mystical experiences" in the contemporary sense; rather they represent the spiritual self's grasp of its real nature. Neither temporality nor the feelings of the soul are central to this state, only the immediate "presence of the One, which exceeds knowledge" (VI.9.4, 4). The duration of the state is not significant to Plotinus, nor are its phenomenological characteristics relevant. These would be distractions to the soul's true task, for they lie, in Plotinus's taxonomy, at the level of sense-perception. Only the inner, moral condition of the contemplative soul matters.

Yet the soul is transformed in contemplation, something that may be evinced in time by the ethical countenance of the soul and its moral behavior. But it is fundamentally a development interior to the spiritual self. It might be described as an epistemic shift and, to an extent, an enrichment of the life of the soul. But contemplation does not effect an ontological change in the soul. The One is always the omnipresent source of the self, and the nature of the self always is what it is within Intellect. The progressive unification that the soul enjoys is epistemic, not the establishment of something essentially new. The soul comes to recognize its true, higher life in connection with the One. But it does not become something else, nor does it become absorbed into the One. Its union with the One has always obtained, but it had failed to grasp this fact adequately. When the soul is able to remove the external distractions that impede its concentration on this connection to the One, then it can come to understand this hidden "communion." As we saw already,

> the soul must let go of all outward things and turn altogether to what is within, and not be inclined to any outward thing, but ignoring all things (as it did formerly in sense-perception, but then in the realm of forms), and even ignoring itself, come to be in contemplation of that One, and having been in its company and had, so to put it, sufficient converse with it, come and announce, if it could, to another that transcendent union. Perhaps also it was because Minos attained this kind of union that he was said in the story to be "the familiar friend of Zeus."
>
> (VI.9.7, 16–26)

We notice here both the characteristic Plotinian theme of interiority, one which had such impact on Augustine, and the weaving in of a traditional religious reference. But what does the real work in this passage is Plotinus's ontology, in particular the omnipresence of the One. When the soul attends only to what is interior within itself, it discovers, not its own independent nature, but rather the One, at the depth of the soul. To be a "familiar friend" of the One is to concentrate on this presence. That allows the center of the self, though still embodied, to do what "the souls of the gods always do," to center on this link to the ultimate "center of all things" (VI.9.8, 7–8 and 20).

Our problem as souls is that we fail to pay attention to the One. This is not so much a function of our embodiment as it is a result of our spiritual condition. This culpable failure to recognize the Good is the basis for our separation from it. But we can change this, restoring our vivid association more fully. Plotinus explains this overcoming of "otherness" as follows:

> That One, therefore, since it has no otherness is always present, and we are present to it when we have no otherness; and the One does not desire us, so as to be around us, but we desire it, so that we are around it. And we are always around it but do not always look to it; it is like a

choral dance: in the order of its singing the choir keeps round its conductor but may sometimes turn away, so that he is out of their sight, but when it turns back to him it sings beautifully and is truly with him; so we are always around him – and if we were not, we should be totally dissolved and no longer exist – but not always turned to him; but when we do look to him, then we are at our goal and at rest and do not sing out of tune as we truly dance our god-inspired dance around him.

(VI.9.8, 33–45)

The shift in focus that removes the "otherness" separating the One from the contemplative self is, once again, fundamentally epistemic. The soul does not become something that it was not before, nor does it lose something essential to itself. It is neither transfigured in the One, nor absorbed by it. The earlier separation is dissolved because it is only an accidental and adventitious element, the result of the soul's conferral of a false individuality upon itself. Since the One is not itself a delimited and finite being, there is nothing to forestall the soul's recognition of the One's presence. For this reason Plotinus is reluctant even to use "one" in reference to it, since this might suggest numerical distinct-ness or exclusivity (VI.9.5 and 6). Thus the progressive unification or centering described above is not the unity of two distinct substances, the One and the soul, but the discovery by the contemplative soul of its share in the One. The One is its source, the conservator of the soul's existence, so that this "ground of being" is not something to which the prodigal soul needs to re-unite. The One is the foundation of the soul's reality, that to which the soul is always connected or united. This is an awesome truth which the soul has the "shock" or the "good fortune" to recognize (VI.9.11, 4; V.5.8, 24). It is a salutory, indeed salvific, realization; a moment of spiritual enlightenment.

Contemplation, while fundamentally epistemic, does have an ontological dimension in the *Enneads*, although not one that can be construed to suggest wholesale change in the soul's character or essence. The soul becomes more real as it concentrates on the source of its reality more intently. This is clear in the following passage, in which Plotinus develops the image of a choral dance of the soul around the Good. Once again, we see the use of several different modes of discourse, both metaphysical and religious:

And in this dance the soul sees the spring of life, the spring of intellect, the principle of being, the cause of good, the root of the soul; these are not poured out from him with the result that they diminish him; for there is no bulk otherwise the things generated from him would diminish. But as it is they are eternal, because their principle remains the same, not divided up into them but abiding as a whole. So they also abide; just as the light abides if the sun abides. For we are not cut off from him or separate, even if the nature of body has intruded and

40

drawn us to itself, but we breathe and are preserved because that Good has not given its gifts and then gone away but is always bestowing them as long as it is what it is. But we exist more when we turn to him and our well-being is there, but being far from him is nothing else but existing less.

(VI.9.9, 1–13)

The contemplative soul finds no answer to its prayer except the discovery that its own eternal nature is in the presence of the Good. It need only abide in this interior communion. To do so is to become more real than the soul now is, and thus to be itself more fully. This is the promise of contemplation in the *Enneads*, the native ability of the human soul to find rest in the presence of the supreme divine being. Moreover, as Plotinus says in a later passage that reverts back to the language of the mysteries, "our true life is there, for our present life, our life without God, is a trace of life imitating that life" (VI.9.9, 15).

Plotinus goes on to remind us that this act of contemplation is what constitutes the life of the gods; to exist in contemplation of the Good is the apotheosis of the spiritual self. Having had its beginning in the One, it has its return there, when it restores its connection to that ultimate "spring of life." In this context Plotinus introduces the notion of the soul's desire for the Good. Through contemplation, the soul can put off its false self and discover its true nature in the presence of the Good. "And when it comes to be there it becomes itself and what it was, for what it is here and among the things of the world is a falling away and an exile and a 'shedding of wings'" (VI.9.9, 22–24). Having been restored to the transcendental world through contemplation, the soul's true nature comes to recognize that Good is the true object of its longing (VI.9.9, 24 ff.).

It is the basic logic of pagan monotheism that Plotinus is trading on in these depictions. The Good is distinct from the soul, in its awesome power and dignity, but its difference from the soul is not characterizable as a form of separation. Its continual conferral of existence on all things entails its omnipresence. Not having been defined as a distinct entity, however exalted, the Good excludes nothing and is never cut off from anything. Souls have only to grasp this to discern the presence of the One within themselves. Although not a finite person or thing, the Good is the proper focus of the soul's love, for the soul recognizes that it emerged from the perfection of the Good, adorned by whatever slim share of beauty it has received. To love the Good is thus a higher love, distinct in its very logic from the love we can accord to any finite thing, whether an intelligible form or an embodied soul. It is the most noble and inexorable desire, the lure of souls:

For since the soul is other than God but comes from him it is necessarily in love with him . . . The soul then in her natural state is in

love with God and wants to be united with him; it is like the noble
love of a girl for her noble father.

(VI.9.9, 26–27 and 33–34)

These images help to clarify the special theism of Plotinus, in which the Good
is at once immediately present and yet also a distant goal. To exist is to be drawn
to the Good, for to exist is to be associated with it. Contemplation heightens
this unification, as the soul purifies itself of all that is extraneous to its ultimate
love, the Good. Plotinus trades off both the image of erotic closure and the logic
of omnipresence as he explains what being "united" with the One entails:

> But there is our true love, with whom also we can be united, having
> a part in him and truly possessing him, not embracing him in the flesh
> from outside. But "whoever has seen, knows what I am saying", that
> the soul then has another life and draws near, and has already come
> near and has a part in him, and so is in a state to know that the giver
> of true life is present and we need nothing more. But quite otherwise,
> we must put away other things and take our stand only in this, and
> become this alone, cutting away all the other things in which we are
> encased; so we must be eager to go out from here and be impatient
> at being bound to the other things, that we may embrace him with
> the whole of ourselves and have no part with which we do not touch
> God. There one can see both him and oneself as it is right to see: the
> self glorified, full of intelligible light – but rather itself pure light –
> weightless, floating free, having become – but rather, being – a god;
> set on fire then, but the fire seems to go out if one is weighed down
> again.

(VI.9.9, 44–61)

The "other life" of the soul comes about by excising all the accretions of
its embodied existence. Then is the self revealed to be divine, having come to
grasp both its own true nature and the Good directly and without distortion.
The soul's embrace of the One requires concentration on its inner core, in order
to discern fully its share in the One. In contemplation, the soul takes on a kind
of lucidity, becoming transparent to itself in the translucent presence of the One.
It becomes "pure light" and "a god." These images are classically Hellenic and
traditionally Platonic: the soul's apotheosis, its share in the divine, its destiny
to associate with the gods, its place in the intelligible corona of the divine Sun.
They are balanced against the language of unification used throughout the
chapter.

Plotinus intensifies this notion of union with the Good in Chapters 10 and
11 of *Ennead* VI.9. The entire discussion is a splendid example of Plotinian
interweaving of ontology with religious discourse, combined with a deep
suspicion of the very images he is employing. These passages invite the reader

to focus on the soul's deep association with the Good that the contemplative self has discovered. In the foreground of previous analysis has been the self-disclosure that the contemplative soul enjoys as a result of its interior association with the One. Now Plotinus considers this union from a quite different standpoint:

> When therefore the seer sees himself, then when he sees, he will see himself as like this, or rather he will be in union with himself as like this and will be aware of himself as like this since he has become single and simple. But perhaps one should not say "will see", but "was seen", if one must speak of these as two, the seer and the seen, and not both as one – a bold statement. So then the seer does not see and does not distinguish and does not imagine two, but it is as if he had become someone else and he is not himself and does not count as his own there, but has come to belong to that and so is one, having joined, as it were centre to centre. For here too when the centres have come together they are one, but there is duality when they separate. This also is how we now speak of "another". For this reason the vision is hard to put into words. For how could one announce that as another when he did not see, there when he had the vision, another, but one with himself?
>
> (VI.9.10, 9–21)

This *tolmeros logos*, this bold statement, suggests that the duality of seer and seen is not really appropriate to contemplation of the One. And indeed, we should not expect that it would be, for the One is not an entity that can be seen, even intelligibly. It is not a thing, but the first principle; as the infinite foundation of the seer, it cannot be seen. For the soul cannot secure any vantage point from which to inspect the ground of its own being. When the seer discovers its root within the One, the soul is not contemplating the One as something distinct from itself, but is rather discovering its deep fundamental unity with it. The contemplative soul concentrates on this closure with the One. This is the apex of contemplation, which can only to be articulated in the dualistic imagery of finite human discourse.

Union with the One is extraordinary in Plotinus, not because it occurs, but because it is usually neglected by our souls. The basic ontological relation upon which this recognition is based is continuous and eternal. Yet this failure to realize the presence of the One is partly a function of bodily existence for the "vision" might more easily be continuous when the soul is liberated from the body by death (VI.9.10, 4). But it is also a matter of moral attention. The soul changes only to the extent that it comes to learn about its place in the hierarchy of being and its immense dignity, the latency of the Good within it. This is accessible to the soul whenever it wishes. Then it can first see itself in relation to the One, and then find its point of union with that "spring of life." This is a quiet transition, one that uncovers the deep ontological structure underlying the self. There is no real journey to be made, only attention to the soul's divine source.

Plotinus reiterates this theme of the union of the seer and seen and underscores the quietude of contemplation in the final chapter of the treatise:

> This is the intention of the command given in the mysteries here below not to disclose to the uninitiated; since the Good is not disclosable, it prohibits the declaration of the divine to another who has not also himself had the good fortune to see. Since, then, there were not two, but the seer himself was one with the seen (for it was not really seen, but united to him), if he remembers who he became when he was united with that, he will have an image of that in himself. He was one himself, with no distinction in himself either in relation to himself or to other things – for there was no movement in him and he had no emotion, no desire for anything else when he made the ascent – but there was not even any reason or thought, and he himself was not there, if we must even say this; but he was as if carried away or possessed by a god, in a quiet solitude and a state of calm, not turning away anywhere in his being and not busy about himself, altogether at rest and having become a kind of rest.
>
> (VI.9.11, 1–16)

Privileged access is invoked because contemplation is a performative sort of knowledge, a moral and spiritual transformation that is non-transferable to other souls. Plotinus begins by introducing the image of sacred disclosure. But once again, it is the underlying union of the soul and the Good that is under review. Plotinus uses the term "united," *henōmenon* (VI.9.11, 6), but at the same time he rejects any suggestion of essential change. The "ascent" is, paradoxically, static, free of movement by the soul or even emotion. The unobserved union of seer and seen is discovered, not effected, by contemplation. This state is first described in vibrant religious language, such as "possession" and "abduction," but these images are then corrected in the static light of the ontology of the One.

We are then invited to reflect on a temple sanctuary, and in its vestibule there is the statuary of the god (VI.9.11, 16 ff.). But within the inner shrine one can encounter the god himself. But this is still an inadequate visual image, since Plotinus is discussing is "another kind of seeing, a being out of oneself and simplifying and giving oneself over and pressing towards contact and rest and a sustained thought leading to adaptation" (VI.9.11, 22–25). This is the only certain use of ekstasis, ecstasy, in the *Enneads*. Plotinus reminds us again that these are all images, and that the "wise priest" will know that the sanctuary is actually invisible. The vision of its "source and principle" is possible only if the soul has been transformed. The wise priest understands "that he sees principle by principle and that like is united with like" (VI.9.11, 28 ff.). Contemplation is no adventitious episode, but is the result of a moral transformation of the soul, leading to this unitive knowledge of the Good.

Plotinus concludes this great treatise on contemplation with a reprise of its major themes. Moral advance and cognitive disclosure are to the fore, while the language of psychic movement is again a variation over the dominant ontological theme:

> it [the soul] will arrive, not at something else but at itself, and in this way since it is not in something else it will not be in nothing, but in itself; but when it is in itself alone and not in being, it is in that; for one becomes, not substance, but "beyond substance" by this converse. If then one sees that oneself has become this, one has oneself as a likeness of that, and if one goes on from oneself, as image to original, one has reached "the end of the journey". And when one falls from the vision, he wakes again the virtue in himself, and considering himself set in order and beautiful by these virtues he will again be lightened and come through virtue to Intellect and wisdom and through wisdom to the Good. This is the life of gods and of godlike and blessed men, deliverance from the things of this world, a life which takes no delight in the things of this world, escape in solitude to the solitary.
>
> (VI.9.11, 38–51)

Recognition of its underlying union with the One confronts the soul with the paradox of contemplation: discovery of the true self in relation to the One reveals it to be but an image of its source. A reverberative dualism thus echoes throughout the *Enneads*: union with the One reminds the soul that it is not the infinite One. Contemplation cannot erase the underlying facts of ontology; indeed, it exposes them. The One is the infinite ground of the being; the soul a finite and eternal emanation, ever linked to its source, ever removed in its finitude from the One. This gulf defines the theology of Plotinus. And while the soul is said to fall away from its vision of the One, this is not the basis for Plotinus's distinction of the soul and the One. Rather the soul's loss of vision merely follows the tracks of Plotinus's monotheistic ontology, for the soul is not the One. However tightly bound to the One, however united to the Good, it remains eternally finite.

The *Enneads* articulate, therefore, a coherent version of pagan monotheism. Behind the manifest image of earthly life, Plotinus discerns an ultimate divine Good. The foundation of all reality, it is that from which all finite entities emerge. There are always levels of reality emergent and distinct from the One. Yet the very fact of their existence betokens the Good's continued presence. Each human soul has within it the capacity, at least in principle, to discern the presence of the divine One within itself. For the spiritual self can grasp the recondite harmony of reality, the eternal symmetry of procession and return.

This is what contemplation initially offers: recognition of the self's eternal place in the nature of things. Contemplation begins with discovery of transcendence by the soul, along with some measure of visionary dreariness, the simultaneous discernment of eternity juxtaposed with exigencies of embodied existence. It culminates in a deeper transcendence, as the soul discovers the presence of the Good, beyond even the eternal and intelligible self.

Thus in the *Enneads* contemplation is a matter of cognitive disclosure and metaphysical insight. The Good is discovered to be immediately present to the soul. Moreover the enlightment that contemplation confers upon the soul is also salvific, for the soul learns that it is among the intelligibles in their eternal station around the One, and hence that it is in union with the One. Only the degree of this recognition can change. Contemplation thus ennobles the soul by revealing a personal eschatology already realized. Neither a "turning" nor an "activity," contemplation is a "quiet solitude," a "state of calm," a "kind of rest." The soul needs no savior beyond itself. It is saved by its very existence in the presence of the Good. When freed by death from embodied existence, the contemplative soul can remain as a god among the intelligibles, there to enjoy the closest possible relation with the Good. In the *Enneads*, this is "the end of the journey," to be alone with the alone.

Part II

VISION AT OSTIA

The *Confessions* is perhaps the most compelling work of patristic literature, at once religious autobiography and narrative theology. It is a piece of a larger project of Christian self-definition, a first-person depiction of the pilgrim's importunate encounters with a level of being that transcends the fallen world and with the author of all reality. *Confessions* is an essentially Christian text, a Catholic reading of the soul's capacity to discover wisdom and to recognize with felicity its deepest hopes. And it is a story that unfolds with personal intensity unprecedented in ancient literature, compelling the reader to weigh the cogency of its spiritual claims and to assess the state of the reader's own soul. That too seems part of Augustine's purpose. For the *Confessions* is – in the end – about God and the soul. It is the dialogue of Augustine's soul with God overheard for our benefit. He tells us, in his *Soliloquia*, written at Cassiciacum in 386 before his baptism, that he sought only to know two things: God and the soul (*Soliloquia* I.ii.7). The great ascension texts of the *Confessions* chart the geography of that relationship and articulate Augustine's mature Christian grasp of the depth of the soul and the presence of an immaterial God. We shall begin with these accounts and watch closely Augustine's treatment of Platonism.

4

BOOKS OF THE PLATONISTS

"At that time, after reading the books of the Platonists and learning from them to seek for immaterial truth, I turned my attention to your 'invisible nature understood through the things which are made'" (VII.xx (26)). Platonism was the intellectual catalyst that initiated his conversion to orthodox Christianity. On Augustine's account, he had been unable to conceive of a reality that transcends the physical world until he discovered these books. It is telling that he could plausibly make this claim. Despite his acquaintance through the years with orthodox Christianity, it had failed to convey to him a firm recognition of immaterial truth. He found that insight instead, he says, in pagan philosophy.

The historical details of Augustine's early theological development are difficult to recover. But it is clear that the very idea of God's transcendence of the physical cosmos was something that came to him with some effort, either through a direct encounter with pagan Platonism, or through its mediated exposure under the direction of Ambrose and his Christian Platonic circle in Milan. However this story is written, one fact is salient: divine transcendence is portrayed by Augustine as a discovery, something that he had not grasped through his exposure to orthodox Christianity throughout his youth and early adulthood. This larger fact must be kept in view, for it lurks behind Augustine's growing disenchantment with the religious materialism that he had adopted during his student days, Manichaeism. The Manichees were not alone in their inability to recognize a transcendent God.

Augustine had been a Manichee until he found the Platonist books. He had practiced an esoteric, heterodox, and formally proscribed Christian sect. Manichaeism had Persian origins and proposed as its salient credendum a type of "conflict dualism," that is, a thesis about two opposite principles at the core of reality. A power of goodness and light was locked in a cosmic clash with the power of evil and darkness. Curiously the light was a passive principle, unable to resist in a forceful way the powers of darkness. But this cosmology was not meant metaphorically. It was as much physics as metaphysics. The two powers were identified literally as the actual forces that make up the physical cosmos, with the sun as the central locus of goodness. Manichees understood themselves to contain a ruined fragment of that primal light within themselves. They could escape at death by means of this inner energy and rendezvous with other light-filled souls on a post-mortem journey through the physical heavens. Their coalescence at the moon occasioned its periodic waxing; their subsequent departure to brighter heavenly stations produced its waning. As Peter Brown has observed: "No religious system, indeed, had ever treated the visible world so drastically, and with such literalism, as an externalization of an inner, spiritual conflict" (Brown 2000: 46).

For Augustine it was this attenuated materialism of Manichean theology that was its most misleading feature. As he matured intellectually, Augustine came to believe that Manichean dualism was a deep conceptual failure of the religious imagination:

> When I wanted to think of God, I knew of no way of doing so except as a physical mass. Nor did I think anything existed which is not material. That was the principal and almost sole cause of my inevitable error.
>
> (V.x.19)

What Platonism offered was a philosophically sophisticated and culturally prestigious account of an immaterial level of reality. The school of Plotinus had refined its Platonism with Stoic materialism in view. Its theology was also explicitly developed in opposition to some other types of ancient dualism, maintained both within the Platonic tradition and by "gnostic" sectarians who attended the lectures of Plotinus (Armstrong 1966: 45–47). The Platonists books that came to him were thus ideally suited as an antidote to Manichaeism and especially well qualified as authoritative sources for its refutation.

Not to Manichaeism alone were those pagan books a palliative. For materialism was not confined to exotic Christian sects like the Manichees. The notion that Christianity was about events that have occurred or will occur entirely within the physical cosmos was common enough among sophisticated and uneducated Christians alike. Tertullian, the North African rhetorician of the late second and early third centuries, is a good example of a refined Christian materialist. Several trajectories within early Christianity, especially among the more apocalyptic schools like the Montanists, were naturally conducive to such thought. There was a burden of proof for Christians like Augustine to articulate with persuasive clarity how the core credenda of orthodox Christianity were really about a world beyond the reaches of the physical cosmos, that the "things visible and invisible" of the Creed of Nicaea referred to immaterial things beyond space and time. This was Augustine's task in the *Confessions*, not only to refute the determined materialism of the Manicheans but to render transcendentalism convincing for orthodoxy.

He was not alone in this Christian transcendentalist program. Along with other Catholic intellectuals of his age, like Ambrose or the Cappadocians, Augustine found in pagan Platonism a powerful metaphysics, one that made the Christian scriptures intelligible and personally compelling. The "almost sole error" of materialism was thus made not just by Manichees but also by those Christians whose literalist readings of the Bible had so offended him (V.xiv (24)). They too were caught in the net of his argument in the *Confessions*, if only indirectly and in a politic fashion. But the effort to secure a transcendentalist reading of Christianity was a much larger one than it appears on the polemical surface of Augustine's text. This fact helps to explain the significance he assigned to the *libri Platonicorum*.

There is another point that bears reflection regarding Augustine's some-times puzzling emphasis on pagan Platonism. For modern readers the spiritual equation of Augustine's spiritual life never seems to balance, at least as he tells it. At face value this is the story of a precocious North African rhetorician who begins life with a mixed pagan and Catholic parentage, becomes a heterodox Manichean Christian, encounters pagan Platonism, and is so impressed that he then becomes a Catholic Christian. The missing value behind the perplexing surface of this tale is the transcendentalism of the Platonists. The equation of Augustine's spiritual life only balances if this shift from Christian materialism – whether orthodox or heterodox – to transcendentalism is kept in view. Yet pagan Platonism itself is never represented in the *Confessions* as being a live religious option, nor is pagan polytheistic cult depicted as having any appeal. Platonism's significance was in offering decisive philosophical and cultural support for belief in immaterial reality.

The great peripety in late antique culture was the apparently sudden transition from polytheism to monotheism. This too can be seen beneath the surface of the *Confessions*. Once again the Platonism of the Plotinian school was an ally and a resource in Augustine's portrayal of orthodox Christian monotheism. The Platonic theology of Plotinus provided a philosophical endorsement of monotheism, and its theodicy provided a direct refutation of Manichean dual-ism. The Plotinian notion of degrees of reality emerging from the One helped Augustine to grasp the insubstantiality of evil. This "privation theory of evil" held that evil is not a substance or energy separate from the Good. Evil is not independent or real in its own right. Its existence depends entirely on the Good. Various theses were then advanced to explain the emergence of evil as a fact of life. Several related accounts can be found in the *Enneads*, notably the fall theory mentioned in Chapter 1 from V.1. On this thesis, evil is the result of the audacity of souls who chose to distance themselves from the One. This "free-will" explanation for evil relies on the primary insight that evil is not a substantial power independent from the Good, but only an epiphenom-enon. The riddle of evil was thus solved for Augustine by Plotinus and the plausibility of Manichean dualistic theology, with its warring powers, was dissolved. The monotheistic Plotinian system of degrees of reality culminating in the One obviated any need to postulate an evil substance opposed to the Good. Platonism provided to Augustine the metaphysics and the theodicy needed to make monotheism coherent and intelligible. As in the case of immateriality, Platonism offered the conceptual foundations for Augustine's turn to Christian monotheism.

"Plotinus was an immortal wound for Augustine . . ." (Bloom 2002: 88). Yet Augustine's *Confessions* is not a Neoplatonist treatise. What Plotinus offered him was the philosophical underpinnings from which to begin his articulation of transcendentalist Christianity and the cultural warrant for some of the main outlines of monotheism. How deep was this immortal Plotinian wound? The answer is complex. The short response is that Augustine did not follow the Platonism of Plotinus in his theology; indeed, he developed an alternative theology in explicit contrast to it. We do not find Plotinus's theology of the ineffable One in evidence in the *Confessions*, nor an undescended self upon which salvation rests, nor the salvific efficacy of contemplation. In short, Augustine's theology in the *Confessions* is not Platonism baptized. Yet the Plotinian wound was real enough. It challenged Augustine to reflect deeply upon the most sophisticated philosophical theology of late antiquity. From this experience he derived the conceptual basis to refine his own thinking. The most obvious element of this encounter was his adoption of a Platonic transcendentalism, the commitment to degrees of reality that was the common property of all the late antique Platonist schools. In addition was the Plotinian assertion of a single first principle, the acceptance of monotheism. When combined, these two Plotinian insights dissolved the problem of evil, making it possible for Augustine to move beyond Manichaeism. Yet both of these metaphysical doctrines would be substantially revised in the *Confessions* under the force of Augustine's new theology.

While the books of the Platonists came to Augustine from an unnamed pagan thinker "puffed up with monstrous pride" (VII.ix(13)), they also came with the sponsorship of Saint Ambrose and his Catholic circle in Milan. They had been translated by Marius Victorinus, the aristocratic rhetorician whose conversion to Catholicism became paradigmatic for Augustine. So the Platonist books were themselves multivalent, already approved within the Christian intellectual elite and understood as forming a philosophical alliance with their brand of orthodox Christianity. Augustine read the works of the Plotinian school, and not those of its Platonic rivals. This fact matters considerably. When Porphyry began his *Life of Plotinus*, he announced that his master was "the philosopher of our times." Yet this was a partisan claim, for there were several other Platonic schools scattered around the Roman world. Each offered its own strain of Platonism, with slightly variant theologies and different degrees of enthusiasm for pagan cultic observances.

Within the school of Plotinus, however, there was general agreement on the main outlines of Platonic philosophy and support for the innovations of the master. These included in particular the doctrine of the undescended soul, the theory that the forms are not outside the divine intellect, and the postulation of an ineffable One. While religious practices varied among members of the school, there was a foundational level of doctrinal orthodoxy which served as the basis for further individual variations. We can see this in Porphyry's *Life of Plotinus* 18 (Armstrong 1966: 49–51), where Porphyry describes how he changed his previous position on the relation of the intelligibles to the divine intellect when he came to Rome from the school of Athens. He then wrote a recantation of his earlier views, read it to the members of the school, and thereafter "believed in Plotinus's writings."

All this matters for the study of the *Confessions* because we need to be clear on the school that served as the sounding board for Augustine's discussion of Platonism in Book Seven. One would like to know exactly what his Platonic syllabus was as an historical matter. But from the standpoint of Augustine's theology, the issue can be overstated with respect to the school of Plotinus itself. There were, of course, some minor differences between Plotinus and Porphyry, but none were really fundamental. Porphyry developed his own thought during the years after Plotinus's death in opposition to the rival Platonic school of Iamblichus. While Iamblichus emphasized a more hierarchical version of Platonism, Porphyry emphasized the continuous relationships that obtain among levels of reality.

Porphyry "telescoped" the hypostases, and concentrated on their mutual inherence (Lloyd in Armstrong 1967: 287–293). Thus he treated the soul, the intellect, and the One as being closely interconnected, rather than considering them to be sharply distinct. This approach is consistent with that of Plotinus. Indeed later pagan Platonists largely followed the more hierarchical model of Iamblichus and considered Plotinus and Porphyry as together defining a common, alternative approach. The doctrinal differences within the school of Plotinus seem then to have been negligible, in comparison with its scholastic rivals.

Behind the divergence in metaphysics between the schools of Plotinus and Iamblichus lies a more significant issue: a debate about the efficacy of philosophical contemplation, *theōria*. Was contemplation, achieved through the practice of the philosophic life, sufficient for the soul's re-association with the eternal world of the forms and with the One? For Iamblichus it was not. He and his influential followers, who would include the Emperor Julian the Apostate, regarded the Plotinian school's notion of a higher, undescended self as a mistaken innovation. For Iamblichus the soul did descend entirely into the material world. In consequence the soul required much greater assistance to restore it to its original level than the practice of philosophy could furnish. The true means to salvation was "theurgy," the practice of pagan ritual designed to effect the soul's return to a higher realm.

"The philosopher is the savior of himself." Such was the view of Porphyry, articulated in his *De Abstinentia* (11.49.2). That was the position of Plotinus as well. For Plotinus, theurgy was of no interest to the philosopher and of no help for the salvation of lesser souls. Porphyry generally agreed with his master on this larger point, but admitted a slightly more significant role for theurgy. Unlike Plotinus, Porphyry did not regard the soul's descent into matter as partly a product of its *tolma*, its moral culpability. The soul for Porphyry did not so much fall into the world as decline to this lower level because of the inherent pattern of emanation from the One. It was on account of the primordial rhythm of reality that souls find themselves embodied. The great coils of the psychic declension and ascension were eternal and the individual human self fit into the pattern. The soul could slowly make its way back to its source through its many incarnations. Theurgy had a place in the life of lesser souls who were not yet ready to practice philosophy. It might prepare them for that culminating spiritual task or enhance the moral quality of their lives here below. Even so, Porphyry agreed with Plotinus on the salvific efficacy of contemplation, even if he is less sanguine than his teacher about the ability of lesser souls to succeed at it unaided. Thus he allowed a role for the pagan sacraments of salvation, apparently to aid souls in their conversion to contemplation. But Porphyry, like Plotinus, denied that the soul can ascend to the One through theurgy. That higher ascent was reserved for philosophical contemplation alone.

There was, therefore, a significant debate among the Platonists of late antiquity regarding the salvific efficacy of contemplation. Augustine was aware primarily of the Plotinian school both in 386–387 and at the time he wrote the *Confessions*. We find a pejorative reference to theurgy, as a catalyst for contemplation, at X.xlii (67). But we are not in a position to achieve a finely grained picture of Augustine's understanding of this great scholastic division within paganism. We do not know what he knew and when he knew it (O'Donnell 1992: xlv–xlv(11)). Yet one intriguing by-product of the debate relates directly to Augustine's depictions of his own contemplative experiences in the *Confessions*. Porphyry is at pains in his *Life of Plotinus* 23 to demonstrate that Plotinus achieved the highest levels of contemplation during his lifetime and that he was, in fact, united with the One through contemplation while Porphyry was present. "To Plotinus 'the goal ever near was shown': for his end and goal was to be united to, to approach the God who is over all things. Four times while I was with him he attained that goal, in an unspeakable actuality and not in potency only." Moreover Porphyry offers further autobiographical witness on his own behalf that he had succeeded in being united with the One. "I, Porphyry, who am now in my sixty-eighth year, declare that once I drew near and was united to him." The polemic point is quite apparent. Porphyry can certify the efficacy of contemplation because he can cite the occasions when he and Plotinus each achieved this goal. His opponents underestimated the power of contemplation, at least for great-souled philosophers like himself and his master.

These personal descriptions of specific occasions of contemplation and their dramatic success became part of the lore that established the reputation of Plotinus as the great pagan "holy man." Augustine may well have discovered this portrait by reading a translation of the *Life of Plotinus*. But even if he did not, he surely would have known about Plotinus's reputation as the philosopher whose contemplative life had brought him into the immediate presence of the

One. Thus a subtle trajectory can be traced back from the *Confessions*, with its autobiographic episodes of contemplation, to Porphyry's story of Plotinus. It is to Porphyry's portrait of his own contemplative experiences and those of Plotinus that we can trace the special focus that Augustine gives to specific episodes as warrants for the veracity of his theology.

Augustine's accounts of contemplation, introduced in Book Seven, nest in the larger Platonic discussion about the nature of human transcendence and the capacity of the soul to renew its grasp on eternity through contemplation. The issues were momentous in the larger religious culture of his time, and Augustine offered his ancient readers an orthodox Christian depiction of contemplation in sharp contrast to that of the Plotinians. In doing so he was allying Christian orthodoxy with the school of Plotinus on the larger questions of transcendence and monotheism. But he was also breaking from it regarding the nature of contemplation, aligning his views with the opponents of the Plotinians who represented the wider consensus among the Platonists of the period. We cannot tell to what extent he was aware of this recondite harmony.

"And I had come to you from the Gentiles" (VII.ix (15)). In Augustine's retrospection, the story of his conversion seems inexorable, yet its theological progression is odd. This peculiarity is not disguised, but featured. For pagan texts catalyze his change of religious conscience from heterodox to orthodox Christianity. Augustine is at pains to underscore the tacit alliance that he has discerned between Platonism and Christianity. He insists that the books of the Platonists were a mixture of cultic polytheism together with philosophical monotheism. At VII.ix (15) the text contrasts two aspects of the pagan heritage: the Egyptian, representing polytheism, and the Athenian, representing pagan monotheism. Recalling Saint Paul's address to the Areopagus, he suggests that the better aspect of paganism was its commitment to "the unknown God," understood as the One or Good of Platonism. In reading the books of the Platonists Augustine believes he has found the golden, Athenian element of the pagan tradition, one that demonstrates that God had called the Gentiles into his inheritance. As Augustine puts it: "Athens is where the books (of the Platonists) came from" (VII.ix (15)).

Thus Augustine employs the books of the Platonists to sketch out the alliance of Athens and Jerusalem, of two sorts of monotheism. The enemy is the polytheism of Egypt. The *Confessions* are, in this respect, a record of a momentous confluence in late antique culture between Christian and pagan monotheism. The success of monotheism was the result, therefore, not of the efforts of Christianity and Judaism alone. It was the Athenian element in the Greco-Roman tradition, its pagan monotheism, which bore a share in this transition. Augustine makes this alliance with Platonism a particular token of Book Seven, using both the ideas and their cultural origins to singular effect. He had suggested, in his encounter with the Manichean bishop Faustus in Book Five, that it was his reading in the philosophers that led him to doubt the intellectual adequacy of Manichaeism even while he was still a member. Repeatedly he maintains that he had been unable to think of God except in material terms (V.x (19)). This text bears repeating:

> When I wanted to think of my God, I knew of no way of doing so except as a physical mass. Nor did I think anything existed which was not material. That was the principal and almost sole cause of my inevitable error.

Transcendentalism – belief in an immaterial world at a higher level of reality – is the principal and sole solution to his Manichean materialism. The Platonist books offered not just intriguing metaphysical theories, but also the support of rational arguments, and an ethical program to realize within the soul the promise of transcendence. It is remarkable that Augustine so explicitly attributes the source of his crucial understanding to pagan Platonism. Clearly his ingenuousness in this regard fits a larger purpose: to supply a culturally prestigious ally for transcendentalist Christianity. Yet what is also surprising about the *Confessions* is how little actual Platonic theology can be found there. Rather than presenting a christened version of Plotinus, Augustine proceeds instead by asserting the congruence of Platonism and Christianity, but doing so through the use of largely Christian language. He insists, moreover, that this Christian reading was his understanding of the *libri Platonicorum* at the time that he first read them.

Augustine gives an inventory of his discoveries in the Platonist books at VII.ix (13–15). Each Platonist thesis is given in correspondence with a Christian one, and in a predominantly Christian key. As he says in reference to the *libri Platonicorum*: "There I read, not of course in these words, but with entirely the same sense and supported by numerous and varied reasons. . . ." Some of the elements he discerns are the following:

(a) The Platonists teach the existence of God and his creative Word. Augustine refers to John 1:1–5.
(b) They hold that the human soul is not this light, which is the Word.
(c) The Word is a direct product of God.
(d) The Word is, by nature, God.
(e) Souls are renewed by participation in this Wisdom abiding in them.

This is an unusual collection of ideas to derive from readings works from Plotinus and his followers. It indicates how thoroughly Augustine's understanding of Platonism was Christian and driven by his own acute desire to understand the issues before him. We must not forget that he was never a scholar, nor was he ever formally trained in a Platonist school. Both his reading and his representation of Platonism were idiosyncratic and intensely Christian. Nor can that Christian reading be easily dismissed as a retrospective one. It is not only firmly presented in the *Confessions* as his means of understanding

Platonism, it is also consistently found in the earliest discussions that we have of Platonism in his first works. We will discuss this issue in the initial section of Chapter 3.

This catalogue of Platonic elements is presented by Augustine simply as the personal preparation of his pilgrim's soul for conversion. These were the ideas that helped him to break from Manichaeism and gave him the rudiments of a philosophical monotheism. That metaphysical framework was subsequently filled in as he learned more fully about the Christian revelation. Platonism seems at this point in the text less as a rival theology than as a stripped down form of monotheism, without the fullness of Christianity. Christianity is the fulfillment of the metaphysical promise of pagan Platonism, which it has now superseded. But an underlying sense of competition is also present, for the Platonists are still "those who, like actors, wear the high boots of a supposedly more sublime teaching" (VII.ix (14)). Nonetheless it was this Athenian element of paganism which set the stage for the first ascension episode recorded at *Confessions* VII.x (16).

Confessions VII.x (16) is commonly read as an unsuccessful mystical experience, as a failed attempt at Plotinian ecstasy. But in the narrative of the *Confessions* its place is at once less dramatic and more significant than that. Unlike the later Ostia episode in Book Nine, it is not given high relief. We are told neither the exact time nor location, but are instead located largely conceptually. This is what transpired in the life of a disaffected Manichee when he read the books of the Platonists. That approach lends the account a rather general character and a certain prescriptive force, suggesting that the theological transition from materialism to transcendentalism is universalizable. To understand the passage we might examine it in three parts, beginning with the initial introspective ascent:

> By the Platonic books I was admonished to return into myself. With you as my guide I entered into my innermost citadel, and was given the power to do so because you had become my helper. I entered and with my soul's eye, such as it was, saw above that same eye of my soul the immutable light higher than my mind – not the light of everyday, obvious to anyone, nor a larger version of the same kind which would, as it were, have given out a much brighter light and filled everything with its magnitude. It was not that light, but a different thing, utterly different from all our kinds of light. It transcended my mind, not in the way that oil floats on water, nor as heaven is above earth. It was superior because it made me, and I was inferior because I was made by it.

We are reminded directly of the *Enneads*: the awakening to the interior self, the inner light beyond the surface of consciousness, the sense of interior depth and disclosure. This act of deep introspection also exhibits the self's ontological dependence on a deeper source. All this can indeed be found in the books of the Platonists. Yet there are several immediate differences. The *oculus animae* achieves a revelatory insight not into its own transcendent self, and then into the One, but directly of a light that is clearly distinct from it and also productive of it. Nor are the intimacy of direct address and the sense of personal divine guidance Platonic. And divine intervention is involved at the incipience of transcendence, suggesting a much greater degree of removal from the eternal world. For the soul has no native claim on the *lux incommutablis* and no natural means of attaining it. Here the inner ascent is plainly to a power separate from the soul, yet still distant enough to have heard the plaintive prayers of the pilgrim soul. Even in this initial instance when the power of Plotinian Platonism is most direct, transcendence is presented in accordance with the logic of a different type of monotheism. It is the God of the Psalter who is the helper of the soul.

Augustine then continues his depiction of this instance of Christian interiority as follows:

> The person who knows the truth knows it, and he who knows it knows eternity. Love knows it. Eternal truth and true love and beloved eternity: you are my God. To you I sigh "day and night." When I first came to know you, you raised me up to make me see that what I saw is Being, and that I who saw am not yet Being. And you gave a shock to the weakness of my sight by the strong radiance of your rays, and I trembled with love and awe. And I found myself far from you "in the region of dissimilarity," and heard as it were your voice from on high: "I am the food of the fully grown; grow and you will feed on me. And you will not change me into you like the food your flesh eats, but you will be changed into me."

The text offers a critical cognitive advance: the soul now grasps fully its own contingency, and this leads to the shocking recognition that it has an eternal source. Moreover, that source is known through love and discovered to be the power of love that has drawn the soul to this very moment of discovery. That realization means that the source of the soul has, as it were, a metaphysical location sufficiently distinct from the soul to permit this expression. And it means, moreover, that the God who loves the soul can reveal his existence in a mode that the soul can recognize. This aspect of the Augustinian account differs fundamentally from Plotinian contemplation. The logic of Plotinian theism does not permit this sense of distance, yet that is the salient element in Augustine's depiction. "Beloved eternity" and "true love" describe the referent of this contemplation, intimating what God may be said to be. The Augustinian soul trembles with love and awe, awakened to the promise of eternity by an act of God. Raised up to a level of reality not its own, the soul simultaneously and forcefully grasps both the eternal being of God and the contingency of its own existence. Thus the shock of contemplation proceeds as much the recognition of the soul's fundamental distance from God as from the disclosure of being itself. And so the essential nature of contemplation for the pilgrim soul consists paradoxically both of dissimilarity and association. It is also an act that has a direct source in the intervention of its transcendent object. In language charged with eucharistic imagery, the divine voice promises that the soul will be changed into God. Here hope is found that the soul may, at the behest of God, close the distance that separates them. None of this can be found in the books of the Platonists.

Augustine concludes this passage with the distant voice of the God of Exodus and a consequent rejection of the Manichean notion of divine extension.

> And I recognized that "because of iniquity you discipline man" and cause my soul to waste away like a spider's web and I said: "Surely truth cannot be nothing, when it is not diffused through space, either finite of infinite?" And you cried from far away: "Now, I am who I am." I heard in the way one hears in the heart, and all doubt left me. I would have found it easier to doubt whether I was myself alive than there is no truth "understood from the things that are made."

The passage's transition from the divine discipline of souls and the diffusion of truth in space is initially opaque. Augustine's point is that God exists as a power outside the physical cosmos, who acts upon the soul from afar. God is not a power or energy diffused within space, as Manichees conceived the Good to be. This recognition of the reality of God is the central insight of this contemplative episode. From it Augustine emerges with an absolute conviction that God – as true being – is the core of reality. In comparison his existence pales in its contingency. The truth of contemplation is thus immediate, non-inferential, apodictical, and indubitable.

As it stands this initial ascension narrative defies phenomenological analysis. What could be identified as the raw data of this experience, or as a simple description of the experience? Even the emotions mentioned, like love or awe, are themselves embedded in the cognition that Augustine achieves. No doubt there are levels of interpretation here, but there is no self-evident rule that could disclose which concepts or phrases were the result of incorporated interpretation, which emerged as spontaneous interpretations at the time of the event, and which came later, during the composition of the *Confessions*. We have only the account that is before us. What it records is a powerful experience of a transcendent God, whose intervention into the life of the soul makes the existence of that God indubitable. It is clearly a successful moment of direct understanding which dispels completely both the Manichean view of reality and dissolves any lingering skepticism that Augustine entertained while his convictions as a Manichee were waning.

The modern critical judgment that this episode is a failed attempt at Plotinian ecstasy is strangely misguided. Although Platonic metaphysics defines Augustine's representation of transcendence, the basic structure of this instance of contemplation is not fundamentally Plotinian, but Christian. For the God that emerges as indubitable has an ontological location sharply distinct from the soul, yet he is also active in closing that gap. Moreover contemplation is not an act of recovery, not the awaking to a forgotten but eternal self, not the reassuring discovery of the presence of the One at the depth of the soul. It is instead profoundly disquieting, exhibiting the soul's state as a contingent and fallen being. Yet there is reassurance here as well, as the soul discerns the voice of God calling at its depth. The God who calls from afar is also attentive to the soul's plight. Contemplation is thus represented according to a different theistic grammar than that of Plotinus. Augustine succeeds in discovering a God of Being and of Love, whose existence he will never be able thereafter to doubt. It is upon this critical insight – catalyzed by the books of the Platonists – that the subsequent theological narrative will be constructed.

5

A TREMBLING GLANCE

In the first chapter of Romans, St. Paul recounts his indebtedness to the wisdom of the ancient Greeks. Although salvation is only available through the gospel of Christ, nonetheless the Greeks had access to the truth. This truth had been made manifest to them by God. "For the invisible things of him from the creation of the world are clearly seen, being understood by the things that are made, even his eternal power and Godhead, so that they are without excuse . . ." (Rom. 1:20). Despite their natural knowledge of God, the Greeks lacked real wisdom, for they practiced idolatry and abandoned themselves to immorality and sexual license. Their knowledge was vain for salvation.

This text was chosen by Augustine as the lodestone for his encounter with Platonism throughout Book Seven. In its light the grasp of transcendence achieved at VII.x (16) was seen to be Janus-faced. While it was the foundation of his rejection of Manichean materialism, it also disclosed the soteriological inadequacy of the pagan Platonism. Romans 1:20 was invoked repeatedly by Augustine in his discussion of the "Athenian" legacy. To Augustine this text referred to the cognitive significance of Platonism, while also reinforcing its spiritual deficiency. However powerful knowledge of transcendence might be to the embodied soul, it was insufficient to sustain the soul in its association with the divine. The accuracy of this Pauline thesis was represented by Augustine as something he discovered before turning to the study of Paul. We are left to conclude that Platonism has cognitive merits only.

As we have noted, the dominant reading of the Confessions finds in Book Seven a sequence of failed attempts at "mystical experience," beginning with VII.x (16), which were catalyzed by the *libri Platonicorum* (Courcelle 1950; 1963). This approach assumes that Plotinus defined for Augustine an experiential standard of mystical experience, and moreover, that achievement of this momentary state was the goal of the philosopher in the *Enneads*. But as we discovered in Chapter 1, such an episodic and ecstatic understanding of Plotinian contemplation is quite selective and is belied by most depictions of *theōria* in the *Enneads*. These describe a deepening of spiritual understanding and an intensification of the spiritual self's connection to the transcendent world. When that cognition appears to be momentary, its episodic character is a result of the soul's embodiment. The brevity of spiritual recognition is itself significant only when understood in light of the enduring truths revealed, especially the soul's abiding connection to the eternal forms. The adventitiousness of contemplative awakening exhibits both the descended state of the soul and also uncovers its capacity for renewed association with the forms both now and in its future life after death.

Augustine evidently understood these essential points from his readings of the *libri Platonicorum*. In the text of Book Seven he does not represent himself as seeking an ecstatic state of consciousness and failing to achieve it. Nor does he contrast a failure to achieve ecstatic consciousness at this stage in his life with subsequent success after his conversion or baptism. These readings are modern impositions upon the text. Rather the *Confessions* describe a sustained effort to analyze and assess the pilgrim soul's practice of contemplation. And that contemplation is directed toward the soul's cognitive elevation, not toward a special psychological state. To use an analogy rooted in the Platonic tradition, contemplation is like grasping a mathematical proof. It is – in minimalist terms – an experience, a state of consciousness which may be brief in duration, surrounded by a sense of joy in discovery, and so on. But none of those psychological characteristics are what is sought; they are epiphenomenal. The goal is to encounter truth directly and immediately, not to achieve ecstasy.

In Book Seven of the *Confessions* Augustine has read the Platonist treatises and come to recognize quite vividly the truth about the nature of things proposed within them. His goal is knowledge of reality, not a special state of consciousness. That much is clear – only our own preoccupation with psychologized approaches stands in the way of understanding Augustine. Yet there is one element of disanalogy in this example of mathematics. For Plotinian Platonists not only spoke of the soul's capacity to achieve certain knowledge of the intelligibles, they also recognized in this epistemic advance the soul's own capacity to participate in the eternal world of forms and even to discover its true nature there. The moment of grasping the truth about these transcendentals would also be an instance of discovering the stable foundations of the self. For Plotinians, the certainty of contemplative knowledge leads to the surety of an eternal self.

When Augustine speaks of failure in Book Seven, it is neither a failure at contemplation nor a failure to reach an ecstatic state of consciousness. It is rather a curious lack discovered in the very success of contemplation that troubles him. The pilgrim soul recognizes that knowledge of the intelligibles is ultimately disappointing, for it does not, in fact, lead to the soul's transcendent stability. Augustine presents this Pauline thesis quite clearly in Book Seven and in doing so exhibits an accurate grasp of contemplation as taught by the Plotinian school. Contemplation is both cognitive and salvific: that is the Plotinian view. For Augustine, contemplation is only cognitive in its significance. The failure uncovered in Book Seven is not an inability to achieve ecstasy, to reproduce a Plotinian state; rather it is a disappointment at the contemplative achievement itself. For contemplation, in laying out the transcendent cosmos behind the manifest world, fails to recover the soul's fixed connection to that world. Only a mediator can do that for the Augustinian soul. This Pauline proposition is set out in the narrative as part of the pilgrim's own recognition, as he grows in his understanding of that transcendent world first manifest at VII.x (16).

One of the exegetical imperatives that has followed from reading Book Seven as a record of attempted ecstatic experiences has been a tendency to break up the continuous narrative from VII.x (16) through the end of VII.xx (26). But the entire section is a seamless discussion of the impact Plotinian Platonism. Read as a continuous piece, Augustine's text develops a notion of contemplation in which the soul's purchase on wisdom is directly proportional to its spiritual condition. Both a grasp of the intelligibles and moral reform are preconditions for knowledge of the eternal. These are the notions from the *libri Platonicorum* that form the soundboard for Augustine's sustained assessment of contemplation in Book Seven. It is clear throughout this discussion of Platonism that its promise of transcendence through contemplation was a success. Augustine, beginning as we have seen in VII.x (16), does not just entertain, as it were, a metaphysics different from Manichaean dualism. Rather, he depicts himself as verifying the truth of Platonic transcendentalism. Since his narrative purpose here is to advance beyond Manichaeaism he must represent Platonism as effective in this regard. Moreover, the dramatic autobiographical account of VII.x (16) is followed by meditation on its significance. These comprise sections VII.xi (17)–Xii.xvi (22) and they confirm and expand upon the dawning of transcendence in the depths of the pilgrim's soul.

In VII.xi and VII.xii Augustine explains several critical elements of his recognition of a transcendent God. The first is the unchanging character of true being: "that which truly is is that which unchangeably abides," but the things "below" God can, in contrast, "be said neither absolutely to be or absolutely not to be." These are derivative from real being but unlike it are susceptible to corruption. Moreover, all existence is a good, for degrees of reality and degrees of value must be correlated. Hence "whatever things exist are good, and the evil into whose origins I was inquiring is not a substance, for if it were a substance, it would be good." All contingent substances are derived from God and are good. Recognition of the full import of this transcendental level of reality precludes the independent existence of evil. This cluster of ideas is repeated in VII.xv (21). All things are finite and owe their existence to God, who abides immutably: "For all periods of time both past and future neither pass away nor come except because you bring them about, and you yourself permanently abide."

Whatever one might think of these sketchy arguments, it is clear that they are meant to exposit what contemplation uncovered in the innermost part of the pilgrim's soul. They are the discursive representations of the pilgrim's immediate recognition of divine presence within the soul. These are not a record of failure. As such, they establish an explanatory context for the next autobiographical sequence, the ascension narrative of VII.xvii (23). This is not so much a separate incident, distinct from VII.x (16), as it is a restatement of the stages of contemplation. It does not so much supersede the earlier account as explain it.

In preparing us for the great ascension narrative of VII.xvii, Augustine is quite careful to give his reader some antecedent warning of its import. The crux is the fallen nature of the soul. As we have seen, it is the audacity of the spiritual self that offers one explanation for embodiment in Plotinus. Both separation from the Good and incarnation in time limit the soul's present capacity to sustain contemplative association with the One. These Plotinian theses are adapted by Augustine in VII.xvi (22) and VII.xvii (23) in advance of the visionary sequence. Following his grasp of divine transcendence, his acceptance of monotheism, and his rejection of dualism, the pilgrim is depicted as realizing that the source of evil is the soul itself:

> I inquired what wickedness is; and I did not find a substance but a perversity of will twisted away from the highest substance, you O God, towards inferior things, rejecting its own inner life (Eccls. 10:10) and swelling with external matter.
>
> (VII.xvi (22))

This text serves to alert Augustine's reader to the limitations of embodied contemplation. Thus the very recognition of transcendence with the soul becomes a simultaneous disclosure of the soul's distance from God. This is acutely put at the beginning of VII.xvii (23):

> But I was not stable in the enjoyment of my god. I was caught up to you by your beauty and quickly torn away from you by my weight. With a groan I crashed into inferior things. This weight was my sexual habit. But with me there remained a memory of you. I was in no kind of doubt to whom I should attach myself, but was not yet in a state to be able to do that.

What stands in the way of the soul's continuous association with the transcendental and the divine is its moral condition. The body is only a token of the soul's moral state, exhibiting the soul's perversity of will, and not the cause of its falling away from the eternal. The pilgrim soul thus lacks stability and the capacity for sustained enjoyment of its God because of its inherent moral character. It is weighed down by a propensity to the things "below," to carnal things, especially sexuality. Freedom from this awesome weight must be found if the soul is to sustain the promise of transcendence. In the meantime, memory must suffice, memory of the soul's momentary enjoyment of the divine. A sexually grounded disregard for "the higher things" is depicted as a special burden for the pilgrim Augustine. But his vagrant sexuality is not the cause of the intermittence of contemplation. That failure lies deeper.

These observations by Augustine introduce the reader to the fuller presentation of the soul's gradual appropriation of transcendence found in VII.xvii (23). It is especially important to recognize that Augustine's focus is directed in advance to the moral insufficiency of the soul for sustained participation in the transcendent and the eternal. Both the process of ascension and any impediments to this achievement are rooted in the character of the human soul. We are warned in advance by Augustine that it is not embodiment as such that frustrates contemplation, it is rather the inner disposition of the soul. This is a critical point which underscores how contemplation is a complex transposition of the inner self, involving both its moral state and its inner nature. Contemplation, both in its fruition and its disappointment, is far more than a psychological event. It is, to be sure, an "experience," in the sense that all aspects of human sentience can be so characterized. But to understand it primarily as a state of consciousness, however exalted, is to reduce and avoid its full significance.

The richness of Augustine's account and his analysis of its significance belie any such diminished representation. It is Romans 1:20 that dominates the entire passage; mentioned twice, it both initiates the ascension narrative and helps to provide closure. Its presence forcefully articulates the nature of this episode in the narrative. The contemplative soul seeks to discover the invisible things of God, to understand them, and to observe them intellectually, through the things that are made. The contemplative soul is "caught up" to God by his beauty, manifest now in a world discerned to be the creation of a single divine source and not as the product of two opposing powers. Hence the force of Romans 1:20 now becomes evident as a result of the pilgrim's reading of the *libri Platonicorum*. Without the confusion of Manichaean dualism, he can attend to God univocally manifest in the created world. While not yet in a moral state sufficient to do so, he now has no doubt that he should "attach" himself to God.

Significantly, the soul's ascent begins with a query regarding the basis for normative judgments about values. In the context of this discussion, Augustine determines that truth is independent of the mind. This becomes the epistemic catalyst to the ascension narrative. The text in full reads as follows:

In the course of this inquiry why I made such value judgements as I was making, I found the unchangeable and authentic eternity of truth to transcend my mutable mind. And so step by step I ascended from bodies to the soul which perceives through the body, and from there to its inward force, to which body senses report external sensations, this being as high as beasts go. From there again I ascended to the power of reasoning to which is to be attributed the power of judging the deliverances of the body senses. This power, which in myself I found to be mutable, raised itself to the level of its own intelligence, and led my thinking out of the ruts of habit. It withdrew itself from the contradictory swarms of imaginative fantasies, so as to discover the light by which it was flooded. At that point it had no hesitation in declaring that the unchangeable is preferable to the changeable, and that on this ground it can know the unchangeable, since, unless it could somehow know this, there would be no certainty in preferring it to the mutable. So in the flash of a trembling glance it attained to that which is. At that moment I saw your "invisible nature understood through the things which are made" (Rom. I:20). But I did not possess the strength to keep my vision fixed. My weakness reasserted itself, and I returned to my customary condition. I carried with me only a loving memory and a desire for that of which I had the aroma but which I had not yet the capacity to eat.

(VII.xvii (23))

This is an ascension through fixed cognitive levels. The basic scheme is:

1 body;
2 soul that perceives body;
3 the inward force of soul;
4   the power of reasoning;
5 intelligence itself; light;
   that which is unchangeable;
   that which is.

The second through fourth states represent epistemic activities of which the soul is capable. The second stage is the basic capacity of sensation, the third is the capacity for sense perception; both are shared with animals. The fulcrum of the scheme is the power of reasoning or judgment which is both mutable and yet capable of improving its discernment. By self-withdrawal, by removal from the contradictory storm of the impressions of the sensory world, the soul's rational power can discern intelligence itself, the light which floods the soul. That is the point at which the individual soul discovers the immutable power of intellect. This is being itself, that which is. The soul has thus discerned what it sought, the foundation of necessary judgment. It is the unchangeable and authentic eternity of truth "that transcends the mutable mind." Thus the soul has achieved its initial goal, finding the certainty it sought for its judgments regarding mutable things.

But there is more to the story than this cognitive advance, however important it may be. For the soul encounters something beyond itself, paradoxically disclosed by this interior reflection. That new element is the unchangeable, intelligible light, through which sense perceptions can be made intelligible. And that light is divine, the eternal truth that is distinct from, though present to, the mind. Mutable things can only be known through the immutable light of truth.

The invisible things of God, his "power and divinity," are revealed as well through this epistemic ascension.

And what of this "flash of a trembling glance" in which the soul "attains to that which is"? Here the soul "reaches" the invisible things of God with the swiftness of insight. This is clearly a cognitive success, since access has been attained to Intellect itself. The soul moves beyond the confusions both of its immediate sensory perceptions and its fallible judgment. In doing so, it raises itself to that power of reason which is beyond the vicissitudes of personal embodiment and moral confusion. This transition, from personal capacity to a power beyond the self, is at the core of Augustine's ascension narratives.

Yet there is failure here as well, for the contemplative soul loses its immediate contact with this light. We need to be quite precise about this loss. The text reiterates the account which began the chapter: the soul lacks the strength necessary to maintain visionary association with the divine light. It is the soul's moral infirmity that weights it down, so that it returns to its antecedent and habitual state. This indicates that it is the soul's moral condition that forces its severance with the higher power beyond itself.

Whatever else may be said of this event, it is not a failed attempt at "Plotinian ecstasy." Nor is this a mystical experience, in the modern, Jamesian sense. We are, in fact, not told little about the characteristics of this experience, but much about the soul's moral instability. Augustine's concern is to underscore the soul's moral imperfection, something that the brevity of its attention exhibits. Augustine's soul suffers not from the transiency of mystical experience but from its moral insufficiency. The defining axis of this episode is not temporal but ethical.

Our contemporary tendency to describe this text as a mystical experience and to assess its adequacy as an instance of ecstasy must be resisted strongly. It is an act of some exegetical violence to extract from this autobiographical narrative an identifiable "experience." The text itself, from VII.x (16) through VII.xvii (23) has a recapitulatory character. The reader is invited to survey, from a variety of contiguous angles, the same spiritual development. In this case it is the recognition of transcendent being, discovered through the *libri Platonicorum* in the interiority of the soul. As the text stands, we have neither one event, nor two, but a long personal narrative of transformed understanding, punctuated with certain vivid points of subjective reference, such as the "flash" of recognition. But the text itself is much more than an embellished record of an experience, whose outlines are recoverable beneath layers of philosophy and scriptural allusions.

One reason that the contemporary notion of mystical experience does not fit this section of the *Confessions* is that the underlying model of sensory perception upon which this idea is based does not apply. Augustine's insight results in a declaration of the relative superiority of the unchangeable to the changeable. This is the initial recognition that supports his deeper and more immediate contact with the eternal. Augustine believes that he has come to know truth, and that knowledge is not the result of "mystical perception," to use William Alston's term (Alston 1991: 9–43). Augustine does not describe non-sensory perception of something distinct from himself, about which he has gained knowledge. Rather, he has discovered, through a process of interior reflection, certain necessary truths which are immutable and eternal and features of God's nature. Augustine discerns a priori verities, the unchangeable and authentic eternity of truth independent of his mind's fallible judgment. The a priori character of his account sets it apart from any attenuated notion of perception, whose modal character would be a posteriori. Augustine's notion of vision refers, therefore, to a cognitive state in which the contemplative "sees in the sense of 'understands'" (Pike 1992: 63 fn.21). And that understanding yields eternal truth directly grasped.

Augustine's text is unequivocal about the reason for the cessation of contact with divine truth. It is the moral weakness of the soul. This is as we should expect because Augustine is articulating an act of personal transfiguration. The ascension texts of Book Seven depict the struggle of the soul to achieve a type of understanding that requires the transformation of the soul's inner dispositions. In this respect, Augustine makes common cause with Plotinian Platonism; both hold that levels of being knowledge and value are directly correlated. The texts underscore the epistemic success of these instances of insight, which swept away Manichean materialism with their veridical force, while also imprinting a continuing memory of transcendence within the soul. And it is here that Augustine begins to inventory the worth of Platonism. Augustine suggests, not that he had failed in his efforts to be a Platonist, but rather that Platonism had failed him.

The end of Book Seven is preoccupied with this assessment of Platonism. It is a powerful critique, centered on the salvific efficacy of contemplation. Thus Augustine, at the very moment he praises Platonism for providing the conversionary insight of transcendence, also initiates a disparaging review of its soteriological inadequacy. In this regard Augustine understood the Plotinian school accurately, privileging as they did contemplation as a mode of psychic return to the One, as the true means to salvation. Thus the text begins the task of disabusing the Plotinian philosophic religion of its claims to soteriological efficacy. Augustine concentrates on the incompleteness of his moral transformation and its impedimentary role in contemplation. Contemplation is never presented in the *Confessions* as simply a type of experience, however, unusual. It is a type of cognition – indeed the supreme form of knowledge – and a means of association with God. But as a path to salvation, contemplation is inadequate.

This apologetic theme is suggested in part by Augustine's repeated references to Romans 1:20, a text which itself had an explicit polemical context. Romans 1:18–19 argues that pagans are justly in receipt of divine wrath because the truth had indeed been shown to them by God. They ignored that knowledge and so invited their just punishment. St. Paul continues this line and concludes that "they are without excuse." Vain in their imaginations, with their foolish hearts darkened, the ungodly become fools while professing themselves to be wise. Thus the knowledge of God accrued through contemplation becomes a precondition of their judgment as unworthy. Yet, while this outlook is softened by Augustine, it nevertheless remains the scriptural referent for his apologetic strategy. By analogy with Romans, he affirms that pagans have access to knowledge, but they lack the means necessary to achieve salvation. *Theōria* can be successful only as a cognitive act.

The text is quite definite and unequivocal on this point. Immediately following the ascent narrative, VII.xviii (24) insists that the strength necessary to enjoy God was not available to the pilgrim until he embraced "the man Christ Jesus." Only when the reality of the incarnation was understood, with its supreme example of humility, and accepted, could the soul be lifted up by the divine Word. This is set out in a lengthy review of Platonism at VII.xx (26):

> At that time, after reading the books of the Platonists and learning from them to seek for immaterial truth, I turned my attention to your invisible nature understood through the things which are made (Rom. 1:20). But from the disappointment I suffered I perceived that the darknesses of my soul would not allow me to contemplate these sublimities. Yet I was certain that you are infinite without being infinitely diffused through finite space. I was sure that you are, and are always the same; that you never become other or different in any part or by any movement of position, whereas all other things derive from you, as is proved by the fact that they exist. Of these conceptions I was certain; but to enjoy you I was too weak.

This disappointment with Platonism is plainly not cognitive, but relates to an inability of the soul to enjoy God. In many respects, this inventory of Platonic transcendentalism is remarkable for its precision and its generosity. The Platonists have a cognitive grasp of the divine. There are four main elements of their contemplative knowledge:

1 God is non-spatial and infinite.
2 God is true being, that which truly is.
3 God is always the same; God is never different in any part or changed.
4 God is the source of all things.

This is the positive content of Platonism, the truth read in the *libri Platonicorum*. It is depicted as the direct result of Augustine's own efforts at contemplation. Yet contemplation as advocated in the books of the Platonists failed to lead to "enjoyment of God." This is a characteristic phrase of Augustine's. It refers to acquiring the stability of the divine nature and confirming the pilgrim soul's association with God. The Platonists have been unable to provide this completion to the pilgrim's journey and to secure stable habitation in God. That judgment is articulated in two striking assessments at VII.xx (26) and VII.xxi (27) regarding the relative merits of the *libri Platonicorum* and the Scriptures:

> I believe that you wanted me to encounter them before I came to study your scriptures. Your intention was that the manner in which I was affected by them should be imprinted in my memory, so that when later I had been made docile by your books and my wounds were healed by your gentle fingers, I would learn to discern and distinguish the difference between presumption and confession, between those who see what the goal is but not how to get there and those who see the way which leads to the house of bliss, not merely as an end to be perceived but as a realm to live in.

> I began reading and found that all the truth I had read in the Platonists was stated here together with the commendation of your grace, so that he who sees should "not boast as if he had not received" both what he sees and also the power to see. "For what has he which he has not received" (1 Cor. 4.7). Moreover, he is not only admonished to see you, who remain ever the same, but also healed to make it possible for him to hold on to you. So also the person who from a distance cannot yet see, nevertheless walks along the path by which he may come and see and hold you.

Perception without access, vision without habitation, presumption without expiation through confession – these are Augustine's evaluative images of Platonism. All rely on the autobiographical judgment that the Platonic books failed to articulate a true method of salvation. The contemplative path that the Platonists prescribed for both knowledge and salvation was inadequate for the latter task. It is the failure of the philosophical soteriology of the Plotinian school that Augustine decries here. The soul's healing is available only through the grace of Christ.

This annunciation of a Christian apologetic strategy against pagan Platonism establishes one of the major themes of the *Confessions*. It defines a clear contrast between two different theologies. The visionary ascent of VII.xvii (23) is thus nested in a wider cultural debate. Although Augustine's point is apposite only to Plotinian Platonism, it nonetheless is a piece of a larger Christian strategy of self-articulation. Thus this cognition of the invisible nature of God becomes the occasion for a rejection, indeed a theological condemnation, of Platonism. Just as the knowledge displayed by those who profess themselves to be wise in Romans 1 is misused, so the Platonist's have misapplied contemplative knowledge by over-stating its salvific efficacy.

This late antique dispute over the religious value of contemplation sets both sides into relief. In particular, a subtly different sense of interiority or the "place" of God is exhibited in each case. Consider what the interior journey has uncovered for Augustine: not a recessive connection to the intelligibles, a spiritual latency based on the soul's undescended portion in eternity as found in Plotinus. In Augustine there is loss only. The ascension narratives exhibit a movement out of the self and a connection, fleeting and tenuous, with an external, divine wisdom. And the soul meets directly a divine other, not its true self. Moreover, restoration does not lie within the soul's control. Thus depth of the soul's exile is suggested not only by its current captivity to sin, but also by its just extradition into the control of that "ancient sinner," the president of death, who persuaded us to conform our wills to his. The Augustinian soul requires deliverance "from the body of death," something available only through the grace of Christ. As such, contemplation reveals the terrible dilemma of the fallen soul.

Augustine summarizes this sharp theological divergence from Platonism with some of his most splendid rhetoric at VII.xxi (27):

> None of this is in the Platonist books. Those pages do not contain the face of this devotion, tears of confession, your sacrifice, a troubled spirit, a contrite and humble spirit (Ps. 50:19), the salvation of your people, the espoused city (Rev. 21:5), the guarantee of your Holy Spirit (2 Cor. 5:5), the cup of our redemption. In the Platonic books no one sings: "Surely my soul will be submissive to God? From him is my salvation; he is also my God and my saviour who upholds me; I shall not be moved any more" (Ps. 61:2–3).

The depth of the soul's fall in Augustinian Christianity tracks a deeper ontological separation, the sharp ontological difference between God and the created soul. The ambiguous Plotinian fall of the soul, at once an act of audacity and the expression of the Good's self-diffusion, is now unequivocally a disaster. For the fall, whether angelic or human, follows upon an initial ontological separation which conforms to the intent of the creator. Unlike the compatibilism of divine production and fall in Plotinus, the creation and fall are distinct events for Augustine, the latter exacerbating a separation entailed by the former. Hence these texts from Book Seven exhibit a greater sense of loss, a greater need for salvific restitution, and a profound need for the soul to be submissive to God. These are all conceptions foreign to the *Enneads*.

It is easy enough to emphasize in the *Confessions* the soul's abject need for a divine savior, in contrast to the *Enneads*, where the contemplative soul finds salvation through enlightenment. Yet even in the *Enneads*, the soul must wait for the emergence of the One. Enlightenment is never in the exclusive control of the soul. Nonetheless there is a pervasive spiritual confidence in Plotinus. The ascension narratives of Book Seven are starkly different, for the soul must be "lifted up" or "caught up." Nothing is ever easy for the Augustinian soul. Hence the Platonist books also represent a danger, for they describe a vain path to salvation, which can tempt the soul to spiritual pride, and thereby ironically and tragically exacerbate its fallen state:

It is one thing from a wooded summit to find the way to it, but vainly to attempt the journey along an impracticable route surrounded by the ambushes and assaults of fugitive deserters with their chief, "the lion and the dragon" (Ps. 90:13). It is another thing to hold on to the way that leads there, defended by the protection of the heavenly emperor.

(VII.xxi (27))

Given the degree of the soul's fall and the strength of its demonic opponents, only direct divine mediation can suffice. Platonic contemplation, whatever its salutory epistemic influence on the pilgrim soul, is only visionary, an act of ethereal, almost gossamer transcendentalism. Another path must be found.

6

THE PRESENCE OF TRUTH

In a Milanese garden, beneath a fig tree in spring, Augustine hears the fugitive voice of a child from a nearby house: tolle lege, tolle lege; "Pick up and read, pick up and read" (VIII.xii (29)). He does so, opening to Romans 13:13–14: "... put on the Lord Jesus Christ and make no provision for the flesh in its lusts." "At once, with the last words of this sentence, it was as if a light of relief from all anxiety flooded into my heart. All the shadows of doubt were dispelled." With this divine admonition, Augustine decides his future course as a Catholic Christian pledged to asceticism.

Ancient Christian literature describes a religion of personal decisions, centered upon acts of conscience under divine guidance. Augustine cites the example of St Antony, whose abrupt renunciation of the world served as an archetype of conversion through the reading of specific scriptural passages (VIII.xii (29)). For Augustine, his decision to become a Catholic Christian involved three related components: withdrawal from worldly ambition, acceptance of the ascetical life, and baptism into the life of Christ. This composite act resolves the pilgrim's exhortations enunciated at the beginning of Book One (I.v (5)):

> What a wretch I am! In your mercies, Lord God, tell me what you are to me. "Say to my soul, I am your salvation" (Ps. 34:3). Speak to me so that I may hear. See the ears of my heart are before you, Lord. Open them and "say to my soul, I am your salvation." After that utterance, I will run and lay hold on you. Do not hide Your face from me (cf. Ps. 26:39). Lest I die, let me die so that I may see it.

After hearing the ambiguous admonition in the garden, Augustine runs and lays hold of Christ. Having done so, having died to sin, he will then be able to associate with the divine more fully. This act of association will be accomplished in the *Confession's* next garden scene, the culminating ascension at Ostia.

In Book Seven, the contemplative soul achieved a cognitive grasp of God, but was unable to remain with him in the transcendent world. The soul's moral weight intervened. As we have seen, Augustine insists that he would only find the strength to enjoy God when he had "embraced 'the mediator between God and man, the man Christ Jesus' (1 Tim. 2:5)". The removal of this impediment to enjoying God is something that he had failed to accomplish by reading the books of the Platonists. He is now concerned to explain further how Christianity supersedes Platonism, as he develops his story in anticipation of Ostia.

The image of the two wills is instructive in this regard. At VIII.v (10), Augustine clarifies the causal chain that has led to his enslavement to sin. His problem is the passion that drives his engagement with sin, a passion which is rooted in his sexuality but is larger still. This passion was based upon a choice, which led to his soul's alliance with the enemy of God. Augustine expresses admiration for the freedom of the Christian rhetorician and converted Platonist, Victorinus, who gave up his career after an edict by the Emperor Julian the Apostate in 362 forbidding the teaching of rhetoric by Christians:

> I sighed after such freedom, but was bound not by an iron imposed by anyone else but by the iron of my own choice. The enemy had a grip on my will and so made a chain for me to hold me prisoner. The consequence of a distorted will is passion. By servitude to passion, habit is formed, and habit to which there is no resistance becomes necessity.
>
> (VIII.v (10))

The soul's central problem, then, is both volitional and self-created. It needs to discover some means of reversing the process that led to its necessity, its bondage to the habits of sin. But it has not the strength of will. Augustine then contrasts the will in bondage to a new will, one that begins to hope for true freedom. It aspires to the ability to move beyond the apparent choices made by the old will, restricted as it is in its weakness to recapitulation of the habitual. This new will must be strengthened by God in order to succeed in its spiritual intentions:

> The new will, which was beginning to be within me a will to serve you freely and to enjoy you, God, the only sure source of pleasure, was not yet strong enough to conquer my older will, which had the strength of old habit. So my two wills, one old, the other new, one carnal, the other spiritual, were in conflict with one another, and their discord robbed my soul of all concentration.
>
> (VIII.v (10))

It was the benighted old will that prevented continued association of the soul with the divine in Book Seven. Through this "darkness of the soul," the soul had been frustrated in its enjoyment of God. But Platonism was to no avail; indeed, it might have exacerbated the soul's fallen condition. Knowledge

74

of the transcendent could lead to pride and presumption, thus throwing the soul's fallen state into further affliction and deepening its crisis. Thus the epistemic advance of Platonism was in vain, even in part regressive, for the fallen soul's will was conformed that of "the ancient sinner," who had not remained in God's truth. The fallen angelic soul, descended from the vision of divine truth, is thus an archetype for the individual human soul's fallen state. The old man/new man imagery of Ephesians 4 is the regnant Pauline sub-text, itself an anti-pagan passage replete with condemnation of pagan pride. This Pauline passage addresses the condition of the Gentiles, their understanding remaining darkened and their desires misdirected. Both sexual desire and greed are implicated.

Ephesians Chapters 3, 4, and 5 are recurrent Pauline sub-texts in Book Eight and Nine. As with the use of Romans 1 in Book Seven, these texts formed a scriptural sounding board. Indeed Augustine models his own encounter with pagan Platonism upon Paul's encounter with the Gentiles. The result is powerful and compelling indictment. Platonism has failed because it could offer the soul no rest. The discord of the divided wills "dissipates" the soul. The intellect is now obscured, because of the moral disposition within the Gentile's hearts. Alienation from God follows from this moral condition, and the intellect is of no avail to overcome it. But the obfuscation of the fallen intellect can be overcome only if the moral status of the soul could be changed, only if the divided wills are resolved into unity (VIII.x (23–24)).

It is in the garden at Milan that Augustine discovers the strength to assert a new will through divine admonition. The Platonic impasse is resolved, presenting new possibilities for the Christian soul. Monica's reaction to Augustine's conversion in the garden is presented in Pauline terms, again using Ephesians:

> She was filled with joy. We told her how it had happened. She exulted, feeling it to be a triumph, and blessed you who "are powerful to do more than we ask or think" (Eph. 3:20).
>
> (VIII.xi (30))

Once again, an apologetic gesture is made through this reference. Its Pauline context (Eph. 3:16–19) discusses the strengthening of the inner self and the new comprehension of God that is then made possible. The soul can, through the new power of Christ, come to a condition of comprehensive understanding. This new state surpasses knowledge; it is a different sort of knowing, a grasp of the love of Christ leading to the soul's being filled with the fullness of God. Through the use of Ephesians 3, Augustine signals to his Christian reader a context for understanding this deeper dimension to his own story. What Christianity can offer is more than mere vision, more than momentary encounters with the transcendent. It can provide the pilgrim with stability of soul, salvation, and a higher mode of spiritual knowledge. These are the promises of Christ.

Baptism was necessary to become this new man. Augustine tells us little about this event as such, although its necessity and significance are never in doubt. Significantly, the text meditates on the old and new man of Ephesians immediately prior to the baptism episode. Augustine, in retreat at Cassiciacum before his baptism, begins to reflect upon what his new life will include: a turn within to the eternal, redemption from time, and a new sense of spiritual delight in the divine. All relate to his previous contemplative ascension, to his successful overcoming of Manichean materialism, and his failure to achieve divine enjoyment:

> We derive our light from you, so that we "who were once darkness are light in you" (Eph. 5:8). If only they could see the eternal to be inward! I had tasted this, but was enraged when I was unable to show it to them, even if they were to bring their heart to me, though their eyes are turned away from you toward eternal things, and if they were to say "Who wills how us good?" In the place where I had been angry with myself, within my chamber where I felt the pang of penitence, where I had made a sacrifice offering up my old life and placing hope in you. As I first began to meditate on my renewal: there you began to be my delight, and you gave "gladness to my heart" (Ps. 4:7). And I cried out loud when I acknowledged inwardly what I read in external words. I had no desire for earthly goods to be multiplied, nor to devour time and to be devoured by it. For in the simplicity of eternity I had another kind of "corn and wine and oil" (Ps. 4:9).
>
> (IX.iv (10))

By becoming a Christian Augustine believes that he will enjoy profound inwardness. His claim is that once before – in the contemplative ascension described in Book Seven – he had tasted the eternal within himself. The proper spiritual path leads within, toward the transcendent. The new life of baptism will bring an inner renewal, one that cannot be discovered externally, one that is concerned with the interior self. There, within that inner sanctuary, the old divided life was surrendered, and delight in the divine life of Christ began.

This is what was impossible in Platonic contemplation. But by means of Christian penitence, sacrifice, and renewal through divine grace, the soul can begin to take delight in divine things. Moreover, it can achieve real freedom from time, and come into the simplicity of eternity. Augustine describes how he discovers to this eternal stability within the soul:

> At the following verse I uttered a cry from the bottom of my heart: "in peace . . . the self-same", and at the words "I will go to sleep and have my dream" (Ps. 4:9). Who will bar our way when the word is realized which is written "Death is swallowed up in victory" (1 Cor. 15:54)? For you are supremely "the self-same" in that you do not change

(Mal. 3:60). In you is repose which forgets all toil because there is no one beside you, nor are we to look for multiplicity of other things which are not what you are. For "you Lord, have established in hope by means of unity" (Ps. 4:10).

(IX.iv (11))

"*Idipsum*" or the "self-same" is a term that recalls both "*ego sum qui sum*" ("I am who am") of Exodus 3:14 and *auto kath'auto*, "self-sameness," the classical epithet for the Platonic forms. The Augustinian soul seeks the complete stability of the intelligible and eternal world. This is what the soul had tasted before, in the Book Seven ascension: the "simplicity of eternity" and freedom from multiplicity, change, and time.

And this is God – immediately present and intensely close within the inner recesses of the soul. Hidden because of the effects of the fall, but present nonetheless as the author of the soul. Contemplation thus articulates the core logic of monotheism for Augustine, recovering by interior discernment a first principle which is responsible for the soul's continued existence. Augustine, like Plotinus, depicts a cognitive breakthrough to a first principle that is unique, one that excludes all multiplicity. The god of Exodus, first encountered at VII.x (10), is a God who is the eternally abiding source of all things. This the soul discovered through contemplation, although it could not yet remain in this repose. It could not bear such reality, this "simplicity of eternity," for it is itself still lost "in a region of dissimilarity."

This recapitulation of the contemplative advance of Book Seven introduces the quiet, anti-climatic baptism scene in the Milanese basilica of Ambrose (IX.vi (14)). In that ritual moment, "disquiet about our past life vanished from us." The pilgrim soul takes delight initially in reflecting on God's purpose for the salvation of the human race. It then turns to meditation on the future lives of the saints, the contemplative catalyst for the later vision at Ostia. That scene comes shortly after the abbreviated baptism section and after a review of Monica's life. It cannot be said that Augustine's readers are left unprepared.

As we turn now to this famous passage, we might reflect on the argument thus far presented. Both Book Seven and the initial section of Book Nine have given Augustine's reader a vivid and consistent account of his efforts to engage in the practice of contemplation. And he has achieved much, above all an immediate and certain knowledge of transcendent Wisdom. Reprising Pauline critiques of pagan philosophy from Romans 1 and Ephesians 3–5, Augustine has tested Platonism. He imparts his conclusion with clarity: Platonism does indeed provide knowledge of God, but not salvation. That knowledge is salutary but not salvific; it has freed him from the confusions of Manichean materialism, and it has brought him into a momentary association with God's Wisdom. This knowledge endures, even if the intense presence of God at its dawning does not, and it is retained only by the faculty of memory. The vision at Ostia thus occurs after Augustine has succeeded in intellectual vision, in discovering within his soul the certain presence of transcendent Wisdom beyond time and space. But this happens only because that transcendent power has aided the soul in its interior ascension. As in Romans 1, this knowledge of divine truth threw the fallen soul's condition into stark spiritual relief, helping to describe its state in a temporal world vexed by habituation to sin. The soul's visionary association with God displayed its own salvific inadequacy. Thus the contemplative episodes of Book Seven were profoundly ambivalent, at once articulating the surety of divine existence, while revealing the soul's abject state of removal from God in time.

The portrait of Platonism in the *Confessions* is thus carefully balanced, an exercise in theological apologetics. Through it Augustine initiates a claim to the same knowledge of the transcendental and the divine world that the Platonists achieved, while exposing the spiritual limitations of such contemplation from his autobiographical perspective. As such the central books of the *Confessions* recount neither a failed attempt at Plotinian ecstasy, nor indeed a successful Plotinian experience. Rather, they indicate where Platonism succeeds and where it fails, its cognitive value and its salvific inadequacy. The vision at Ostia will now present exactly what salvific value can be discovered through contemplation, and how deeply the baptized soul can reach into eternity. This is the theological purpose of the Ostian narrative.

It is accomplished in a striking fashion. Augustine's rhetorical training is never more effective, nor so hidden from view. The episode is presented in two initial sections, 23 and 24, followed by a further meditation in section 25 on the significance of the ascension. Here is the text of the first two narrative sections:

> The day was imminent when she was to depart this life (the day which you knew and we did not). It came about, as I believe by your providence, through your hidden ways, that she and I were standing leaning out of a window overlooking a garden. It was at the house where we were staying at Ostia on the Tiber, where, far removed from the crowds, after the exhaustion of a long journey, we were recovering our strength for the voyage.
>
> Alone with each other, we talked very intimately. "Forgetting the past and reaching forward to what lies ahead" (Phil. 3:13), we were searching together in the presence of truth which is you yourself. We asked what quality of life the eternal life of the saints will have, a life which "neither eye has seen nor ear heard, nor has it entered into the heart of man" (1 Cor. 2:9). But with the mouth of the heart wide open, we drank in the waters flowing from your spring on high, "the spring of life" (Ps. 35:10) which is with you. Sprinkled with this dew to the limit of our capacity, our minds attempted in some degree to reflect on so great a reality.
>
> The conversation led us towards the conclusion that the pleasure of the bodily senses, however delightful in the radiant light of this physical

world, is seen by comparison with the life of eternity to be not even worth considering. Our minds were lifted up by an ardent affection towards eternal being itself. Step by step we climbed beyond all corporeal objects and the heaven itself, where sun, moon, and stars shed light on the earth. We ascended even further by internal reflection and dialogue and wonder at your works, and we entered into our own minds. We moved up beyond them so as to attain to the region of inexhaustible abundance where you feed Israel eternally with truth for food. There life is the wisdom by which all creatures come into being, both things which were and which will be. But wisdom itself is not brought into being but is as it was and always will be. Furthermore, in this wisdom there is no past and future, but only being, since it is eternal. For to exist in the past or in the future is no property of the eternal. And while we talked and panted after it, we touched it in some small degree by a moment of total concentration of the heart. And we sighed and left behind us "the first fruits of the Spirit" (Rom. 8:23) bound to that higher world, as we returned to the noise of our human speech where a sentence has both a beginning and an ending. But what is to be compared with your word, Lord of our lives? It dwells in you without growing old and gives renewal to all things.

(IX.x (23–24))

This is a Christian account of contemplation, not a Plotinian one. It portrays the personal verification of Christianity, a higher wisdom demonstrated with personal certainty to be true. Augustine's point is subtly made, both by the force of the passage's explicit autobiographical details, and also by the continued use of imbedded scriptural references. As we have seen already, these texts are often references to Pauline arguments that Augustine's own discussion reduplicates. This is especially true in the Ostian narrative, where scriptural sub-texts are effective in securing a deeper Christian resonance. Augustine presents to his readers a moment of Christian contemplation, the realization of aspirations available to those blessed by the grace of God.

The text begins with the dramatic announcement of its poignant context: the conversation that Augustine and Monica have while looking into a garden in Ostia takes place only a fortnight before her death. This is a scene of earthly repose amid the tumult of the earthly city during a respite from the long journey between northern Italy and Africa. It is a providential interlude, before Monica's removal to the transcendent world. The reader has already been alerted to her great moral strength, as well as her minor shortcomings, such as a fondness for wine. Augustine sketches the garden scene in the hope of Monica's heavenly future. He surmises her future salvation and devises his setting accordingly. Mother and son converse about the eternal life of the saints, establishing a dialogue which frames the ascension narrative, one that is superseded only at the apex of contemplation. This dialogue links Augustine's depiction to the practice of classical dialectic and to the antecedent period of catechumenal dialogue at Cassiciacum, when Alypius, Monica, Augustine's son Adeotus, and others, engaged in Christian dialectic. Then, before the "antidote" baptism, this period of leisured discussion yielded insight, not immediate association with God. But Ostia will be different, after the medicinal effect of the baptismal ritual.

We are introduced to Augustine and Monica's discussion by Philippians 3:13, a resurrection text. This Pauline references serves to secure a specifically Christian outlook on this episode; the wider context of the reference clarifies its Christocentric character. The use of Philippians 3:13 is no fugitive reference. Not only does it remind the Christian reader of Monica's aspiration for resurrection, it also gives a forceful sanction for Augustine's pilgrimage. He too has now given up his life – ambition, marriage, sexuality – in order to gain Christ. He is about to be "in Christ," although not through his own efforts. Adapting Paul's rejection of legal righteousness to his own ends, Augustine now portrays himself as seeking God, not through the willed perfection of Platonic philosophy, but through the power of Christ. The law thus becomes a symbol for classical philosophical ethics and its promise of self-perfection for the sage, the *spoudaios*. Both the law and philosophy are superseded by Christ. Thus, lacking in perfection or any means save grace to attain it, the pilgrim soul presses on toward its goal: the surpassing worth of knowing Christ through God's upward call.

Monica and Augustine begin their discussion "in the presence of truth." They are both baptized Christians, conformed now to the divine image and apprised of the truths of the Christian revelation. Their conversation pertains to the "eternal life of the saints," a topic that directly anticipates the forthcoming death of Monica, when "this religious and devout soul" will be "released from the body." The promise of a higher Christian wisdom, superior to that of the pagans, is suggested by the use of 1 Corinthians 2:9. Monica and Augustine attempt to reflect on this eternal life; their efforts are not, however, unprecedented or misguided. For 1 Corinthians 2:7 speaks of "a secret and hidden wisdom of God, which God decreed before the ages for our glorification."

The ancient Christian reader of the Ostian narrative's preamble would thus have a set of scriptural resources for interpreting what transpires. Here again Augustine makes reference to a Pauline text that contrasts the wisdom available to Christians through the divine Spirit with the wisdom which non-Christians can obtain. Human wisdom is of no avail in this regard; spiritual truths are obtainable only to those who possess the Spirit. For the Spirit alone can search the depths of God. Because the Spirit comes upon them at Ostia, mother and son will know each other's inner thoughts and achieve for a moment the mutual lucidity of the saints. And they will together come to comprehend immediately the eternal thoughts of God through the Spirit.

Augustine then presents a formal pattern of ascent, although here it is pursued jointly by both souls. They include:

1   the bodily senses;
2   corporeal objects;
3   the heavens (sun, moon, stars);
4   the mind;
5   Divine Wisdom; eternity.

The primary ontological fault line comes between 4 and 5, between the temporal level and the eternal; this maps as well the separation between the human and the divine. The pilgrim souls begin with the levels of temporal existence: body, the objects of sense perception both corporeal and heavenly, and finally the human mind that exercises dialectical reasoning in time. This last level is that to which the souls return upon completion of the ascent; it is the stage of internal reflection, dialogue, and reflection upon empirical knowledge.

This shift to eternity invites scrutiny. The entire ascent is conducted "in the presence of truth which is you yourself." Augustine and Monica move beyond their own speech into silence, into the quietude of wisdom. This wisdom is eternal and has never come into begin; in it there is neither past nor future. It is life, the principle by which all things come into being. Hence it is the source of all entities that emerge from it into time. To reach this ontological level requires that the soul reverse its own course of life, returning to its source. There is no effort to distinguish the level of being – or divine wisdom – from a higher level, the One, through the use of apophatic theology. At Ostia the contemplative souls ascend from discursive reasoning directly into eternity and to divine Wisdom. In doing so, they transcend their own minds and move beyond the temporal self. Divine Wisdom is present and immediately available to the contemplative soul whenever the soul can make the interior turn to its inner sanctuary.

The text then discusses the soul's intimacy with Divine Wisdom. "And while we talked and panted after it, we touched it in some small degree by a moment of total concentration of the heart. And we sighed and left behind us 'the first fruits of the Spirit' bound to that higher world, as we returned to the noise of our human speech where a sentence has both a beginning and an ending." The first phase is of special interest: "we touched it in some small degree by a moment of total concentration of the heart" – *attingimus eam modice toto ictu cordis*. The use of *ictus*, a stroke or beat, recalls the apex of the ascent found at VII.xvii (23) – *in ictu trepidantis aspectus*: "in the flash of a trembling glance." Both suggest that the soul's association with God is limited. The phrase can be read intensively as well: "in some small degree (*modice*), by the total force of the heart, we touched it." Use of "heart," the Biblical seat of moral affection and decision-making establishes a point of contrast with the earlier ascent of Book Seven. While in Book Seven there is language of the soul "reaching" the eternal (VII.xvii (23)), the Ostian account emphasizes that contact with wisdom is a matter of the heart, of the moral self. As we have seen, the discourse of Book Seven was rather more abstract, relying on a Platonic model which emphasized the soul's capacity for a priori judgments regarding necessary truths. But here in Book Nine, it is *sapientia*, wisdom as such that is touched by the pilgrim souls, if only to a small degree. A moral transformation of the soul through baptismal grace has occurred in the interval, changing the inner resources of the self.

This is evident in the next phrase, as the contemplative souls sigh and leave behind "the first fruit of the Spirit," bound to that higher world. They return to discursive reasoning, to the level of temporally bound human discourse. In doing so they also leave behind, as it were, a spiritual place mark. Augustine's theological point seems clear enough. Some account must be given of the contemplative soul's relation to the reality that it has just contacted. In the *Enneads* the ascending soul discovers its intelligible and undescended self in the eternal world of being, as it moves from dialectical reasoning in time into intellect. After this transformative discovery, embodiment has no charm. But Augustine countenances no such direct access to an unfallen self. His help-lessness, his habituation to sins, his tears of self-betrayal have taught him otherwise. And so has the importunity of divine grace and the providential emergence of Christ in his life, whose power effects the conversion of his wholly fallen soul. Thus the contemplative soul cannot discover its real self within eternal wisdom, for there is no eternal self there to be recovered. Contemplation can only be an exercise in hope, the discernment of where the self may one day rest, if it should achieve its salvation. Thus, for Augustine, contemplation is inherently eschatological, and unlike Plotinus, that eschatological hope is never realized by the embodied soul. It can only be actualized after death.

The use of "first fruits of the spirit" from Romans 8 underscores the escha-tological nature of contemplation. Its employment fundamentally changes the metaphysical scope of the self. The Christian self has no native grasp on the transcendental world and no natural kinship with it. This association was conferred by the creator at the soul's initial generation and restored after the fall by a savior. Contemplation is a momentary insight into the nature of this ontology and the salvation history that is spooled around it. It is a momentary glimpse from a fallen world through an aperture opened by the grace of Christ emergent within the soul, but not naturally found there. Interior contemplation is the necessary means to that moment of understanding, but it is a singular gift, not a natural capacity to be exercised from deep within the soul. The valence of contemplation has thus been radically changed in Augustine's new Christian context.

As we have seen throughout these central books, Augustine constructs his own theological arguments over against Pauline texts. Here the reference to Romans directs the reader to Paul's meditation on the foundations of Christian hope in verses 8:22–24. Paul's text speaks of the whole creation and the souls of Christians groaning in travail in expectation of the resurrection of the body. Monica and Augustine thus achieve in contemplation an initial hold on wisdom, and discover their place of hope, their true place within the divine wisdom. But this option cannot be exercised until the soul has followed Christ into both death and resurrection. How Augustine understands the condition of resurrection is not articulated, although the prevailing need for divine intervention to catalyze this transformation is emphasized.

Augustine then reflects anew upon the ascension that he and Monica enjoyed at IX.x (25):

> Therefore we said: If to anyone the tumult of the flesh has fallen silent, if the images of earth, water, and air are quiescent, if the heavens themselves are shut out and the very soul itself is making no sound and is surpassing itself by no longer thinking about itself, if all dreams and visions in the imagination are excluded, if all language and every sign and everything transitory is silent – for if anyone could hear them, this is what all of them would be saying, "We did not make ourselves, we were made by him who abides for eternity" (Ps. 79:3, 5) – if after this declaration they were to keep silence, having directed our ears to him that made them, then he alone would speak not through them but through himself. We would hear his word, not through the tongue of the flesh, nor through the voice of an angel, nor through the sound of thunder, nor through the obscurity of a symbolic utterance. Him who in these things we love we would hear in person without their mediation. That is how it was when at that moment we extended our reach and in a flash of mental energy attained the eternal wisdom which abides beyond all things. If only it could last, and other visions of a vastly inferior kind could be withdrawn! Then this alone could ravish and absorb and enfold in inward joys the person granted the vision. So too eternal life is of the quality of that moment of understanding after which we sighed. Is not this the meaning of "Enter into the joy of your Lord" (Matt. 25:21)? And when is that to be? Surely it is when "we all rise again, but are not all changed" (1 Cor. 15:51).
>
> (IX.x (25))

The contemplative souls at Ostia seek to discover the authentic voice of a divine being wholly distinct from their souls, yet directly concerned with them. The God that the pilgrim souls discover at the end of their interior journey at Ostia is clearly distinct from them. The God discerned at Ostia is not just the source of the soul, a power like the One distinct from its products, but never significantly removed from them. There is a fundamental difference of theological location involved. Here at Ostia God is at once an omnipresent source and sustainer of the soul, yet also a separate God whose voice is heard from afar. The logic of this theism demarcates God off from the beings that have been produced by him and who seek to touch him. There is no sense, even in this most intense instance of contemplation, that God is "a long line stretched out." For this reason, the language of contact and audition seem particularly salient, establishing the dominant imagery of differentiation, closure, and finally renewed divorce. Such is the underlying logic of Augustinian contemplation.

In section 25 the distinction between the two sorts of voices, that of creatures and that of the creator, helps to define the passage. The text contrasts mediated reports about Wisdom, whether through human, angelic, or symbolic form of representation, with direct encounter. In contemplation, the soul closes the gap of its separation from God. But that, for Augustine, is both its promise and its anguish. The soul only hears directly the God for which it yearns momentarily, and only achieves unmediated contact with him for a limited time. Here again temporal duration is used to underscore ontology, the fundamental distinction of God and the soul. The embodied soul, even after baptism and under the direction of divine grace, can only achieve an instance of unmediated association with God. When it has imitated Christ through death, then it will be saved. Then the vision of God will ravish and absorb and enfold it in inward joy. But contemplation cannot accomplish this in our present life, for it is not an act of salvation.

How should we understand the silence of the soul in IX.x (25)? It must involve surpassing both discursive thought and rational conceptualization. But there must be more included as well. Souls are said to revert to wisdom in silence, and in this silence the contemplative soul also surpass itself. This is connected to a loss of self-conscious reflection. By no longer thinking of itself, it can achieve the contact with eternal Wisdom that it seeks. And by transcending itself, it transcends time and transiency. The announcement by transitory things makes this clear: "we did not make ourselves, but he who abides eternally made us." The contemplative soul is apparently able to recognize its original place within the eternal world of being and redress the cognitive effect of the soul's declension into the becoming of time. This requires putting off one element of that psychic fall: ordinary consciousness. Augustine represents this as a moment of rapid, even violent, mental activity, a type of mental process distinct from conscious reflection. The soul extends itself in order to touch eternal wisdom. But most striking is Augustine's concluding claim that if this perception of eternal being were to last, then this would be the mystery of the resurrection of the dead, when "we all rise again" from 1 Corinthians 15. But the vision at Ostia is conducted without the body, which is transcended. Yet the contemplative self, when revealed at this supreme moment of understanding, has none of the characteristics of bodily resurrection.

This text thus defines a fecund tension which goes directly to the limited value of contemplation. Augustine draws his Christian reader's attention to this through the use of a Pauline resurrection text. Augustine closes the Ostian narrative with 1 Corinthians 15:51. Augustine's treatment of the import of contemplation at Ostia is quite evident. The major Pauline references in the Ostian narrative are resurrection texts: Philippians 3:13, 1 Corinthians 2:7 and 15:51, Romans 8:23. These texts juxtapose a model of our final state, which is both psychic and corporeal, over against the merely psychic character of the vision at Ostia. Contemplation at Ostia leaves the body behind; Christian resurrection does not. Thus salvation is once again shown to be distinct from contemplation. The first fruits that contemplation reaps are at best harbingers of a more complete and final state to come.

What Monica and Augustine achieve at Ostia is the highest state available to human beings: an unmediated vision of God, direct understanding of him, contact with him. They are able to enjoy God, something that Augustine depicted as unavailable to him in the earlier ascent of Book Seven. Thus this fully Christian event succeeds to the extent that Augustine believes it is possible in this life. Unlike the ascent of Book Seven, the vision at Ostia allows the pilgrim souls to find joy with God in anticipation of their final state of eternal association with him. But beyond this they cannot go, for their souls are still human, still in need of redemption, still in the need of prayer. This is even true of Monica, for whom Augustine prays after her death at IX.xiii (35). Despite enjoying this vision at Ostia, her soul still is in need of divine absolution. Whatever occurred at Ostia, it was not apotheosis.

As was the case in the ascension narratives of Book Seven, we do not find in this passage the language of direct description. Indeed Augustine tells us that he is giving an approximate account of their dialogue: "I said something like this, even if not just this way and with exactly these words" (IX.x (27)). The result is a meditation on the conditions under which souls can encounter the transcendent as well as a record of a particular religious experience. That process of meditation includes for Augustine an array of religious ideas and scriptural phrases. All are so deeply ingrained into the record of the event that none can be convincingly labeled as merely retrospective, as opposed to those which are original to the experience. Even the scriptural references might have been incorporated contemporaneously into the event, since they formed the shared and remembered religious vocabulary of Monica and her son. These texts themselves may have been the subject of their discussion about the eternal life of the saints and so partially framed their experience of contemplation. And even if the specific texts referred to were retrospective inclusions by Augustine, they might have been elaborations on Christian conceptions that were incorporated into the episode itself. The conversation that catalyzed the ascension was, after all, about Christian ideas of the afterlife. The text of the *Confessions* should therefore be seen as continuous with the episode at Ostia itself, rather than a later theological imposition upon it. It is part of a complex and lengthy process by which Augustine sought to give meaning to the events of his life. There are no means at our disposal to pinpoint what was original to that interlude at Ostia, no way to discover the original characteristics of the experience itself, no discourse free from the religious language that Augustine uses. Indeed all of these efforts are philosophically suspect. As Augustine relates it, the vision at Ostia is a Christian experience and its character is irreducibly Christian.

Augustine maintains in this text that he and his mother together encountered an importunate presence that has quickened and multiplied their consciousness of what is real and their understanding of what is true. And they have done so as Christians and because they are Christians. The passage thus accomplishes several things. It confounds any effort to treat its salient features as merely retrospective theology. And it also certifies for Christians, both learned and uneducated, the capacity for immediate knowledge of the divine. Through this autobiographical account, Augustine was thus able to provide to his ancient readers a vivid and manifest warrant of the truth of Christianity. He could demonstrate that the Platonic ascent of the soul was accessible to Christians, although not in the terms to which Platonists would subscribe. What he and Monica have encountered in their mutual journey within themselves is not the presence of the One but the creator of their souls. They have discovered an eternal source whose transcendence is compatible with acute concern for themselves as persons. And it is this eternal wisdom that they attained at that moment of understanding, a personal One who calls from the eternity in which he abides.

Yet it was the fruit of experience, and not experience itself, that was the end for Augustine. For this reason, the category "mysticism" helps us little in analyzing Augustine's account of contemplation at Ostia. There is a cold friction between this notion and the text itself. Augustine is not primarily concerned to record his subjective feelings, nor does he build theological inferences from these sensations or emotions. In these texts the presence of truth is depicted as a lucid stillness, but it is this cognitive lucidity that is salient, not the moment of stillness. But if we put aside our contemporary tendency to discern mystical experiences in the *Confessions*, we can discover Augustine's own categories of reflection. And when properly read in the context of the late antique discussion regarding the nature of *theōria*, the significance of contemplation in the *Confessions* can be seen to be strikingly different from that found in the *libri Platonicorum*. The Augustinian soul is able to grasp the nobility of its creation, but also to recognize the enormity of its spiritual estrangement. Contemplation for Augustine is thus transformed into a double-edged recognition of the certain existence of transcendent Wisdom together with the soul's tragic loss and fall. Contemplation has thus secured the transcendental hope of the soul at the expense of its equanimity.

Part III

A LIVING SOUL OF THE FAITHFUL

"With him the beginning of life has all the characteristics of resurrection." Such was Pater's judgment of Michelangelo (Pater 1980: 59). Much the same is true of human life in the *Confessions*, whose beginning and end is drawn in reference to resurrection and eternal life. This arresting truth is revealed through the Christian practice of contemplation. It offers a momentary and immediate sense of God's presence to the fallen soul and intimates its final end. The soul yearns for the perpetuation of the divine presence, drawn by the force of God's love. "The storms of incoherent events tear to pieces my thoughts, the inmost entrails of my soul, until that day when, purified and molten by the fire of your love, I flow together to merge into you" (XI.xxix (39)). Contemplation discloses the "amazing depth" of the soul – its deep recesses and its innate potential to discover the stability of truth through the illuminative strength of divine grace. Yet contemplation also betrays the shallowness of the soul, the contingency of its existence, the poverty of its fallen state, its native inability to associate eternally with God. But it is Christ whose resurrection offers power and hope, and confession of Christ can renew and deepen contemplation itself. This Christian understanding of contemplation emerges more explicitly in the later discursive books of the *Confessions*. These sections form a theological coda to the personal narrative of the first nine books. In them we hear the voice of their author as a participant in the act of confession, speaking out of the depths of fallen existence to God. Confession is an act whose significance transforms contemplation. For Augustine tells us in Book Seven how God had taught his pilgrim self to discern the difference between the presumption of Platonic contemplation and the grace of Christian confession. In the later books of the *Confessions* Augustine reflects on contemplation, reformed by grace and by his confession of Christ. His initial experiences of contemplation engendered their prolongation in the memory and constrained the soul to continue these experiences in a retrospective mode.

The final chapter of our inquiry will begin by following these reflections in Books Ten through to Thirteen, tracing the deepening of contemplation. Discussion then turns in the second section of the chapter to taking stock of the over-all view of Christian contemplation that we have identified in the *Confessions*. The final section is devoted to consideration of some texts written after the *Confessions* that shed further light on it and confirm its representation of contemplation.

7

A HOME OF BLISS

The *Confessions* is built on the armature of an evolving yet consistent theology. By the time Augustine came to write it, the main lines of his thought on contemplation and human transcendence were already in place, even if tentatively so. Some central notions had formed within the crucible of his conversion experiences, and these contemporaneous interpretations provided the foundation for the subsequent reflections that characterize the finished work. The *Confessions* is thus the expression both of Augustine's account of Christian contemplation and of the autobiographical context in which it emerged. The theory and the events are deeply bound together. Those ideas that frame the personal narrative give it notional shape, but seem transposed into a more personal key in that very process

The *Confessions* offers its readers a sharply drawn portrait of contemplation. It is a momentary act of transcendence, when the soul is lifted up by God's grace and freed from the confines of bodily existence in space and time. And it is a brief occasion of access to the self's potential place in the heavenly world, to which it may hope to journey. There the soul may enjoy unmediated contact with God. But all that is only momentary and fleeting, crashing to an end in an instant, as the soul's embodiment floods back upon it and its mortal condition reasserts itself. Moreover, the soul realizes that there is no heavenly future guaranteed by this glimpse into eternity, for it ends so abruptly precisely because the soul is fallen, an exile lost from this transcendent home, powerless to effect its own ascension. Contemplation does not yield surety of salvation; it does not complete a safe passage to eternity for the soul. It only describes the depth of the soul's fall and gives clarity to its hopes.

We are in a position to understand Augustine's theology of contemplation in the *Confessions* not only because of the intense scrutiny that the notion receives in the text itself, but also because we can observe the development of this assessment in earlier works. Remarkably we possess the works that he wrote at Cassiciacum in the autumn of 386 and the winter of 387, while in retreat prior to his Easter baptism in 387. These works were thus written just prior to the vision at Ostia. They include *Contra Academicos*, *De Beata Vita*, *De Ordine*, and *Soliloquia*. We also possess his first theological depiction of contemplation in the treatise *De quanititate animae*, written at Rome in 388. These can help to frame the Ostian narrative. While we have no privileged access to that experience itself, we are at least in a position to follow the early development Augustine's depiction of contemplation. That process of reflection and interpretation leads directly to the definitive account that we find in the *Confessions*.

We shall look closely in this section first at the texts written after the events described in Book Seven but before Ostia, and then at the first discussion of contemplation written subsequent to that event. We will turn next to *Confessions* Books Ten to Thirteen, when the narrative voice becomes explicitly that of the bishop reflecting on his earlier experience a decade or more after the vision at Ostia. This will allow us to consider the model of contemplation that formed, as it were, the backdrop of expectation before Ostia, along with those concepts that were incorporated into the description of that event. We can also review the explicitly retrospective interpretations that formed Augustine's theology of contemplation as it emerges in the later books. So our first subject will be interpretations of contemplation – prior and posterior to Ostia.

Contra Academicos is a treatise directed against the moderate skepticism of the Platonic New Academy, which flourished in the second and first century BC and had a significant influence on some learned Romans, especially Cicero. Augustine tells us that he had begun to entertain a skeptical outlook on theology as his disaffection with Manichaeism grew. He needed to dispense with this perspective and purge its worries about the foundation of human knowledge if he was to proceed toward baptism. We find his first account of his conversion in Book Two, Chapter 5, recalling the impact that philosophical reading had upon his life and ambitions, and emphasizing in particular the writings of the Apostle Paul. These he snatched up and studied – "trembling, irresolute, and impatient." *De Beata Vita* describes his theological development in a fashion familiar from the *Confessions*: the early impact of Cicero's *Hortemsius* when he was 19, the Manichean years, the importance of the skeptical Academy – here more prominent than in the *Confessions*, the discovery of Ambrose and the novel idea of incorporeality. And he recounts reading a few books of Plotinus and comparing them with a Christian authority, evidently Paul. These are the regnant texts in his reflections before Ostia, some treatises of Plotinus and the epistles of Paul.

We can see what emerged from this bivalent reading in *De Ordine* and *Soliloquia*. In the former work, at II.viii.25 and ix.26, Augustine presents an ideal of the contemplative life in which the soul lives more fully to the extent that it contemplates the law of God and transcribes it into its own life. Those who follow the percepts of the perfect life come to grasp what intellect is, in which all things are, or better, which is the summation of all. But beyond intellect the soul can discern the source or first principle of all. The text then states: "In this life few reach this knowledge, but no one is able to go beyond it even after this life." This suggests that a type of contemplative knowledge may indeed be possible for some highly disciplined souls in this life. Moreover, that knowledge is not surpassed even when the soul is freed from the body.

Soliloquia present a similar thesis. In this novel work Augustine engages with reason in an inner dialogue within his own soul. We discover that the eye of the mind can exercise reason whenever it is free from the body and mortal desires have been purged. Faith is necessary to resist the senses and to believe that the mind has access to a better world. Hope sustains that project, which is completed by love. Love longs to see and to enjoy God, a longing which is completed by the vision of God. After this mortal life, only love of God remains; faith and hope are unnecessary. When the soul is released by death, the soul can give itself wholly to God, to whom it clings. Thus the vision of God in this life is an abbreviated form of what the soul can achieve continuously in the next. That is Augustine's judgment and expectation before Ostia. Contemplation is already based on a Christian model, assuming in particular that the ascent to God emerges from a relation of mutual love. The abstractive logic of Plotinian negative theology, in which the soul ascends by the removal of predication from its image of the One, is not in view. Indeed contemplation in *Soliloquia* resembles most the account of *Confessions* VII.xvii (23), and appears to be an initial representation of it.

In late 387 or early 388 Augustine wrote out his first treatment of contemplation after the vision at Ostia. This retrospective interpretation is found in a work entitled *De quantitate animae, On the magnitude of the soul*. While the texts that precede Ostia give us a sense of Augustine's culturally conditioned ideas about contemplation, this work is quite specific about what he now believes. Two points are particularly striking. First, Augustine identifies seven levels within the soul, seven degrees within the range of its existence. And the highest level, contemplation, is a culminating and enduring state accessible within this life. Second, Augustine indicates that some great souls now achieve this supreme spiritual state, although he indicates rather intriguingly that in some cases this is achieved quickly, while in others slowly.

The seven degrees of the soul include:

1. *animatio*, animation. The soul is the animating force of the body.
2. *sensus*, sensation. The soul is capable of sensing its surrounding environment, of movement, and of memory.
3. *ars*, art. The soul as maker, through thought and language, of the entirety of human culture.
4. *virtus*, virtue. The soul as moral and ethical aesthetic interpreter, capable of moral discernment and progress. This is only possible through the help of God's justice.
5. *tranquillitas*, tranquility. The soul, in a state of moral self-possession grasps its worth and begins to seek contemplation of God as Truth.
6. *ingressio*, entrance. Here the soul is so morally purified that its yearning to understand what is true and best leads into intellectual vision.

7   *contemplatio*, contemplation. The soul is now in a state of settled enjoyment
    of God.

Here is the description of this final degree of the soul:

> Now we arrive at the vision and contemplation of truth, which is
> the seventh and highest degree of the soul, not exactly a degree but
> a dwelling place to which the other degrees have brought it. What shall
> I say are the joys and what is the enjoyment of the perfect and true
> good? What breath of serenity and eternity? The great and incom-
> parable souls have spoken of these things to the extent that they
> determined that these things could be discussed, great souls who, we
> believe, saw and now see these things.
>
> *(De Quant.* XXXIII (76))

In this early exposition, contemplation is primarily a matter of moral and
spiritual progress, culminating in an intellectual vision or direct understanding
of truth. That is also an unmediated enjoyment of God, a final station of settled,
eternal peace. This enjoyment is not a momentary event or sudden episode,
although the pace of spiritual progress toward it may vary. And it is a level that
great souls can and do achieve in this life, and moreover, it is a station that
endures. There is no sense of a fugitive moment of spiritual vision here. Instead
we find a majestic ascension through the powers inherent in the soul itself.

We do not know the scope of the phrase "great and incomparable souls," for
no names are mentioned. Perhaps the pagan Platonic sages are intended, perhaps
not. What is clear, however, is that this process, while it actualizes forces inherent
in the soul, proceeds through the power of God. Augustine also underscores
that the soul is a creation of God, its author, father and creator. As the maker
of the soul, God acts to mold and restore it. Moreover, that process of seven-
fold ascension occurs through the spiritual nourishment of the Church, the
soul's mother. It is through the incarnation of Christ that humans have been
provided with an exemplar of this process and a start toward salvation. Thus
the first account that we have of contemplation after Ostia is a fundamentally
Christian one.

This text is the high watermark of spiritual optimism in Augustine's accounts
of contemplation and the human condition. It assumes, to be sure, the necessity
of divine intervention for ascension to the enjoyment of God. Christ and the
Church have a role to play, as yet undeveloped. But the text is also explicit that
the achievement of contemplation proceeds from a program of spiritual perfection and represents its completion. And that fruition is a sustained condition,
one that great souls do indeed accomplish in this life, as they come to enjoy the
peace of the divine presence. Death will afford an escape from the body, easing
the path to God and removing "a stumbling block to the soul's complete union
with truth itself." Yet some souls accomplish this even in this life. There is

nothing episodic about the magnificent spiritual condition of these great souls, who know no moral recidivism. Contemplation is thus the seal of the soul's spiritual development. In his later thought, Augustine will never deny the soul's capacity for intellectual vision of God. That becomes the lodestone of his later theology. But the notion of a sustained condition of spiritual perfection in this life, betokened by contemplation of God, will soon become suspect. A decade or more later, when he writes the *Confessions*, this claim will change.

This text from *De quantiate animae* is Augustine's first retrospective consideration of contemplation and the soul's capacity for spiritual ascension after the events of 387–388. Yet Augustine's description of these levels in the soul's approach to God is not explicitly an interpretation of any specific autobiographical event, only a theoretical appraisal of the powers of the soul. Its tenor is established by two significant aspects. First, it shares with the later ascension texts from *Confessions* Seven and Nine a preponderantly epistemic character. It is about the soul's ability to come to know God, a knowledge which leads to the soul's unmediated association with the supreme author of reality. Second, it sketches a transformation of the inner self that restores the soul to a state which allows it to contemplate God. Augustine is describing the content of what is revealed and the nature of this supreme mode of cognition. Significantly the substance of contemplation is said to include a grasp of the certainty of the resurrection of the body (at *De Quantitate* 76). Moreover, as in the *Confessions*, contemplation leads to an ability to measure mortal things properly, and recognize the positive character of death.

It is the endurance of this spiritual level which Augustine will come to deny in the *Confessions*. As we have seen, in contemplation the soul will achieve knowledge of truth at Milan, and will be prepared at Ostia for the death of Monica. But this spiritual level once achieved does not endure according to the account in the *Confessions*. The reason might be found in the strands of interpretation that combine within the depiction of contemplation in the *De Quantitate*. Ascension through these seven levels involves several related but distinct elements: the enhancement of the soul's capacity for knowledge, the moral conversion of the innermost self, and the refurbishment of its very nature which was designed by God for association with him. In the later analysis of the *Confessions*, Augustine comes to realize that his own development in 386–387 failed to conform to this model, and more important perhaps, that his moral condition continues to fall short. But in *De quantitate*, the three strands of contemplation – the epistemic, moral, and ontological, were correlated and this conduced to direct knowledge of God and to the endurance of that sublime condition. Through contemplation the soul comes to "a dwelling place" where it can "enjoy" God in a stable state of undisturbed peace. Augustine will modify this aspect of the earlier account of contemplation in the *Confessions*. His focus will be upon moral conversion and the part it played in his own story. Most decisively he insists that he achieved the highest level of contemplation at Milan and Ostia, but concedes that this level was not sustainable. Moreover, he will come to see this not as a personal failure, but as one that is universal to all fallen souls.

Two prominent features of the *Confessions* manifest this revision of his earlier understanding of contemplation: the admission of his unresolved passions, and the character of Monica. Both emerge to startle the reader, though in different ways. It is fair to say that general understanding of contemplation was the received cultural heritage for a reader of Cicero and the books of the Platonists. And that model assumed a gradual moral reform of the soul through its own efforts at philosophical dialectic and moderate asceticism. Estimates varied regarding the pace of that project. But the final purpose of contemplation was the emergence of a soul restored to its inner divine purity, in a state of moral self-control, and at an advanced level of intellectual advancement. This was the wisdom that emerged through the practice of contemplation, and set the stage for the soul's final association with the divine. At its height, contemplation brought the soul to "a dwelling place," to use the phrase of *De quantitate animae*. For Plotinus, as we have seen, the philosopher's soul could secure rest in the deeper recesses of its intelligible self, and there await the deepening presence of the One. This entire philosophical process was arduous, lengthy, and, except for its ultimate stage, largely the product of the inner self's own efforts. It is a contemplative program whose foundations still rested on the Platonic portrayal of Socrates, especially his representation of moral progress as grounded in intellectual knowledge, and ethical failure in cognitive error.

Yet Augustine will challenge this understanding of contemplation, first in incipient ways in his earliest works and decisively in the *Confessions*. At Cassiciacum, for example, the practice of dialectic among Augustine and his students is shown to yield no greater results than those already attained by Monica, an unlearned woman. At the finale of *De Beata Vita*, it is Monica who offers a fitting admonition and a succinct summary of the happy life from the foundation of her faith. Even at this stage in Augustine's development, his mother had become an exemplar of the moral wisdom available to devout Christians unschooled in the classical practices of philosophy. As we have seen in *De quantitate animae*, Augustine suggested that the process of contemplative development could be either lengthy or short. Thus, even in his earlier writings, the Plotinian model of *theōria* was already qualified.

Confessions makes a formal break with antecedent tradition. Now the limitations of contemplation are recounted, not so much to deny the Platonic account of contemplation, as to enlarge it, transforming its meaning through the depiction of his experience of *theōria*. As *Confessions* VII.20 (26) insists, Platonism failed to offer what it clamed: a spiritual realm for the soul to live in, "a home of bliss." The grounds for this claim are presented with arresting candor in Book Ten. One of the most disconcerting aspects of the *Confessions* is Augustine's lengthy and detailed admission of his continuing struggle with the temptations that continue to affect him. That soul is spiritually unfinished, even after its baptism and the vision at Ostia. In contrast to the serenity of the contemplative sage in Porphyry's *Life of Plotinus* or the conspicuous sanctity of the holy man in Athanasius's *Life of St. Antony*, Augustine presents himself in an initially unfavorable light. Neither conversion nor vision could fully amend his fallen nature. Like Saint Peter, for whom the transfiguration of Christ was insufficient to forestall later apostasy, Augustine is plagued by moral recidivism. Having been admitted into the hope of salvation through Christian baptism, having been converted to a new understanding of the divine, having even achieved momentary contact with divine Wisdom, Augustine's soul is nonetheless still scarred by the effects of the fall and his moral stability is not wholly secured. This is a remarkable admission, one that deliberately undercuts antecedent notions of contemplative sanctity, both pagan and Christian. In this respect, the *Confessions* are not an autohagiography, or perhaps a very sly one.

One striking example of this novel confessional demeanor is found at X.xxx (41), where Augustine admits to continued sexual desires in his dreams even after baptism and the adoption of an ascetical life:

> You commanded me to abstain from sleeping with a girl-friend and, in regard to marriage itself, you advised me to adopt a better way of life than you have allowed (1 Cor. 7:38). And because you granted me strength, this was done even before I became a dispenser of your sacrament. But in my memory of which I have spoken at length, there still live images of acts which were fixed there by my sexual habit. These images attack me. While I am awake they have force, but in sleep they not only arouse pleasure but even elicit consent, and are very like the actual act.

While Augustine distinguishes between the moral condition of the conscious and the sleeping self, he is nonetheless puzzled by the continued functioning of reason within the sleeper's mind along with the degree of consent and culpability involved. The impression conveyed is of a soul not yet purified of sexual desire and in need of divine grace to cure the "sicknesses of the soul." What distinguishes this text of Augustine is both the self-report of his condition and the palpable sense that there are opaque elements of the self that evade the power of reason. The self's conviction and conversion ride on the surface of deeper, unresolved energies.

The elements which conduce the soul to sin are by no means only sexual, although it was the weight of lust that had prevented his soul from finding a stable place in which to enjoy God in Book Seven. Thus their continued presence is especially noteworthy. While sexual desire manifests itself through his memory and in sleep, there remains an element of consent to sin that cannot be denied (X.xxx (42)). Even after the most profound moment of contact with divine Wisdom, nothing seems to have changed in the depth of the soul. Augustine relates in Book Ten a whole series of continuing temptations and shortcomings, all of which are the product of his soul's consent. We are given a moral inventory of his soul, a review of the senses and their relative power over him. He is afflicted by a creeping gluttony, since food, unlike sexual relations, cannot be simply renounced (X.xxxi (44–47)). He thinks that he is largely indifferent to perfumes, although even here he worries that this judgment is mistaken and a secret weakness may lurk within (X.xxxii (48)). But regarding the pleasures of the ear, he believes that he may err on the side of severity (X.xxxiii (49–50)).

Moreover there are more complex tendencies toward sin within the self which rely upon the senses but go beyond their immediacy. Curiosity in particular concerns him (X.xxxv (54–56)). It draws the soul to use the senses in a lust for novelty and experimentation. Thus humans are drawn to the spectacle of the theatre, to magic, to astrology, to the occult – although these have no hold over him. Yet he cannot pretend to be indifferent to praise and remains unable to remove the sting of criticism and with it a tendency toward self-justification. (X.xxxvii (60)). Life is an "immense jungle of traps and dangers" (56). Only the "God of my salvation" can offer him hope. And it is through that divine assistance that the soul comes to grasp its flaws and to acknowledge them to itself, to God, and to its neighbor. That is the purpose of confession, something that alone can be accomplished even imperfectly with God's aid.

The act of confession, the daily recognition of the soul's precarious and unceasing struggle for salvation, becomes for Augustine an integral and necessary element in the practice of contemplation. Contemplation is to be reformed by confession, restructured to conform to what Augustine believes is a Pauline conception of the human soul. His public confession is part of this continuing task of personal moral renewal, the effort to remove the "weight" which continues to hold him, his unresolved will to sin. Augustine reflects on this suspicion of innocence and the practice of authorial and private confessions at X.iii (4)–iv (5):

> My Lord, everyday my conscience makes confession, relying on the hope of your mercy as more to be trusted than its own innocence. So what profit is there, I ask, when, to human readers, by this book I confess to you who I am, not what I once was? The profit derived from confessing my past I have seen and spoken about. But what I now am at this time when I am writing my confessions many wish to know, both those who know me and those who do not but have heard something from me or about me; their ear is not attuned to my heart at the point where I am whatever I am. So as I make my confession, they wish to learn about my inner self, where they cannot penetrate with eye or ear or mind. Yet although they wish to do that and are ready to believe me, they cannot really have certain knowledge. The love which makes them good people tells them that I am not lying in confessing about myself, and the love in them believes me.

But what edification do they hope to gain by this? Do they desire to join me in thanksgiving when they hear now, by your gift, I have come close to you, and do they pray for me where they hear how I am held back by my own weight? To such sympathetic readers I will indeed reveal myself.

A Christian revision of contemplation, a blending of spiritual ascension with continual confession, becomes the central task of the later books of the *Confessions*. Augustine is at once engaged in retrospective analysis of his past life, and also reconsidering the role of contemplation in his present life as a baptized Christian. He recognizes that he still has limited knowledge of God, and surprisingly of himself. The inwardness of contemplation has uncovered much that is opaque, in particular the darkness of his prevailing spiritual nature. But this aspect of the self, now known only to God, may one day be revealed; in the meantime only confession will suffice:

> Without question we see now through a mirror in an enigma, not yet "face to face" (1 Cor. 13:12). For this cause, as long as I am a traveller absent from you (2 Cor. 5:6), I am more present to myself than to you . . .
>
> Accordingly, let me confess what I know of myself. Let me confess too what I do not know of myself. For what I know of myself I know because you grant me light, and what I do not know of myself, I do not know until such time as my darkness becomes "like noonday" before your face (Isa. 58:10).
>
> (X.v (7))

The practice of interiority, which was the hallmark of contemplation, is now understood in conjunction with confession to involve the recognition and declamation of the spiritual self's opacity. Eschatological self-knowledge is the only sort worthy of the name, for at that final moment both God and the self will be mutually translucent. "Know thyself" is an injunction doomed to failure without the divine light, something fully available only at end of time.

The interior path to transcendence remains, however, of central spiritual significance. Augustine makes this apparent in his long review of the earlier ascension narratives at X.vi (8) ff. Romans 1:20 is again the master text, although its significance is perhaps now clearer. Augustine affirms that the plea by which he began the *Confessions* has been answered with certainty. In the prologue of Book One we find:

> What a wretch I am! In your mercies, Lord God, tell me what you are to me. "Say to my soul," I am your salvation (Ps. 34:3). Speak to me so that I may hear. See the ears of my heart are before you, Lord. Open them and "say to my soul, I am your salvation." After

that utterance I will run and lay hold on you. Do not hide your face from me (cf. Ps. 26:9). Lest I die, let me die so that I may see it.

(I.v (5))

Augustine has died to himself through baptism and "seen" what can be "seen" of God at Ostia. His love for God was first manifest through God's own call in a garden in Milan. Now he understands his past contemplative ascensions to have been exercised with salvific purpose and to have bound the soul to God:

My love for you, Lord, is not an uncertain feeling, but a matter of conscious certainty. With your word you pierced my heart, and I loved you. But heaven and earth and everything in them on all sides tells me to love you. Nor do they cease to tell everyone that "they are without excuse" (Rom. 1:20). But at a profounder level you will have mercy on whom you will have mercy and will show pity on whom you will have pity (Rom. 9:15). Otherwise heaven and earth would be uttering your praises to the deaf.

(X.vi (8))

Contemplation emerges as a contributing element in the Christian soul's return to God. The visible things are but the tokens of the invisible things of God. This the baptized Christian can now recognize more fully than did the pilgrim Augustine in Book Seven. It is reaffirmed once again that knowledge of God through the visible world remains a reproach to all those who ignore it, for they are without excuse in their willful rejection of transcendence. Yet, as Augustine now notes, it is finally God's act of mercy that can convert this knowledge into salvation. Thus the knowledge derived or occasioned by contemplation of the world contributes to the salvation of some, the ears of whose hearts have been opened.

This sort of contemplation, centered on the beauty of the world, is the subject of one of the most finely wrought passages in the *Confessions*, in which Augustine reiterates the need for divine intervention in order to make contemplation transformative of the soul. It is found at X.xxvii (38):

Late have I loved thee, beauty so old and so new: late have I loved you. And see, you were within and I was in the external world and sought you there, and in my unlovely state I plunged into those lovely created things which you made. You were with me, and I was not with you. The lovely things kept me far from you, though if they did not have their existence in you. They had no existence at all. You called and cried out loud and shattered my deafness. You were radiant and resplendent, you put to flight my blindness. You were fragrant, and

I drew in my breath and now pant after you. I tasted you, and I feel but hunger and thirst for you. You touched me, and I am set on fire to attain the peace which is yours.

Here Augustine sets out a movement of the soul from external enjoyment of the lovely things of the world – while in a state of sin – to an interior love and enjoyment of God. The shift is abrupt; conflating what is elsewhere described as a multi-staged transition, for example at VII.xvii (23). It is divine intervention that initiates the interior discovery of God within the soul. And that presence is immediate and direct. Augustine's descriptive images convey both the power of God and the directness of the soul's association with him. The language of the spiritual senses is invoked: smelling the divine fragrance in contrast to worldly perfume; tasting God rather than earthly food; touching God, rather than feeling tactile pleasures. This contrast is used elsewhere in Book Ten; it describes the immediacy of love for God over earthly delights:

But when I love you, what do I love? It is not physical beauty nor temporal glory nor the brightness of light dear to earthly eyes, nor the sweet melodies of all kinds of songs, nor the gentle odour of flowers, and ointments and perfumes, nor manna or honey, nor limbs welcoming the embraces of the flesh; it is not these I love when I love my God. Yet there is a light I love, and a food, and a kind of embrace when I love my God – a light, voice, odour, food, embrace of my inner man, where my soul is floodlit by light which space cannot contain, where there is sound that time cannot seize, where there is a perfume which no breeze disperses, where there is a taste for food no amount of eating can lessen, and where there is a bond of union that no satiety can part. That is what I love when I love my God.

(X.vi (8))

Neither of the two texts is a description of sense experience. None of these images denotes physical sensations. All describe – through the attenuation of physical imagery – a transcendental state that the soul undergoes when freed from time and space, when it comes into immediate association with God. The point of this language is analogical: it intends to intimate how much greater is the soul's joy in the presence of God than is its enjoyment of earthly delights. In each case, Augustine's argument is a relative one, presenting this contrast to a protreptical end. For God is an infinite being, and a soul that discerns the source of beauty finds itself in the presence of infinite beauty. To suggest that state of awareness, the soul is presented as enjoying paradoxical states of enrapturement: hearing sounds that time cannot seize, perfumes impervious to wind, unquenchable hunger and thirst, etc. All are analogues of transcendence, attempting by finite discourse to draw the soul onwards in its salvific return – by analogy to anagogy.

This strategy is Christian in its content, underscoring the prevalence of divine love and concern. In another discussion of contemplation in Book Ten, Augustine provides a lengthy account in two major stages, coupled with an attack on the Platonist understanding of contemplation. The first stage sets out the practice of exterior and interior contemplation, in which the soul remains distinct from God. The second stage then discusses the Ostian type of contemplative closure, as the soul comes closer to God. The first level reads:

> Truth, when did you ever fail to walk with me, teaching me what to avoid and what to seek after when I reported to you what, in my inferior position, I could see and asked your counsel? To the best of my powers of sense-perception, I travelled through the external world. Starting from myself I gave attention to the life of my own body, and examined my own senses. From there I moved into the recesses of my memory, manifold vastness full of innumerable riches in wonder-ful ways, and "I considered and was afraid" (Hab. 3:2). Without you I could discern none of these things, and I found that none of these things was you. Nor was I you, though I had made these discoveries. I traversed everything, and tried to make distinctions and to evaluate each entity according to its proper rank. Some things I observed in interrogating the reports of my senses. Other things I felt to be mixed with my own self. I identified and numbered the senses reporting to me. There in the wide riches of memory, I examined other things, hiding some away, drawing out others. But as I did this, the eye, that is the power by which I was doing it, was not you. For you are the abiding light by which I investigated all these matters to discover whether they existed, what they were, and what value should be attached to them. I listened to you teaching me and giving instruc-tions. This I frequently do. It gives me delight, and I take refuge in this pleasure from necessary business, so far as I am able to take relief. But in all these investigations which I pursue while consulting you, I can find no safe place for my soul except in you. There my dispersed aspirations are gathered together, and from you no part of me will depart.
>
> (X.xl (65))

Contemplation of the world, the reflective division of things according to their nature, is presented here as significant but not spiritually satisfying. The interrogation of human memory, that vast "stomach of the mind" (X.xiv (21)), does not provide access to God, for it is no different in kind from external things. Interiority discloses no inner connection to the One, as the Plotinian school had supposed. Memory is an empirical faculty yielding knowledge of the world, not God himself. The soul does not, then, come to God by its own efforts at contemplation. There is no safe place for the soul except in God,

and this can be found only through divine intervention. The next segment of
X.xl (65) brings this out clearly:

> And sometimes you cause me to enter into an extraordinary depth of
> feeling marked by a strange sweetness. If it were brought to perfection
> in me, it would be an experience quite beyond anything in this life.
> But I fall back into my usual ways under my miserable burdens. I am
> reabsorbed by my habitual practices. I am held in their grip. I weep
> profusely, but still I am held. Such is the strength of the burden of habit.
> Here I have the power to be, but do not wish it. There I wish to be,
> but lack the power. On both grounds I am in misery.

Affective language is again used to indicate the deepest sort of interior
contemplation. The soul's condition is exhibited as it is drawn out of its habitual
state of sinfulness into a state of association with God. Its strangeness is the result
of the spiritual self's being brought into a new condition in relation to God.
It is "most unusual," an interior state of remarkable perhaps unknown delight.
That delight is the direct result of the soul's freedom from the misery of sinful
habituation, the joy of its release from servitude. The passage is defined by this
moral conversion, this sloughing off of the misery and burden of sin. What
Augustine presents here is another portrait of the Ostian vision, the turning of
the soul to God and its momentary entrance into a state of freedom from the
moral weight of its fall. The focus of the passage is the representation of the
soul's spiritual conversion. If this state were to be perfect, then the soul would
indeed be beyond human life. He uses the language of human delight to
describe a moral and spiritual change in the soul, one that renders it capable
to exist before God within that place of safe refuge. But the soul lacks both the
power to enter this state without God, and it is powerless to sustain it. Just as at
Ostia, the soul falls back under the weight of its flawed moral condition. Once
again, brevity underscores spiritual distance, for the soul is both a creature
distinct from God and a self not yet freed from its habituation to sin.

Only God can "cure all the sicknesses" of the Augustinian soul. Only
divine grace can lose the glue of lust and extinguish its impulses. It is the soul's
divided loyalty, to God and the world, which is the source of its failure. This
is what stands between the soul and that state of delight and release: the
divided will:

> You are the truth presiding over all things. But in my greed I was
> unwilling to lose you, and wanted to have you at the same time as
> holding on to a lie, in much the same way as no one wants to become
> such a liar as to lose all awareness of what the truth is. This is why
> I lost you: you do not condescend to be possessed together with
> falsehood.
>
> (X.xlii (66))

The imperfection of the soul is not found in its lack of knowledge of reality, but in its inability to act upon the divine truth it knows. Its carnal desires are both sicknesses within the soul and a dissemblance before the truth. This is the prevalent character of the human condition, eradicable except through divine mercy. That must come through a mediator, one who is both divine and human, an "immortal righteous one, mortal like humanity, righteous like God" (X.xliii (68)). It is precisely this that the Platonists have missed in their notion of contemplation. Here in Book Ten, the indictment is broadened to catch not just the Plotinian Platonism, with its emphasis only on philosophy as a means to contemplative release, but also other sorts of Platonism, those that engage in ritual practices in pursuit of contemplation:

> Who could be found to reconcile me to you? Was I to beg the help of the angels? What prayer should I use? What sacred rites? Many have tried to return to you, and have not had the strength in them-selves to achieve it, so I have been told. They have attempted these methods and have lapsed into a desire for curious visions, and have been rewarded with illusions. For in their quest they have been lifted up by their pride in their high culture, inflating their chest rather than beating their breast.
>
> (X.xlii (67))

"A desire for curious visions" – this notion not only rehearses the image from Book Seven of the Platonists as arrogant visionaries, it also reminds us anew of Augustine's single-minded interest throughout the *Confessions* in soteriology. Moreover, the very phrase here indicates a pejorative attitude to the desire for such visions for their own sake, as a prideful spiritual diversion. The reader is invited to realize that contemplation may be attempted in a fashion that is illusory, even demonic. The desire for such visions is a species of curiosity, a vain inquisitiveness that Augustine had condemned as another form of lust at X.xxxv (54). It bears mention that Augustine seems aware in this passage of the fissure among the Platonic schools on the proper path to contemplation discussed earlier. The passage suggests that Augustine was alert to this pagan dispute regarding the nature of contemplative and the competing accounts of philosophy and theurgy, at least in outline. It is likely that he grasped Porphyry's position on theurgy, and perhaps had some sense of the larger debate with the school of Iamblichus. But the latter point is at best speculative. He would later be highly critical of theurgical Platonism in the *De Civitate Dei* IX, at a point in his career when he had a broader understanding of that school. Porphyry seems the principal target there. Yet it is intruiging that in the *Confessions* Augustine offers a critique of the Plotinian school's account of contemplation that parallels interscholastic Platonic criticisms.

These intimations of a new Christian representation of contemplation are developed more thoroughly in Book Twelve. Its revisionist project follows two main tracks. The first completes the logic of the Romans 1:20–21: that knowledge of God provides the basis for God's just judgment. Sin is conditioned by knowledge; it is an act of volition against what the soul knows to be true. With this text in mind, Augustine comes to understand contemplation as a component of Christian confession. The second element of Augustine's revisionism presents contemplation as most fully pursued within the structure of the Church and related to God's definitive revelation in scripture.

Contemplation of the invisible things of God offers certain and indubitable knowledge. The ascensions of Book Seven had already established that. And the vision of Ostia had offered direct if fleeting access to God's wisdom. Yet the soul, in the very process of coming into contact with God, recognizes that it is not saved, but fallen. Contemplation is an act which lays bare with exquisite accuracy the full truth of the soul's state in reference to God. The soul has slipped away from the source of its existence and embraced a debased condition. Contemplation, far from exhibiting the soul's fundamental connection with the One, bares instead the deep fissure that obtains between it and God. Thus contemplative knowledge is critical to the framing of the soul's spiritual location. This line of reflection can be seen at XII.xi (11):

> and you said to me, Lord, with a loud voice to my inner ear, that you created all natures and substances which are not what you are and nevertheless exist. The only thing that is not from you is what has no existence. The movement of the will away from you, who are, is movement toward that which has less being. A movement of this nature is a fault and a sin, and no one's sin harms you or disturbs the order of your rule, either on high or down below. "In your presence" (Ps. 18:15) this truth is clear to me. Let it become more and more evident, I pray you, and as it becomes manifest may I dwell calmly under your wings.

Contemplation, conducted "in the presence of truth," exhibits both the scope of the soul's declension and its need for divine assistance.

Augustine has thus succeeded in making contemplation propaedeutic to confession, to the salvific return of the soul through Christ. That is the nature of contemplation in this present life. Confession, salvation, and contemplation will converge, perhaps after death, certainly at the last day. Augustine uses Paul as a witness to his case at XIII.xiii (14). He begins disassociating the salvific path of faith from contemplative sight, using the authority and the figure of Paul. A final state of eschatological vision is hinted at:

> Nevertheless we still act on faith, not yet on sight, "For by hope we have been saved" (2 Cor. 5:7). "Hope which is seen is not hope" (Rom. 8:24). "Deep" still "calls to deep," but now "with the voice of your cataracts" (Ps. 41:8). In this life even he who says "I could not

speak to you as spiritual but as carnal" (1 Cor 3:1) does nothing that he himself has comprehended.

The force of this claim is considerable. The language of the vision at Ostia is recalled – once again contemplation is represented in terms of Romans 8:23:

> For that city the bridegroom's friend (John 3:29) sighs, having already the firstfruits of the spirit within him; but he still groans within himself "waiting for the adoption, the redemption of his body."

Yet contemplation can only anticipate the final vision enjoyed by the saints, when salvation and direct knowledge of God are one.

> "What a beautiful light that will be when 'we shall see him as he is' (1 John 3:2), and there 'shall pass away the tears which have become my bread day and night, while it is daily said to me, Where is your God?' (Ps. 41:4)."

This final conjunction of eternal life with truth remains, despite its eschatological remoteness, a paradigm for our present state. For Christians, contemplation is indeed a worthy task, even if while in this life we are "saved by hope" (Rom. 8:24). Augustine summarizes this connection between contemplation and confession at XIII.xiv (15):

> We were "once darkness" (Eph. 5:8), the remnants of which we bear in the body which "is dead because of sin" (Rom. 8:10), "until the day breathes and the shadows are removed" (Cant. 2:17). "Hope in the Lord. In the morning I will stand up and I will contemplate you. I will ever confess to him. In the morning I will stand and I will see the salvation of my face" (Ps. 41:6–12), my God "who shall vivify even our mortal bodies through the Spirit who dwells in us" (Rom. 8:11).

Book Thirteen expands on this Christian view of the practice of contemplation. As Augustine's practice throughout the *Confessions* demonstrates, Christian contemplation is scriptural in character. This "solid firmament of authority over us" provides the soul with a foundation more sure than philosophical dialectic. And the solidity of scripture is linked to the surety of Christ's spiritual people on earth. For Christians, contemplation is rooted in the Church, in its scriptures, and in the capacity for theological discernment found there. The Christian contemplative life is founded on the knowledge and delight that emerge from scriptural reflection, which is a form of divine dialectic (XIII.xviii (22)):

Passing from the lower good works of the active life to the delights of contemplation, may we "hold the word of life" which is above and "appear as lights in the world" (Phil. 2:15) by adhering to the solid firmament of your scripture. For there you hold conversation with us to teach us to distinguish between intelligible and sensible things as between day and night, or between souls dedicated to the intelligible realm and souls dedicated to the material world of the senses. Then it is not only you in the secret place of your judgement who divide between light and darkness as you did before the making of the firmament; it is also your spiritual people established in the same solid firmament and distinguished by your grace manifested throughout the world.

This ecclesial dimension is essential to Augustine's final representation of contemplation. It is an unmistakable theme in Book Thirteen, drawing out formally the scripturalism of the entire work. Christian contemplative practice must be grounded in reflection on scripture. It supersedes Platonic dialectic, having a stronger, more authoritative basis in the gospel and in the church (XIII.xxii (32)). Christian contemplatives are spiritual persons who exercise spiritual judgment. These contemplatives may or may not be ordained, and may be either male or female (XIII.xxviii (33)). Dialectic is no longer a necessary feature of spiritual discernment, having now been superseded by reflection on divine word in scripture. The language of audition, prominent in Augustine's reflection on Ostia, comes more clearly into focus in the late books, as the soul's listening to scripture is made the foundation for Christian contemplation (XIII.xxx (45)): "I listened, Lord, my God; I sucked a drop of sweetness from your truth, and I understood."

There is a larger Christian thesis behind this scriptural imperative. Augustine is committed to the notion that the fallen soul can engage in a return to God through the Spirit active in the church. There are several aspects to this pattern of contemplative "turning around" to God. The presence of the Spirit in the Christian soul is the motivating force behind the soul's conversion. This presence provides the capacity to attend to God, and, in so doing, helps to draw the soul more tightly to the divine nature. The need for this divine presence, essential to the contemplative love of God, is put forcefully at XIII.xxxi (46):

When people see these things with the help of your Spirit, it is you who are seeing in them. When, therefore, they see that things are good, you are seeing that they are good. Whatever pleases them for your sake is pleasing you in them. The things which by the help of your Spirit delight us are delighting you in us. "For what man knows the being of man except the spirit of man which is in him? So also no one knows the things of God except the Spirit of God. But we (he says) have not received the spirit of this world, but the Spirit which is of God, so that we may know the gifts given us by God." (1 Cor. 2:11–12). I am moved to declare: certainly no one knows the things of God except the Spirit of God. Then how do we ourselves know the gifts which God has given? The answer comes to me that the statement "No one knows except the Spirit of God" also applies to the things we know by the help of his Spirit. "Just as it is not you that speak" (Matt. 10:20) is rightly said to those who are speaking by the Spirit of God, so also the words it is not you that know "may rightly be said to those whose knowing is by the Spirit of God." Therefore it is no less correct that "it is not you that see" is spoken to those who see by the Spirit of God. Whatever, therefore, they see to be good by the Spirit of God, it is not they but God who is seeing that it is good.

1 Cor. 2:9 ff. was the Pauline reference used in reference to the eternal life of the saints in the Ostian narrative. It was a text to which Augustine returned at X.v (7), in the context of self-knowledge. Here in Book Thirteen its implications are more fully developed. Now we discern more clearly that Christian contemplation, far from being an autonomous act of the pilgrim self, is actually a result of the indwelling of the Spirit of God. It is not the exercise of a native capacity discovered within the soul; it is directly the expression of divine reflection. The contemplative ascent is initiated by the recognition of God's creative presence in creation. This was critical to the narrative of Book Seven. Here in Book Thirteen, Augustine maintains that the very act of knowing is not just an instance of divine illumination, it is an act of divine knowing. The text follows from a discussion of Manichaean cosmology (XIII.xxx (45)), so that the truths discovered would seem to be not so much facts of observation as theoretic claims about the value of things in the world. The world can only be properly valued when it is understood to be as it is seen by God: as a direct product of God under his continual observation. This is the initial stage of contemplation, now understood to be a direct participation in the divine intellect's knowing of created being. And this is an extraordinary power that the contemplative soul participates in, for God's knowledge of created things is the continuing basis for their existence (XIII.xxxviii (53)): "We see things you have made because they are. But they are because you see them."

These are remarkable claims, dignifying the Christian soul both with the inhabitation of the Spirit of God and with a share in the sight of God through which all created things exist. It is a startlingly original position. For Augustine maintains that God, while remaining in himself, also engages in an outflow, first to create the world, second to know and appreciate it, and finally to save souls fallen from their proper state. Contemplation is the sight of God directed outside himself in creation and then back upon himself through contemplation. God's contemplative presence is the active force holding reality in existence, and the

Christian soul can come to connect up with that divine intellection. Moreover, Augustine discerns a trinitarian dimension to contemplation. This is the second, specifically Christian element in his account. The contemplative soul, as this text from XIII.xxxi (46) indicates, it is inhabited by the Spirit and knows "the things of God" only through the Spirit. Renewed in its mind, the Christian soul has an ability to understand and "judge" created things, since such a "spiritual person" begins to grasp "the Trinity in Unity and the Unity of the Trinity." Even aspects of human psychology are indicative of the inner life of God. Being, knowing, and willing are functional analogues of the trinitarian life of the Godhead. While this theme in the *Confessions* is not systematically elaborated, nevertheless the activity of the Spirit is clearly viewed as the agent of divine self-contemplation. It is this divine contemplative motion, out into creation and back through the "things of God," that establishes the great rhythm of creation. It is this majestic spiritual movement that spiritual persons discover in contemplation.

The church emerges in Book Thirteen as the vehicle for Christian contemplation. Augustine views it not as the mere aggregation of those souls that have been called or predestined by God to salvation (XIII.xxiii (33)). Rather, it is "a living soul," a society of contemplative souls whose occurrence is not a natural element in the structure of reality, but a result of human reformation. It is the divine Word, taught in the Gospels, that brings this "living soul" into existence:

> But the Word, O God, is fount of eternal life (John 4:14) and does not pass away. A departure from God is checked by your Word, when it is said to us "Be not conformed to this world" (Rom. 12:2) so that the "earth may produce a living soul" through the fount of life. By your word through your evangelists the soul achieves self-control by modeling itself on the imitators of your Christ.
>
> (XIII.xxi (31))

Augustine believes that the declension of souls is arrested by the Church, whose "head and body" are the Word (XIII.xxxiv (49)). It is this society of the spiritual that teaches and exemplifies the Word. They constitute an integral unity, modeling their lives on the evangelical record of Christ's life. This model of the church, of the spiritual body inhabited by Christ as its head, allows Augustine to describe an ecclesial locus for contemplation, nesting it within an institutional structure. At the same time, the cosmic significance of the Church is drawn out in reference to God's own act of knowing. Thus the Spirit of God is immediately present in the act of contemplative knowledge for Christians, who see by that Spirit. These spiritual Christians constitute the true Church, and establish a society of souls that await their deliverance, morally renewed in conformity with Christ. This notion, of the church as "the living soul," is iterated fully at XIII.xxxiv (49):

Hence you kindled lights in the firmament, your saints, "having the word of life" (Phil. 2:16), shining with a sublime authority made manifest by spiritual gifts. And then to instruct the unbelieving peoples, you produced from physical matter sacraments and visible miracles and the sounds of the words of your book, symbolized by "the firmament". Believers also are blessed by them. Then you formed "the living soul" of the faithful with their affections disciplined by a strong continence. Then you renewed the mind (Rom. 12:2) after your image and likeness (Col. 3:10) to be subject to you alone and in no need of human authority as a model to imitate.

This entire line of reflecting in Book Thirteen draws together contemplation in all its aspect – contemplation of the created world, of the holy scriptures, of the divine Word, and finally of the Trinity – and nests it within the church. In so doing, Augustine has rejoined contemplation to the path of salvation. Unlike the world soul of the Platonists, "the living soul of the faithful" is not a feature of the natural order, but a function of grace. The recursive contemplation of human souls is catalyzed by the activity of the Trinity, specifically the Spirit which acts through them. Augustine has not only provided, as it were, a field theory of contemplation in response to the Platonists, he has sketched as well a Christian conception of deity in contrast with Neo-Platonism. In the *Confessions*, contemplation is exercised by human souls through the direct intervention of the Spirit of God.

In the late books of the *Confessions*, the contemporaneous voice of the Christian bishop is heard, setting the earlier narrative into a more systematic, theological relief. This retrospective analysis suggests a final summary observation regarding contemplation and the vision at Ostia. In constructing his nuanced Christian account in the *Confessions*, Augustine has secured a Christian claim to contemplative knowledge of the transcendent. At the same time, however, he has preserved orthodox soteriology. His theology of contemplation bears the mark of Paul's proleptic eschatology of Romans 8: the belief that contemplation betokens the presence of the Spirit within the world, the firstfruits of the future kingdom. Contemplation prefigures the final state of Christians, even if a soul who enjoys it is still not yet saved, but prone to the vicissitudes of its fallen state, as Augustine relates so candidly in his own case. It is this careful balance, of cognitive realization over against salvific inadequacy, which is the theological hallmark of contemplation in Augustine's *Confessions*.

Contemplation is effective only when it is conjoined to confession. Only then does the soul contact God and grasp the true nature of its present condition. Thus contemplation supports the practice of the Christian religion in the account of the *Confessions*. There its true significance and final purpose emerge. For confession is a distinctively Christian practice – admission of the fallen and culpable state of the soul, recognition of the reality of God's presence, and finally, submission to the saving power of Christ. Contemplation serves to prepare for

this practice, giving visionary insight, certitude, and even momentary association. But contemplation is only completed by confession. Contemplation
without confession is futile and empty. But with it, contemplation offers the
beginning of Christian hope that the soul will find the "home of bliss."

8

TOTAL CONCENTRATION OF
THE HEART

"Nothing is distant from God, and there is no ground for fear that he may not acknowledge me at the end of the world and raise me up." These are Monica's final words in the *Confessions* (IX.xi (28)). Hers is the story of a life well lived, for hers is a story that ends in the certain hope of resurrection. She is, as much as her son, an exemplar of the Christian contemplative. It is time now to reflect on the full account of contemplation that Augustine offers in the *Confessions*, and to explore some of its most salient features. Two aspects require further consideration: its depiction of transcendence and its conception of deity. Clarification of these will help us answer a question that is perennially intriguing: how are we to understand the contact with God described in the vision at Ostia? Indeed, Augustine's depiction of contemplation sometimes perplexes contemporary readers because it makes no reference to union with God. In his recent study of the Christian mystical tradition, Bernard McGinn raised this issue, pointing out that Augustine appears to have intentionally avoided the language of mystical union. He says:

> It is difficult not to think that this deliberate avoidance of the language of union in someone who knew Plotinus so well as a conscious choice and an implied criticism of the limitations of non-Christian mystical effort.
>
> (McGinn 1991: 231)

To address this issue, we must first come to terms with Monica. In the account of Ostia, she too touched divine Wisdom through the total concentration of her heart. In many respects, Augustine's representation of contemplation becomes clearer when we study it from the standpoint of Monica. Above all, attention to Monica provides a basis for separating off Augustine's account of contemplation from that found in the *libri Platonicorum*. If contemplation in the *Confessions* should be read neither as a failed instance of Plotinian ecstasy nor as a successful one, then what is the distinctive nature of Christian contemplation according to Augustine's text?

Monica had no place in an ancient Platonic school like that of Plotinus and no access to the discipline of contemplation as the *libri Platonicorum* understood it. Her dispossession from the Platonic schools was not so much a matter of gender as caste. There were female members of the Plotinian circle, such as Gemina and Amphiclea, who were said to be devoted to philosophy (Armstrong 1966: 31). Hypatia was the most celebrated woman philosopher, a member of the Alexandrian Platonist school and a pagan martyr who died about 415. But Monica was not formally educated, coming as she did from a provincial background of some means but not from the rarefied aristocratic world where an exceptional daughter might receive an education in the *artes liberales* and in philosophy. Monica at Ostia is thus an unpromising candidate for high contemplation in the Plotinian style, even a counter-example to the Platonic ideal of transcendence acquired through dialectic and the refined, ascetic life. Augustine accentuates this fact, portraying her instead as an unlearned, married woman of earned and infused wisdom. The formation of her moral character is, in fact, a sub-tonic theme throughout the *Confessions*. We repeatedly see her minor failings and also her false compromises with family ambition for the sake of her brilliant son's career: her acquiescence to Augustine's concubinage, her acceptance of his secular education in the liberal arts (II.iii (8)), her promotion of an arranged and socially advantageous marriage with an underaged daughter of a noble Catholic family in Italy (VI.xiii (23)). And then there is her fondness for wine (IX.viii (18)). Yet through all this we also see her nobility of character and a wisdom which grew beyond the merely practical. For Monica is not an archetype of the worldly wise woman. It is the practice of her faith that ennobles her, nurturing an inner sanctity that matures throughout the story of the *Confessions* and manifests itself in her relations with the little platoon of people who surround her. The traits and dispositions of her character bear evidence of the grace of the Spirit. Indeed she appears in the narrative as perhaps more prepared for those contemplative moments at Ostia than her son is, still green in his new religion.

That is because she had long been a confessor. Hers was a life of confession. She had risked it to stand before the Catholic cathedral with Ambrose, bishop of Milan, in the face of Imperial troops who were intent on enforcing a pro-Arian edict. As Augustine describes the scene:

> The devout congregation kept continual guard in the Church, ready to die with their bishop, your servant. There my mother, your handmaid, was a leader in keeping anxious watch and lived in prayer.
>
> (IX.vii (15))

Less dramatically she had endured the difficulties of her marriage and the vicissitudes of her children's upbringing with Christian steadfastness, even guiding her wayward pagan husband Patricius into her faith before she died (IX.ix (19–22)). Her servants, we are told, "felt your presence in her heart, witnessed by the fruits of her holy way of life" (IX.ix (22)). As Augustine tells the story, hers was a life lived through continual confession – of her faults and of her savior – that led to a moment of total concentration of her heart at Ostia.

In this light we would do well to notice Augustine's narrative framing of the vision at Ostia. It is embedded in the story of Monica's life, which begins at IX.viii (17) and continues through the end of the chapter and the close of the autobiography. But there is no dramatic emphasis upon the vision or any great spiritual change in either Monica or Augustine because of it. It is a quiet deepening of their souls into the transcendent, an instance of premonitory grace before Monica's death. And it is an occasion in which the nearness of God, which had been the watchword of Monica's life, is transformed into the immediate presence of Wisdom. There both are prepared for her impending death. For Monica, the vision at Ostia confers a sense of completion to her life, and freedom from worldly concerns. Augustine reports that "at the time of their conversation at the window . . . she said 'What have I to do here now?'" Later she "spoke of her contempt for this life and of the beneficence of death" (IX.xi (28)). For Augustine himself, Ostia offers the courage to face her passing.

The vision at Ostia is, then, both remarkable and quotidian. It is, to be sure, an extraordinary spiritual moment. But it nevertheless has its place within the practice of Monica's Catholic faith. It endorses that path of salvation; it does not supplant it. It deepens the meaning of her Christianity and certifies its truth. Its fruits are yielded thereafter by the moral demeanor of Monica in the face of death, by the disposition of Augustine's life, and by their shared hope for the eternal life of the saints. It is in this respect that Monica represents an affront to the Platonic contemplative ideal. However unpromising she may be as a philosopher, she achieves certain knowledge of transcendental Wisdom, consummating contact with being itself within her soul. That is what we are told. Her success is not a function of her intellectual preparation, nor, given her own story of gradual moral development, is it a result of some special sort of ethical insight. It is instead a function of the Spirit within her, whose presence was prepared by her life in the Church. That was her training for contemplation's fruition, the church of Ambrose. And, in light of Augustine's subsequent reflections in Books Ten to Thirteen, we can see how this should be so. The Church, as the living soul of the faithful, sets the foundation for a life of grace and for the drawing of the soul into the presence of God. Monica's moment of concentration in love is an ecclesial moment, one that emerged in the schoolhouse of souls that is the Church. For there is no other explanation for Monica at Ostia; hers is an ecclesial soul perfected into the presence of God by the power of the Spirit.

Monica's vision at Ostia also exhibits one curious similarity with Plotinian contemplation, however removed she may be from the intellectual culture of the Platonic schools. Monica's soul is unchanged at Ostia. Just as in Plotinus, *theōria* at Ostia changes nothing. Monica's soul achieves no new ontological condition as such. Her status as a creature of God remains, even if she enjoyed a measure of deification by her contact with divine Wisdom. She does not become something wholly new at Ostia in a strictly ontological sense; the spiritual renewal of which she was capable had already been accomplished long ago through baptism. This fact invites further reflection on what might be called the architecture of the spiritual universe revealed at Ostia. What did Ostia disclose about the transcendental world which Monica's soul traversed in those moments of distracted vision? Answering that question will take us some way toward understanding the meaning of that "moment of understanding" at Ostia.

Perhaps the passages in the *Confessions* that best exhibit Augustine's distinctive transcendentalism are those which relate to the *caelum caeli*, the heaven of heaven, in Book Twelve. Augustine read the *caelum* of Gen. 1:1 in reference to the *caelum caeli* of Ps. 148:4. The first creation is the heaven of heaven, in contrast to the visible and material world. On this exegetical opening Augustine constructed an account of a foundational level of created but immaterial reality. One critical passage is found at XII.ix (9):

> That is why the Spirit, the teacher of your servant (Moses), in relating that in the beginning you made heaven and earth, says nothing about time and is silent about days. No doubt the "heaven of heaven" which you made in the beginning is a kind of creation in the realm of the intellect. Without being coeternal with you, O Trinity, it nevertheless participates in Your eternity. From the sweet happiness of contemplating you, it finds power to check its mutability. Without any lapse to which its createdness makes it liable, by cleaving to you it escapes all the revolving vicissitudes of the temporal process.

We can discern several key claims:

1 The *caelum caeli* exists within the level of intellectual existence, outside space, time, and materiality.
2 It is a primordial form of creation.
3 As such it is not within the uncreated Godhead, nor eternal along with the Trinity.
4 It exists by participation in the eternity of the Trinity.
5 This participation takes the form of continuous contemplation.
6 This continuous contemplation prevents the mutability, to which it is liable as a created being, from taking hold.

Moreover Augustine attributes to the "heaven of heaven" both the capacity for contemplation and the capacity for decision making. The conditions of its existence could be worse, if it chose the vicissitudes of temporality.

Another revealing passage also bears analysis, one of the "dominical voice" texts that take on a special emphasis and authority. At XII.xi (12), Augustine recounts his recognition of the nature of the heaven of heaven.

> Again you said to me, in a loud voice to my inner ear, that not even that created realm, the "heaven of heaven", is coeternal with you. Its delight is exclusively in you. In an unfailing purity it satiates its thirst in you. It never at any point betrays its mutability. You are always present to it, and it concentrates all its affection on you. It has no future to expect. It suffers no variation and experiences no distending in the successiveness of time. O blessed creature, if there be such: happy in cleaving to your felicity, happy to have you as eternal inhabitant and its source of light! I do not find any better name for the Lord's "heaven of heaven" (Ps. 113:16) than your House. There your delight is contemplated without any failure or wandering away to something else. The pure heart enjoys absolute concord and unity in the unshakeable peace of holy spirits, the citizens of your city in the heavens above the visible heavens.

Created and contingent beings have the capacity to move away from God, toward less reality. But the heaven of heaven is coeternal with God because, though created, it has not chosen distance, and so is not distended into temporality. Moreover the heaven of heaven is described by the use of a related notion, the House of God, the heavenly city. There is a collective act of volition by the holy spirits that dwell within the *caelum caeli*, and this secures its adherence to God. At XII.xiii (16) Augustine further indicates that the pilgrim soul's grasp of the heaven of heaven comes about through meditation upon scripture. He also defines the contemplative state associated with the heaven of heaven in reference to Genesis 1:

> My provisional interpretation of that is that "heaven" means the "heaven of heaven," the intellectual, non-physical heaven where the intelligence's knowing is a matter of simultaneity – not in part, not in an enigma, not through a mirror, but complete, in total openness, "face to face" (1 Cor. 13:12). This knowing is not of one thing at one moment and of another thing at another moment, but is concurrent without any temporal successiveness.

In this sequence of passages, Augustine asserts a direct knowledge of the transcendent realm – the *caelum caeli*. He sketches out a scripturally grounded knowledge of the *caelum caeli*, the first, intelligible creation. And the *caelum caeli* is described as an unfallen creature, a collective realm of spirits who have not exercised the option of sin and embraced mutability. Significantly, he concludes his discussion of the *caelum caeli*, the heavenly Jerusalem and the homeland of the soul, with a reference to the firstfruits of the spirit from Romans 8.23 at XII.xvi (23). This scriptural reference recurs from the vision of Ostia, and this passage is, in some respects, a gloss on it. Augustine believes that he has had certain knowledge that the true place of the human self is there in the transcendent realm of the *caelum caeli*. But, unlike Plotinus, that intelligible locus of the human self is not so secure that the soul always remains rooted there in the transcendent world. Rather, the contemplative soul can only identify in anticipation its station within the *caelum caeli*; it does not currently exist at this level of existence – even fractionally.

If we return now from these passages from Book Twelve to Monica at Ostia, we can glimpse how Augustine understands her enjoyment of contemplation. These passages are his refined, retrospective interpretation of the deeper logic of contemplation. They suggest several points about Monica at Ostia which clarify his overall Christian account. The first of these concerns the tacit ontology of the vision at Ostia. When her soul is described as lifted up toward eternal being in the first description of IX.x (24), it is said to move beyond the mind and into the "region of inexhaustible abundance where you feed Israel eternally with truth for food." This region, obscure in an initial reading, begins to come clearer in reference to the concept of the created "heaven of heaven." It is a region that is outside time and space, where reflection is collectively exercised. It is also the foundation for all things that do come into being, the created wisdom of things that emerge by creation into time. It is also a region that is contrasted in the vision at Ostia with Wisdom itself, the uncreated and eternal source of all created beings.

When subsequently unpacked, this initial description contains a barely evident region that Monica's soul moves through without much notice as it goes on to direct contact with divine Wisdom. But it is there nonetheless. And it shows once again Augustine's subtle adaptation of Plotinian accounts of *theōria*. In Plotinus, as we saw, Intellect engages in eternal contemplation of the One, and this is the source for its production of all consequents beings at lower levels of reality. The embodied soul joins in this higher reflection when it rediscovers its deep, intellective self in contemplation. In the *Confessions*, a related account is adumbrated: the "heaven of heaven" is the partial equivalent of Intellect, one that also engages in simultaneous reflection of a first principle. That contemplation is complete and unmediated; it is moreover "face to face." But there are several major differences. The "heaven of heaven," while an inexhaustible region, is not eternal and is created by the eternal Wisdom that it contemplates. While prone to the vicissitudes and mutability of contingency, it never actually suffers them, because of the intensity and immediacy of its focus. But it abides across the gulf of creation from Wisdom, a creature in its nature, wholly distinct from its eternal source. Thus its contemplation, and that of the embodied souls who reach this level, always occur at a distance, at some measure of ontological removal from eternal Wisdom. That is a direct result of the act of creation. The "heaven of heaven" is a "blessed creature," but a creature nonetheless.

Monica's soul can thus be seen to participate in the inner life of this region, this transcendent and heavenly hypostasis. Her soul has, as we saw earlier, no native place in the transcendent, so it can only mark of its place of hope. Yet it has participated in the direct contemplation that is the eternal life of the "heaven of heaven." And it has surpassed even this, by its touch of Wisdom, across the gap between the perfection of creatures and perfection itself. This same ontology of contemplation is restated in the second account of the vision at Ostia (IX.x (25)). Again the forceful and unmediated presence of him whom the soul loves is described, only to be superseded by a moment of closure as the contemplative soul attains eternal Wisdom. This text is stronger, however, than the earlier description in the preceding section (24) in one respect. It suggests that the eternal life of the saints is not only a state of unmediated reflection on divine Wisdom. It is also a "moment of understanding" when the soul closes the gap with its eternal creator. Both unmediated presence and direct association are thus part of the eschatological state of the soul. But neither complete union nor absorption into eternal Wisdom are indicated, only contact with divine Wisdom. The prevailing ontology thus remains strictly monotheistic.

These aspects of contemplation at Ostia emerge when the text is read against the theological interpretation of the later books. They help us to understand more clearly what Augustine only adumbrates in the autobiographical descriptions themselves. Indeed the type of contemplation ascribed to Monica can be seen more clearly to be attenuated and largely transposed from that found in the *libri Platonicorum*. Many aspects of the account confirm this. Monica's ascent is a case in point. The Platonist ascension narrative calls for the soul to grasp fundamental truths and to move up through levels of knowledge which are correlated with levels of reality. The levels iterated at Ostia are not really levels of knowledge, hard-won by the soul through its cognitive efforts. The soul of Monica is simply lifted up past these levels, so that the ascent turns, not on the natural connection between levels of reality and knowledge, but on the power of divine grace. These levels are nonetheless important and they are clearly understood to be real and not fictive or imaginary. But the ascent is not ultimately rooted in them, in what they represent, and in the power that the ascending soul takes from them. At Ostia, physical contingency and mental changeability are levels of reality that Monica's soul traverses as tokens of its movement under the power of divine grace. Thus the veridicality described in the vision at Ostia takes on a distinctive meaning. Monica's ascent begins, we are told, in the presence of truth. And it reaches in the end to that Wisdom upon which all things depend for their being. Ostia is, in this sense, a supremely foundational moment. The highest reaches of reality are disclosed to the contemplative soul. Yet the levels surpassed are ancillary in importance to the real dynamic of the passage, the soul's ascent to its beloved creator. In this the true center of the vision of Ostia lies.

And so Monica's ascension cannot really be said to be about the movement of the self through the natural order of reality which yields its secrets to the philosophically disciplined mind. Nor, as in Plotinus, is it about that a journey into the hidden recesses of a self still securely present to the level of being. It is, rather, about the revelation of divine Wisdom to a created soul. This is importunate and unmerited, though it is presaged by Monica's life within the living soul of the faithful, the church. Contemplation for Monica is, therefore, an act of spiritual transcendence, but it is not an intellectual one or one that follows a discipline for traversing levels of being and knowledge. It is thus a matter of the soul coming into the presence of God, while all else is superfluous. At Ostia, as in the *Soliloquia*, it is only God and the soul that seem, in the end, to matter.

Just here we can begin to see the lineaments of Augustine's distinctive account of contemplation and with it a Christian conception of the soul's relation to God. Monica's soul meets Wisdom, the creative power of God in the vision at Ostia. Or alternatively, he who had been heard from afar in creation is now heard without mediation in the depth of the soul. He who is met directly is the creator of the soul. This means that Monica's soul has accomplished several things at once, against overwhelming forces to the contrary. She has overcome the effects of the fall and stretched out to touch the eternal Wisdom which created all things. This is, as we have seen, only a dispensation, not a permanent condition, and it is the result of divine initiative, not her own. But nonetheless it is described as having happened. The fall is momentarily reversed by the Spirit so that her soul can achieve immediate association with its creator. In this act she discovers that the creator is also the savior of the soul. Contemplation at Ostia follows the inherent logic of salvation, occurring through divine initiative and restoring Monica's soul, even if conditionally, to a direct relationship with her creator. This must be so, for the fall that is redressed has no cosmological value in Augustine's analysis. It was the ruination of initial divine creation and has no positive value in itself. It was a mistake, an instance of cosmic disfigurement. Moreover it is an error that had its origins in the soul itself. It did not proceed from a power opposed to the Good as in Manichaeism, nor did it fit – in some obscure fashion – into the emergence of all things from the Good, as in Plotinus. It was the failure of the human soul to remain devoted to its creator, something that only its creator can reverse.

Monica's discovery of creative Wisdom in the vision at Ostia is thus the discovery of the savior of her soul. Her act of contemplation, while not salvific, is at least the revelation of her savior. So, while contemplation cannot reverse the fall, it does exhibit the architecture of the spiritual universe to her soul, and gives a secure understanding of the nature of her loss. Most importantly, it allows her soul to meet its savior, drawing her soul up to that encounter. Yet there is one thing that contemplation cannot do, and that is to unite the soul eternally to the divine Wisdom. As a creature produced by Wisdom it remains forever distinct from it. Her soul is separated from its source first by the act of creation itself and then by the fall. Yet contemplation changes neither of these facts. That is its admitted poverty, a token of the helplessness of her soul itself. Yet, despite its limitations, contemplation is the revelation of the savior's presence. For this reason contemplation is ecstatic in the *Confessions*, because the soul must be taken out of its fallen self in order to see the possibility of its salvation. And the fallen self is the only self that there is. Thus the act of contemplation has a special power in the *Confessions*, since the soul of Monica is lifted up and out of its fallen self to encounter its author and savior. With neither the means to effect transcendence by itself, nor the power to insure its own salvation, the Augustinian soul must be brought out of itself and shown the conditions of its hope.

Monica at Ostia accentuates, then, the special character of Augustine's transcendentalism, his account of transcendent reality, over against that of Plotinus. If we step back from the texts and survey them, a larger story emerges. For Augustine understands the fault-lines of reality in a subtly different fashion than Plotinus. Consider the intelligible world. For Plotinus it has emerged into finite existence in a process that can be characterized both as an instance of self-manifestation by the One and as an act of culpable self-assertion. The same is true even more so of soul. This over-all movement away from the One has a mixed character, at once the beautiful self-diffusion of the Good and its diminution. Contemplation, in reversing this cascade of being away from the One, is also marked by ambivalence. It is the product of the philosophic soul's self-renewal, and yet it is also part of an eternal process by which all things are drawn back immutably to the One. This august cycle of reality, of unending procession and reversion, is the fundamental credendum of Plotinian Platonism. It means that the transcendent world has a specific place in a larger process. It also indicates that the architecture of the transcendent world must be understood in light of this pattern of spiritual motion, for it is its ontological expression. And contemplation has a role to play in that very architecture and that process. It is by contemplation that Intellect first constitutes itself, looking back, as it were, to the One from which it emerges. So too does soul contemplate Intellect, both in its emergence and also as part of its cycle of return. Thus the structure of reality and the practice of contemplation are directly related. The practice of philosophical *theōria* is an expression of the soul's own deeply felt nature; that is what the soul was always meant to do.

Augustine follows this general line of reflection but with some important shifts in inflection. When Monica's soul ascends to Wisdom at Ostia, a failure is being redressed. This ascension is not part of a larger metaphysical process nor does the soul exercise a natural function. Rather, contemplation is an exceptional aperture into the transcendent. This is because the soul is fallen and the higher world is not its own. It seeks what it does not possess; it is shown what it cannot be in its present state. Contemplation fits, therefore, into the divine economy; that is the larger process in which it plays a part. But this sort of contemplation is not what the soul was originally meant to exercise, for there is an element of distortion and disfigurement that are part of the soul's fall. This is what contemplation discovers, even as it reveals the need for divine aid to restore the soul to its originally intended state. Thus the transcendent world has a place in the theology of the *Confessions* that is quite different from that it occupies in the *Enneads*. It is a world that is the expression of the internal will of the creator and it is the future home for the fallen soul. But the transcendent world exists because it was generated by intention to be a separate creature, distinct from God and endowed with free will. In this sense Augustine has, in his account of the "heaven of heaven," sharpened the theme of the fall and made it central to an assessment of the intelligible world. His is an economic transcendentalism. Contemplation of transcendence has an eschatological value, for it catalyzes the fallen soul's desire to be in the presence of God.

This is why Christian contemplation must involve confession. Only then can the restorative value of contemplation be actualized. When it confesses its need for a savior and its culpability in the fall, the soul can then discern the hope that contemplation discloses. This is also why memory is so important to contemplation in the *Confessions*. Whereas Plotinian *anamnēsis* allows the soul to recall its higher self and is thereby an act of incipient transcendence, Augustinian recollection recovers only the soul's journey in this world. It is the story of a fallen being. In his concentration on the pathology of the fallen soul, Augustine saw more clearly than did Plotinus that psychic flight to a higher realm makes no sense if the enemy is the soul itself. And this aspect of the self must be confronted through memory and expiation, and not just sloughed off as the center of the self shifts to a higher element within the soul. Augustine thus has a more unitary view of the human person than the "cursive self" of Plotinus, capable of choosing its focus from a menu of levels of the soul. The Augustinian soul must confront itself, its history in the world, the factual record of its embodiment. And it must also confess its contingency, its moral insufficiency, its failure to redress the marks of the fall upon it. And then, in consequence, it must confess its need for a higher self beyond the self to save it. That is the premonitory value of contemplation, its disclosure of a God who loves the soul and desires its return to perfection. Then the Christian exercise of contemplation can bring about the sanctification of human contingency.

Love of God, of the eternal creator of the soul, is at the core of Monica's life and it is the underlying force in the Ostian account. It is a moment of concentration in the love of God that brings her into contact with him. That is only possible because the architecture of reality at Ostia is presented by Augustine as being sharply monotheistic. The soul of Monica is something distinct from Wisdom, even if it is dependent upon Wisdom for its existence and could not, for that reason, be wholly separated from it. Yet the Wisdom that the soul meets is understood to be other than the soul. There is no way around this feature of the spiritual universe in Augustine's text. It is fundamental to his account of contemplation. At Ostia the silence of the soul is the silence of presence, of coming immediately into the precincts of God, and finally into some measure of spiritual contact with him.

All this helps to nest the profound sense of divine love that pervades the *Confessions* into a larger context. What was disclosed at Ostia is not just the immediate presence of God, but the direct concern of that God for Monica's soul. The vision would never have happened were this not the case. Her soul could not have generated it by any ritual or philosophical means at its disposal. It was an act of revelation in the strongest sense, for the soul of Monica is given this vision as a function of divine beneficence. Contemplation at Ostia exhibits, then, the nature of a loving God, a God who exists across the fundamental chasm of reality that separates the finite from the infinite, the created and the creator. Yet Augustine believes that at that moment in Ostia God disclosed himself to Monica's soul in an immediate fashion. That is because Monica's soul is part of the divine economy, in which created beings seek the vision of God, impelled by their desire to overcome the imperfection of their finitude and the effects of the fall. We "are a spiritual creation in our souls, and have turned away from you our light" (XIII.ii (3)).

Augustine presents this desire for perfection in a fashion that moves subtly away from his Platonic sources. God is an absolute and infinite first principle, in need of nothing. All finite beings have an innate desire to be perfected, to resolve the incompleteness of their finitude in the perfection of an infinite source. This is the paradox of finite existence, for to exist is to be doubly bound by the limitation of a fixed nature and by individuation as a single instance of that nature. And within the nature of every conscious being is the desire to know the source of its existence, for all beings sense the existence of the infinite. That is a familiar theme in the *Enneads*. Augustine lays this out at XIII.iv (5):

> Even if the creation had either never come into existence or remained formless, nothing could be lacking to the good which you are yourself. You made it not because you needed it, but from the fullness of your goodness, imposing control and converting it to receive form – but not as if the result brought you fulfillment of delight. The corollary of your perfection is that the imperfection of created things is displeasing. So they seek perfection from you that they may please you, yet it is not that otherwise you would be imperfect and need to be perfected by their perfection.

But Augustine recognizes an added paradox, since he has now come to believe that the infinite source of reality also directs attention toward its products. It is absolutely self-sufficient but not wholly self-absorbed or self-directed. While without any need to insure that finite beings reach perfection, God nonetheless seeks to accomplish this. This is the salience of God's perfection for Augustine, his absolute beneficence toward finite beings who are his creatures. God initiates a process that generates the association of imperfect and finite creatures with his absolute perfection. That is the larger valence of the vision at Ostia; it is part of the restoration of souls to a deeper association with God. Here is his presentation, which follows directly from the text just cited at XIII.iv (5):

"Your good Spirit" (Ps. 142:10) "was borne above the waters" (Gen. 1:2), but not borne up by them as if resting weight on them. When scripture says your Spirit rests on people (Isa.11:2), it means that the Spirit makes them rest on himself. But your incorruptible and immutable will, sufficient to itself and in itself, was "borne above" the life which you made, a life for which to live is not the same as living in perfect happiness, because even while in a fluid state in darkness it had life. It remains for it to be converted to him by whom it was made, more and more to live by the fount of life, to see light in his light (Ps. 35:10), and to become perfect, radiant with light, and in complete happiness.

It is by the divine will that finite beings move from imperfect life to perfect life. This is something that God accomplishes, bringing souls ultimately into the "heaven of heaven," where contemplation of divine perfection is immediate. Contemplation at Ostia is the initial advancement of that process, when the souls of Monica and Augustine are said to have seen light in his light, made radiant by the power of the Spirit.

Among the Augustinian images for this state of perfected finitude, when the soul is in contemplative communion with its source, are the heavenly Jerusalem and the "House of God." Like the "heaven of heaven," these help to articulate the nature of the first creation outside of the eternal Godhead, the beginning of finitude. The "House of God" is described as a created realm cleaving to God in pure love, never separating itself from him, never slipping into contingency, change and the successiveness of time. It "rests in utterly authentic contemplation" of him alone (XII.xv (19)). Similarly Jerusalem is beautifully envisioned by reference to the exilic Psalms as the lost metaphysical homeland of the soul. The soul's return to it from its current state of distorted existence will represent the cessation of wandering:

> I will enter my chamber (Matt. 6:6) and will sing you songs of love, groaning with inexpressible groaning (Rom. 8:20) on my wanderer's path, and remembering Jerusalem with my heart lifted up towards it – Jerusalem my home land, Jerusalem my mother (Gal. 4:26), and above it yourself, ruler, illuminator, father, tutor, husband, pure and strong delights and solid joy and all good things to an inexpressible degree, all being enjoyed in simultaneity because you are the one supreme and true Good. I shall not turn away until in that peace of this dearest mother, where are the firstfruits of my spirit (Rom. 8.23) and the source of my certainties, you gather all that I am from my dispersed and distorted state to reshape and strengthen me for ever, "my God my mercy" (Ps. 58:18).
>
> (XII.xvi (23))

Contemplation through the power of the Spirit connects the soul up momentarily with this level of reality. There is a fundamental reason for this temporal brevity. The soul has embraced dispersal into the succession of time and acquiesced to a loss of simultaneity, so that it has no hold on the non-temporal contemplation of this highest created level of existence. Time in the *Confessions* is famously and enigmatically described as the distention of the mind (XI.xxvi (33)). But this is just what the "House of God" is not, for "it transcends all distension between past and future, and all the fleeting transience of time" (XII.xv (22)). The soul has only a fleeting opportunity to participate in this level of contemplation of God before falling back into its distended state, dispersed in the successive patterns of temporality and in the spatial diffusion of the body. Contemplation is a momentary reprieve from its present condition, a dispensation from embodiment.

It happens, as we have seen, because of the Spirit of God. Augustine works hard in the late books of the *Confessions* at expanding his reader's metaphysical imagination to describe this. The idea of an infinite, eternal, and immutable first principle is at the core of the depiction of contemplation in the *Confessions*. This is the still center from which the whole of reality emerges through creation and to which it seeks to return. But how can the soul, distended in space and time and no longer even having its true "shape," discover this eternal principle except through God's own initiative? Yet God transcends change, so that he cannot be said to be a direct actor in time. The answer to this puzzle lies in Augustine's theology of the inner life of God and its outward effects. God has an inner life, which is described in Trinitarian terms as having three aspects: being, knowing, and willing. These are interlocking aspects of the One God, which we can only dimly grasp by analogy to our own created mental faculties (XII.xi (12)). God cannot be known in himself, and his inner life is beyond our knowledge, just as our restoration to his presence is:

> To know you as you are in an absolute sense is for you alone. You are immutably, you know immutably, you will immutably. Your essence knows and wills immutably. Your knowledge is and knows immutably. Your will is and knows immutably. In your sight it does not seem right that the kind of self-knowledge possessed by the unchangeable light should be possessed by changeable existence which receives light. And so my soul is "like waterless land before you" (Ps. 142:6). Just as it has no power to illuminate itself, so it cannot satisfy itself. For "with you is the fountain of life", and so also it is "in your light" that "we shall see light" (Ps. 35:10).
>
> (XIII.xvi (19))

The created soul lacks the capacity to satisfy its own inchoate spiritual longings. But it is the nature of God's inner life that the soul is drawn up to God by the outer force of grace manifested within it through the Spirit. That is, as we saw in the last chapter, part of the very nature of God's inner life. At XIII.xxxi (46), Augustine attributes the soul's capacity to know the things of God to the Spirit. "Whatever, therefore, they see to be good by the Spirit of God, it is not they but God who is seeing that it is good." He goes on to say: "It is a yet further matter to say that when a man sees something which is good, God in him sees that it is good. That is, God is loved in that which he has made, and he is not loved except through the Spirit which he has given."

God's inner life cannot be separated from either the process of creation or from the soul's salvific return to him. When souls come to grasp the good around them in the contingent world, they are participating in God's own consciousness of that fact. They are seeing in some measure as God sees, through the power of the Spirit dwelling within them. Contemplation is the act by which the soul is ennobled beyond its station to see the goodness in all things and the things of God beyond them through the presence of the Spirit in the soul. Another way to put this is that contemplation begins in an acute recognition of God's immanence in all things that are made by the power of the Spirit. And it develops beyond that level of knowledge to a more refined recognition of the inner life of God. This is, in fact, what Augustine believes he and Monica came to understand at Ostia.

The *Confessions* closes on this connection of divine seeing, creation, and redemption. The God discovered at Ostia is wholly good and entirely immutable. The great procession of things into existence is the product of the inner will of God, while that creation was marred by our rejection of the creator. While God remains the eternal and unchanging source of goodness, he is also engaged in attention to his creatures. Indeed their existence is the result of that attention, of his seeing them. So our unstable souls exist over against the stability of our creator, either coming to accord with his divine plan or resisting it:

> As for ourselves, we see the things you have made because they are. But they are because you see them. We see outwardly that they are, and inwardly that they are good. But you saw them made when you saw that it was right to make them. At one time we were moved to do what is good, after our heart conceived through your Spirit. But at an earlier time we were moved to do wrong and to forsake you. But you God, one and good, have never ceased to do good. Of your gift we have some good works, though not everlasting. After them we hope to rest in your great sanctification. But you, the Good, in need of no other good, are ever at rest since you yourself are your own rest.
>
> (XIII.xxxviii (53))

In all these ideas we have come far from the *libri Platonicorum*, so far that it is difficult to understand why Augustine's text is often read as the baptism of the *Enneads*. The basic pattern of Monica's vision at Ostia makes evident how much the fundamental pattern of Augustinian contemplation differs from Plotinus.

The structure of the transcendental world, the power and metaphysical depth of the soul, the method and practice of contemplation all differ from the theology of Plotinus and his school. And taken together these differences cannot be plausibly ascribed to a misunderstanding of the *libri Platonicorum*. They constitute the distinctive approach to contemplation that emerged from the crucible of Ostia as Augustine interprets it. That project of reflection yielded a starkly different account of what the soul ultimately discovers in its interior journey. The conception of deity that Augustine articulates in the *Confessions* is framed in terms that take his theology in a direction far from the Platonism of Plotinus. Chief among these is the nature of the first principle that the soul encounters. In Plotinus, the One's transcendence of the finite universe is secured by an insistence on its ineffability. As we have seen, the One cannot be described in finite terms; the soul can approach it only by a process of stripping off of all putative characterizations. That process underscores that the One is distinct from all its finite products, and that, while not a finite entity itself, it nonetheless constitutes a separate and infinite mode of reality. This is the basis for Plotinus's special form of pagan monotheism, with its emphasis upon a first principle that can only be glimpsed behind the multiplicity of the universe. The One can thus be said to be omnipresent within the finite world; free as it is from any specific attributes, it can more easily be understood to be present to all. Yet it is not the aggregate of all these finite things. Neither is it a single reality of which these finite entities are merely attributes. It enjoys a special sort of infinite existence and emanates into finite existence myriad products, to which it remains intimately present through the very fact of their existence. Paradoxically, the immediacy of the One is thus best articulated through descriptive absence. It is the soul's ability to accentuate the presence of the One that gives his theology its sense of protreptical vigor. The soul can become more what it is, a product of the One in even more immediate contact with the Good at the depth of its being. Yet because the soul is eternal, it does not dissolve into the One.

Augustine understands divine transcendence according to his own logic, which owes its inspiration to the *libri Platonicorum*, but which turns out, upon inspection, to be a departure. He too is emphatic in asserting a level of intelligible reality beyond the sensible world. The intelligible/sensible distinction is fundamental to the theological narrative throughout the *Confessions*. Yet it is also, in the end, superseded by the distinction between the creator and the created. These two dichotomies become for Augustine the joint foundations for his articulation of the nature of God. It is the fact that God is the creator of all finite things that distinguishes him as unique. Augustine underscores the creative nature of God in his descriptions of what was discovered through contemplation. This is what separates God from all his products; and so this is the cornerstone of Augustine's Christian monotheism. That helps to explain one puzzling lacuna in the accounts of contemplation in the Confessions. It is striking that Augustine does not emphasize God's resistance to predication in his descriptions, nor does he construct his accounts according to the Plotinian strategy of progressive levels of predicative abstraction. There is, to be sure, a clear pattern of ascension from the sense world and recognition of the limitations of language in reference to God. But Augustine's ascension narratives do not rely on predicative removal, culminating in the One beyond all description. That is because God's transcendence is initially and fundamentally disclosed in his creative function, and thereafter in his salvific role, as the restorer of creation.

This may be part of the reason that Augustine is a bit vague and suggestive about the geography of the intelligible world in the *Confessions*. He is simply not engaged in the same realist project in theology as the Platonists. The initial theorem of realist theology is the existence of intelligible forms that are perfect instances of the predicates that they define. On that basis the One can be postulated, as that which exceeds this perfect level of predicative description. Augustine adopts the idea of the transcendent world, but it is not the primary or dispositive basis of his theology. His fulcrum of theology rests elsewhere, on the force of a creative first principle made manifest to the created soul in contemplation. The otherworldly geography of the transcendent realm is important to Augustine, but the real focus of his account of contemplation lies in the emergence of the Wisdom of God to his soul. That God is not ineffably perceived behind the perfect intelligibles. Rather, Augustine insists throughout the *Confessions* that God is present as a force of consciousness within all that he has created and all that he sustains in existence. While the creator is disclosed in contemplation to be immutable and impassible, he is nonetheless present to all creatures. That presence is not just ontological, a matter of providing existence to all finite things. It is also the immediate awareness by God of the contingent facts of finite existence. God is the omni-extension of consciousness for Augustine, a power that is first discerned in the core of the soul and then discovered throughout all of created reality. So for Augustine contemplation opens to the soul a new vista of awareness, to the astonishing fact that the world in which it exists is wholly animated by the presence of an omniscient and omnipresent first principle. To be is to be perceived by God.

The "psychological" immediacy of God that is perhaps the most striking feature of the *Confessions*; the sense, disquieting for many readers, that there is no place to hide from the pervasive and even relentless consciousness of God. Omnipresence has thus been revealed through contemplation to be more than just existential presence, more than just the "long life" that stretches out from the One. While the Plotinian One is always present to the soul, it can enter into no direct relations with the soul. That would be a violation of the grammar of Plotinian theology and capture the One in finite description. Since the One transcends such matters, it cannot be said to love the soul. Admittedly it also cannot be said not to love the soul either. But there is none of this in the *Confessions*. Augustine believes that he has discerned a God who has always been present in every facet of his life. No event of his career in the world, no aspect of his inner life has been remote from God. Nothing has been ignored by God; nothing is sheltered from him.

This is root of the special sense of God as a person in the *Confessions*. Augustine is clear throughout the work that God cannot be said, in fact, to be a person in any recognizable fashion. Nor is God an entity in the sense of a finite being. In this respect Augustine's understanding has much in common with that of Plotinus. Yet Augustine's God disclosed himself in terms that exhibit direct regard for human beings. God does not change, yet the outward effect of his inner life plays out in its goodness throughout creation. And God has a direct consciousness of human lives and is active – if unchanged – in the process of changing their moral careers. The Spirit is, as we saw, the power revealed as the consciousness of God. Augustine sees the act of contemplation as connecting up with the mental life of God, of coming to see as the Spirit sees. The inner life of the Trinity is expressed both in the structure of human being, knowing, and willing, and in the human capacity to know as God knows. Human recognition of goodness is itself an act of the Spirit. It is through the Spirit that the contemplative soul comes to recognize that everything that has existence is good. But it is God himself within us who sees that it is good (XIII.xxxi (46)).

Perhaps another way to reflect on this point is to consider the "pointer terms" that Plotinus uses in his contemplative theology to direct the soul in its ascent to the One, while not actually describing the One literally. Terms like "one" or "good" or "beautiful" or "source" have that special function, revealed in the process of contemplation itself. In the *Confessions* God too is an infinite being, but the concepts that direct the contemplative soul are personalistic in character. They include especially God's attention to the soul and his love for it. For Augustine, contemplation verifies and exhibits these values. God is, of course, no more a finite person than the Good is a good thing. But contemplation in the *Confessions* delivers the soul from any doubt about the personalistic character of God, directing it to communion with Wisdom through the Spirit. Moreover the specific values that specify, as it were, the vector of the contemplative soul also change the underlying understanding of what contemplation accomplishes. In the *Enneads* there is an unavoidable naturalistic dimension to contemplation, as the philosopher comes to see the structure of reality as it is and to grasp inchoately its ineffable source. The soul has a worthy place in the larger structure of reality and is engaged in recovering that status and exercising its true function in direct association with the One. But in the *Confessions* the soul discovers its author and creator, and is directed by him to see the path of salvation prepared for the soul. In contemplation the Augustinian soul encounters an unavoidable paradox: that God appears as the active agent of its initial creation, of its recovery of meaning, and of its ultimate salvation, while remaining, in essence, beyond any such direct action. Yet contemplation ultimately brings the soul into the presence of God and beyond any uncertainty. It delivers the soul to the Good that is ever at rest, and gives the soul hope to rest in the greater sanctification that is the eternal communion of saints in God (XIII.xxxviii (53)).

The God of Augustine is discovered through contemplation to be, in the end, a God of the foreground of the soul's life. Augustine's account of contemplative transcendence is strikingly non-hierarchical. It offers the soul immediate access to God, who is present everywhere by the omnipresence of his consciousness. The God of Augustine is directly present to the soul because God is conscious and attentive to the soul, exercising a love that is personal. Contemplation thus has a special value for Augustine, providing the soul with a means to restore a mutual consciousness with God, and to deepen that presence. The soul is, as we have seen, drawn into the intellective power of the Spirit, coming to reproduce in its created consciousness some measure of the reflective life of the Trinity. Contemplation is an exercise in immediacy, as the soul discovers just how intensely present God is to its life as a creature. In this respect contemplation has a very different value from that found in the *Enneads*. There contemplation offered access to a recessive One, whose ontological presence is balanced by its remoteness from its products, about which it exercises no direct concern. That indifference is the price of One's immediacy, as the omnipresent source of existence. But Augustine did not emerge from contemplation at Ostia with this conception of deity. Instead he discerns a God whose role as the omnipresent source of existence is directly correlated with his power of universal consciousness. God is everywhere that there is existence, and he is present as well through the omniscient scope of his divine mind. Thus contemplation in the *Confessions* places a premium on the soul's coming to access this higher mode of simultaneous consciousness, for example, in the second depiction of the vision at Ostia (IX.x (25)). There is, then, a manifest symmetry between Augustine's representation of contemplation and his conception of deity in the *Confessions*. The contemplation exercised by those two souls at Ostia must be seen against the backdrop of God's universal contemplation, into which they have been granted importunate entry. Indeed Augustine has so fundamentally reconceived Plotinian contemplation of the One that its inherent logic has been lost. We have moved into a new theology entirely.

What we have considered in this section goes some way toward understanding why union with God is not part of Augustine's representation of contemplation. The answer is two-fold. First, the *Enneads* do not contain a doctrine of complete union of the soul with the One. As we saw in the first chapter, Plotinus does not endorse a monistic theory, such that the soul is absorbed back into the One at the apex of *theōria*. But he does emphasize that the intelligible self exists in the collective unity of the Intellect, which is engaged in eternal contemplation of the One. Moreover, the intellective self can go beyond this to reassert its deep connection to the One, though without ever losing its identity entirely, for it remains an eternal self at the level of Intellect. The One is therefore a mysterious power at the root of reality, but barely within the frame of human reference. All the more reason for it to be accessible only by an interior journey in which the self strips off finitude and seeks the presence of the One through *theōria*. This helps to clarify why Augustine does not use the conception of union with God in the *Confessions*. Throughout his early writings, Augustine never accepts this Plotinian notion of an ineffable One, of a first principle whose transcendence is articulated by this paradoxical notion of impredicability. Augustine's God, while infinite, is approached in a different fashion. While Augustine too understands the limitations of finite description in reference to an infinite first principle, he takes another route in representing of God's transcendence. He relies instead upon the notion of creation. What separates God from everything else is his unique status as creator of all finite reality. That is the bright line of separation in Augustine's ontology. And as such, no created being can be assimilated fully to its uncreated source.

That is what happened at Ostia. The finite souls of the contemplatives came into the presence of uncreated Wisdom. But the separation between them and the divine Wisdom was complete. It was breeched by divine initiative only to permit some contact between the finite and the infinite, and not to dissolve the former into the latter. Because Augustine seems not to have shared the Plotinian doctrine of the One in his thinking before Ostia, it was never part of his conceptual field at Ostia, nor part of his retrospective interpretations thereafter. Union with the One is thus outside the bounds for a reading of the *Confessions*. It is another feature imposed on the ancient texts by nineteenth and twentieth century theorists whose expectations had been set by the common-core theories of mysticism that we discussed in the Introduction. Augustine might best be said not to have avoided the notion of union with the One but to have never had it as part of his hermeneutical horizon. In understanding the events of his spiritual life, he struck out instead in a different direction, transposing aspects of Platonism into his new Christian theology. Contemplation of the transcendent exposes, therefore, a radically different metaphysical architecture in Augustine, one in which the soul's capacities are much diminished, its created nature deeply contingent and prone to moral loss. Were it not for the power of Christ, the soul's prospects would be dim.

9

SNATCHED UP TO PARADISE

When Augustine wrote the *Confessions* he had already had a decade to reflect upon the events of his conversion. He had come to that garden in Milan a reader of the *libri Platonicorum* and more recently of Saint Paul. Later, in the Cassiciacum treatises, his initial enthusiasm for contemplation is evident and with it a conviction that the soul's sustained access to transcendence was within the scope of human discipline. The accounts of the *Confessions* deny this, for reasons made plain in Book Ten. There the frustrations of continued temptation recall the soul to a more modest sense of its contemplative achievement. For Augustine avers that, whatever he had initially thought, transcendence was at best a momentary excursion for his soul. His moral state was not entirely renewed, nor could it be. He was back where he had begun, changed in his spiritual convictions and bound to a higher understanding at the core of his being, yet still the human person that he was, embodied and on a pilgrim's path in the hope of salvation.

The reading of the *Confessions* offered thus far has relied on the judgment that its ascension narratives do not record mystical experiences that can be plausibly characterized according to contemporary phenomenological typologies. These models fail to capture the depth and cognitive significance of what is recorded by Augustine. Such readings are, in short, too thin. Since the ascension narratives of the *Confessions* emerged from a larger context within the religious and philosophical world of late antiquity, we have read these texts against that larger discussion about the nature of human and divine transcendence, with particular reference to the *Enneads* of Plotinus. In doing so the salience of Augustine's Christian account of contemplation emerges, making evident that the ascension narratives do not simply describe efforts at Plotinian ecstasy in Christian language. Contemplation in the *Confessions* is a new departure, an alternative representation of God and the soul.

It might well be asked whether the portrait of Christian contemplation presented in the *Confessions* is anomalous in the later thought of Augustine. The answer is no. This great treatise of theological self-interpretation yielded an account of the soul's hidden life and of God's beneficence from which he never retreated. Indeed, the works that follow the *Confessions* do nothing to change this understanding of contemplation. They hone it somewhat, ruminating upon its essential features and amplifying it in interesting ways. But Augustine never rescinds the main outlines of Christian contemplation iterated in the *Confessions*. Yet these later texts are helpful in many ways, confirming the *Confessions* account and providing some further nuance. It is worth a look at the most significant of these later treatments, concentrating on discussions of contemplation as such. Then we can return to the *Confessions* and consider it anew.

Throughout his long career, Augustine held that momentary contemplation of God is possible for the human soul through divine grace. This judgment was not a product only of his early days as a reader of the *libri Platonicorum* or of his initial enthusiasm for Platonism. Nor was it something that the *Confessions* served to revise and domesticate, as it were, within his growing orthodoxy. Rather, it was integral to his emergent Christian theology as a whole, part of a larger account of the nature of God and the soul. It was at the core of his adoption of Catholic Christianity, for it was the means by which its account of the architecture of the spiritual universe was verified for him. And that act of verification was something that he believed other souls had experienced, a knowledge to which others too might aspire, even if its accomplishment was not within their control. There are several texts written subsequent to the *Confessions* that assert or develop further its account of contemplation.

Perhaps the palmary text for understanding these later texts is *De Genesi ad litteram* XII. This treatise, an effort to comment on the literal meaning of Genesis, was begun sometime around the time he finished the *Confessions*, between 399 and 404. It was published in 416. Augustine tells us in his *Retractiones* (II, 24) that he added the final book after completing the first eleven in order to develop the subject of paradise more completely. This section was probably written about 415 and contains a lengthy discussion of various types of visions; it is the most illuminating text from Augustine on the subject of unmediated vision of God outside the *Confessions*. It is also a marvelous instance of Augustine at his best as a speculative thinker, in this case beginning with the puzzle of St. Paul's being snatched up (*raptum*) to Paradise from 2 Cor. 12:2–4. There the text relates the apostle's being lifted up to the third heaven, whether in body or not is explicitly left agnostic. There he hears inexpressible words which he is not permitted to speak. This is the perplexing text from which Augustine starts his reflections. He begins by offering a hermeneutical dichotomy (XII.5.14). St. Paul could be understood either as saying that his soul was raised up to heaven along with his living body – whether awake or asleep or in an ecstatic state is unclear – or else that the soul totally left the body for a time and was in effect temporarily dead. This would amount to a resurrection of sorts.

Augustine then distinguishes among three types of vision: bodily, spiritual, and intellectual (XII.6.15 and 7.16). Bodily vision is the actual physical sight of the eyes. Spiritual vision is, despite its name, the exercise of the imagination, by which we see physical things in the mind's eye as if they were present. The example is of a person standing in the dark and picturing the physical features of the surrounding world, even though it is too dark to make anything out. Both of these are rather prosaic forms of vision. But there is a third sort, intellectual vision. This is the exercise of the mental faculties, by which the intellect sees based upon mental images impressed upon the mind. This is the most excellent sort of vision (XII.10.21). It is the sort involved in contemplation of God and is independent from bodily and spiritual vision (XII.24.51). This means that it has no empirical foundations, and is separate from any sense experience. It is removed, therefore, from the context of a posteriori judgment and cannot be deceived. Augustine insists, in fact, that intellectual vision is infallible, for it is an act of interior understanding or intellectual sight. Either the soul understands something which is true, or, if something is not true, it simply does not grasp it (XII.25.52). One might imagine that Augustine is thinking about an incoherent concept like a round square, something that one could never envision mentally. What the soul can envision is logically possible. So the soul can go wrong about things that it empirically sees, but not about the things that it intuits intellectually. Intellectual vision is thus a kind of rapture, in which the soul is entirely removed from the senses and from any concepts that have their basis in empirical sensation (XII.26.53–54). Then the mind is within the intelligible region and directed toward transparent, intellectual truth. There it is free from false opinions, having come to consider what might be described as necessary truths. Such a state of apodictic knowledge is the life of the saints in paradise. It is a condition of undisturbed rest and of unmediated vision of truth. And it occurs for those in this life through divine grace, when God lifts up the soul.

That, at least, is the general idea. But Augustine is commenting on the visions of Moses and Saint Paul, and his Platonist epistemology is not an easy fit with the scriptural texts. The biggest rub is the embodied condition of the contemplator, combined with conflicting representations of visionary association with God in Exodus. As we have seen, Saint Paul's text in 2 Corinthians 12 expresses uncertainty whether his soul remained in the body or not. In Exodus 33:11 God speaks to Moses face to face. But the description of Moses' encounter with God in Exodus 33:12 ff. includes the daunting assertion that no one can see God's face and live. Augustine's solution is straightforward enough: Moses and Saint Paul underwent a virtual death during contemplation. He explains this by noting that the vision of Moses is said to go beyond the sort of intellectual vision he has been discussing, and involves seeing God's substance, clearly in himself, to the extent an intellective being can do so (XII.27.55). At least in the case of God, intellectual vision must become so removed from the context of the body that the soul either completely departs from the body for a time, or at least seems to do so. In the latter instance, the soul is so distant and abstracted from the body and the senses that it enters a condition of nescience regarding its own embodied existence. Augustine reminds his readers that we are strangers to this type of direct knowledge as long as we exist in the world and are living by faith and not by sight (2 Cor. 5:6–7). But the type of intellectual vision he is discussing is clearly the highest achievable by a creature, for it is the substance of God that is seen, although only to the extent that the mind can grasp it (XII.28.56). Augustine thus continues to maintain that intuitive vision of God is in fact possible during this life, even if it is a virtual removal to the next.

Augustine is well-aware that his discussion of intellectual vision involves two different types of intentional objects (XII.31.59). These include ideas and God himself, and they are understood hierarchically. The former is illustrated in reference to the virtues as well their contrary vices. These can only be seen intellectually by the mind and are not physically visible. But they are made mentally visible because of the divine light that enlightens the soul, allowing it to understand things conceptually. Augustine does not develop this notion of illumination further in this context, except to identify this light as divine. This light is something quite different from conceptual ideas, and the mind lacks a natural ability to gaze upon this light directly while in this life. It offers the basis for intellectual knowledge, but it is itself outside the range of that knowledge. However it can be raised up to a higher level and then it can see above its natural range by the help of God, who had enabled it to engage in its usual intellection. That higher vision is a sudden dispensation, the sort of thing reported by Saint Paul. Indeed Augustine asserts that Paul's reference to the "third heaven" at 2 Corinthians 12:2–4 makes sense in reference to the three types of vision that he identified (XII.34.67). The first heaven is the physical heaven of the cosmos, accessible to sense perception. The second heaven is rather obscurely said to be that image of the heavens which the imagination holds. The third heaven is the one grasped by the mind, the intelligible universe. When the soul is raised up by the Holy Spirit, it is then able to see and hear the things of this intelligible heaven. It is even able to perceive intellectually the substance of God and the Word of God. This was the condition of Saint Paul, taken up to the "paradise of paradises," the intelligible world.

Nothing here should come as a shock to the reader of the *Confessions*. We are, in fact, on quite familiar ground. There is, however, one additional and intriguing point that Augustine raises at the end of the treatise which serves as a new departure of sorts. At XII.35.68 he raises an excellent question regarding the resurrection of the body in relation to this rather exalted sort of intellectual vision. Given all that has been said about the ascent from the body to paradise, what is the point of getting a body back at the end of time? Augustine has an ingenious response. He suggests that the soul after death may still not be able to see the immutable divine nature as the angels do. This is because the soul is, by design of its creator, the governor of the body. It thus always bears with it some vestigial attention or residual concern for the body even when it has gone on without it to the higher realms. This causes a diminution of its capacity for undisturbed intellection. But, after the resurrection, the soul will have its complete nature restored, and the body/soul composite that makes up a true human being will then be able to exercise its full powers of intellection. The divine substance will then be more fully accessible to it. Resurrection thus completes the process of intellectual contemplation and is a necessary condition for sustaining unmediated knowledge of God.

There are several initial points that emerge from this text in reference to the ascension narratives of the *Confessions*. The first is suggested by this final discussion of the epistemic function of the resurrection. This is a matter that is never adequately explored in the *Confessions* and, even if only adumbrated here, helps to amplify that concept in reference to its disembodied accounts of contemplation. In addition this account of the highest mode of vision is a thoroughly a priori representation. Augustine does not articulate here a form of sensory or experiential knowledge. In every respect intellectual vision is clearly delineated from either sensory vision or the attenuated version of it that he calls spiritual vision. Neither direct experience nor imaginative visions rooted in sensation are the sort involved in the accounts of Moses and Saint Paul. Their visionary knowledge was one of intellectual perception, of conceptual understanding, of seeing with the mind's rational capacity alone. This is a point of the utmost importance in understanding Augustine's accounts of the human capacity for immediate knowledge of God. We should put down a place-marker here and will return to consider the larger implications of this aspect of contemplation momentarily. Finally, Augustine's treatment of intellectual vision is profoundly veridical, that is, he understands it to be an act of knowledge, indeed, an indubitable and infallible judgment. This is the leading aspect of his reflections on such visionary episodes, that they are acts of knowing. While they have their origins in the human longing for the eternal and the divine, and while they are associated with a dawning love for the God who draws the soul to himself, they are nonetheless not acts of affective piety or spiritual feelings. These visions are about real knowledge of God: direct, immediate, and grounded in the transformation of the individual soul. This is also a point to which we will return.

About 413 Augustine replied at considerable length to a letter from a noble woman, Paulina, who inquired about how the invisible God can be seen. His reply, letter 147, is a mini-treatise on the subject of the vision of God, covering some of the same material found in *De Genesi ad litteram* XII and confirming the perspective articulated there. In Chapter 13 Augustine poses a problem similar to the catalyst for discussion in *De Genesi ad litteram* XII: Is there a contradiction between Matthew 5:8 ("No man has seen God at any time") and Genesis 32:30 ("I have seen God face-to-face") or Isaiah 6:1 ("I saw the Lord of hosts sitting upon a throne")? Indeed Abraham, Isaac, Jacob, Job, Moses, Micheas and Isaiah are all said to have had seen God (147:14). Augustine's response is designed to clarify how God can be said to be known directly in this life, at least in part by certain chosen individuals. He emphasizes that seeing God is promised to the pure of heart after this life (147:18). God may, however, show an aspect of himself, although never his full nature, his plenitude (147:20–21). Yet Augustine raises again the problem of Moses' vision of the substance of God in Exodus 33:20. His solution is the same as in *De Genesi ad litteram* XII. Moses was taken up to an angelic mode of consciousness in a state of removal from the body but before suffering our common fate of death. The same is true of Saint Paul, caught up in a state of ecstasy, when the mind was withdrawn from this life in a virtual state of death. Once again the vision of God is a kind of death, a seemingly rare anticipation of heavenly existence. But it does occur and there are humans beings to whom this state is granted – to this the scriptures attest. There is no obvious autobiographical aspect to this text, just as there was none in *De Genesi ad litteram* XII. Augustine seems intent in both instances to find a way to certify that visionary ascension is indeed something countenanced by Biblical precedent, even if he has to invoke the rather striking idea of virtual death to accomplish this. This indicates the extent to which he remained committed to the soul's immediate knowledge of God.

Other texts that deal directly with the issue confirm this same judgment. *The Homily on Psalm 41* is a particularly good example. Written around 410, it deals with one of Augustine's favorite Psalms, with its powerful image of the deer's desire for running water. The thirst of the soul for God drives it to seek him and to know him as he is. To achieve this, the soul must rid itself of its vices (ch. 3). In a lovely image, Augustine introduces an ecclesial dimension by accentuating the mutual support that deer give one another as they rest their heads on one another while walking (ch. 4). The soul now lives by faith in a God that cannot be physically seen, because God is the creator who cannot be discovered with eyes made for earthly sight. Indeed, only with the mind can God be seen in a limited sense, for the finite mind is fallible. But God is an unchangeable substance and not a finite mind, so there is a restricted basis for analogy between the human mind and God (ch. 7). God is a reality above the world and the soul, so the soul must pour itself out above itself if it is to "touch" God. Once again some form of ecstatic movement of the soul is necessary to reach God. And above the soul there is nothing else except the God who made it. There God the creator dwells, looking down upon the individual person, thinking about the soul, and leading the soul on its journey (ch. 8). On this journey, the tent of the soul is the church, the faithful on earth, filled with examples of virtue and good works. But through the exemplary tent of the church the soul is led to the house of God, the final abode of the just. The soul is said to be drawn by an indescribable sweetness and an inner music while walking in the tent and it follows the inner calling to the house of God.

In an encouraging aside, Augustine remarks on the music of human celebrations and then reports that in God's house there is an unending party. Not an earthy carnival – to be sure – but a celebration generated by the eternal sight of the face of God (ch. 9). This state of joy is available only by anticipation in our present life (ch. 10). We are still embodied and on pilgrimage. But there are moments when we hear that higher music and can come to perceive that unchangeable house of God. But then the weight of our embodied state sends us crashing back into earthly life. The soul walks in the tent of the church and from there into the house of God, impelled by the intelligible music coming from within. But then it returns in a moment to its everyday life. This description corroborates the ascension narratives of the *Confessions*. Many of the essential elements are there, although the role of the church is perhaps more integral.

Brief mention should be made of another passage that confirms this continuity in Augustine's representation of mystical vision. In the *Homily on Psalm 99*, given in about 412, Augustine emphasizes God's omnipresence. It is not that God is absent from us; it is that we are absent from him, being blind to his presence (ch. 5). Augustine then invokes the idea of ineffability to describe the soul's direct encounter with God. By becoming more like God, the soul draws close to him and is in a state of immediate consciousness of God. Because God is love, the soul can deepen its sense of the presence of God through love of its creator. Once this process takes hold, the soul is unable to speak or describe it adequately. Here the concept of ineffability is being applied to consciousness as such, to the mode of immediate knowledge that the souls achieves in relation to God. Inability to describe the experience becomes a token of the consciousness enjoyed by the soul as it comes into a direct relation of love with God.

Sermon 52, preached around 410–412, contains a striking discussion of contemplative vision. Augustine is discussing the Trinity and he begins to comment on Ps. 31:22: "I said in my ecstasy, I am cut off from before your eyes." Once again Augustine employs the idea of the soul being lifted up to God and poured out above itself. He then speaks of the contact that such a soul enjoys with the unchanging light of divine wisdom, followed by its falling back in weakness. Here is the relevant portion from the text of 52.5.16:

> Thus it appears to me that the one who said this has lifted his soul up to God, and poured out his soul above himself, as it is said daily to him: *Where is your God?* and reached to that unchangeable light by a form of spiritual contact, and then being too infirm in his sight to endure this, he fell back once again to his own sickness and feebleness, and compared himself with that light and sensed that he could not calibrate the strength of his mind to the light of the Wisdom of God. And since he had done this while in ecstasy, having been separated from bodily sensation and snatched up to God and then in some fashion returned to a human condition, he then asserted: "I said in my ecstasy, indeed I do not know what I saw in my ecstasy, which I was not able to bear for very long." And having returned to my mortal limbs, and to thinking many mortal thoughts which emerge from the body and burden the soul, I said: "What? I am cut off from before your eyes. You are far above and I am far below."

This description is a fairly faithful reiteration of elements from the accounts of the *Confessions*. Once again Augustine sets out his now settled account of the human soul's momentary dispensation of transcendence. Once again we find that the soul cannot endure this in this state because of its moral condition, and so it returns to its normal consciousness.

All this indicates how much Augustine retained in his later thought the fundamental understanding of contemplation established in the *Confessions*. Yet that understanding was fraught with subtle ambiguities. Consider for example that contemplation as we have discerned it in Augustine has several unusual features, part of the lineage of its development, especially its emergence from Platonism. Contemplation is not something that the soul can initiate on its own. It is meant to have a larger social content in his Christian account, something that begins with its ecclesial dimension and then is amplified by the notion that the soul can enter momentarily into the heavenly Jerusalem, the life of the saints. But all this is unstable and marred by the continued embodiment of the fallen soul. Yet the body too has its value; indeed, as we saw in *De Genesi ad litteram* XII, it is a necessary component of stable and complete contemplation. The body cannot just be jettisoned; it too must be ennobled through the soul's progress toward salvation. Moreover this whole process of contemplative ascension has an ambiguous value for Augustine. He repeatedly recognizes its significance in the lives of heroic figures such as Moses and Saint Paul, for whom visionary access to God certified the very course of their lives and authenticated their missions. This too is what the *Confessions* claims for Monica and for himself. Yet there remains an adventitious aspect of these visionary episodes, since they emerge from no certain discipline. They are prepared, to be sure, by the moral life, but they remain, as it were, outside the range of its promises.

This nest of complexities and anxieties led Augustine in these later works both to confirm his definitive account of intellectual vision from the *Confessions* and also to expand upon it, settling it more firmly into his developing Christian theology as a whole. This process of expansion emerges most clearly in the later books of *De Trinitate*, especially Eight to Fifteen, where the trinitarian hints of *Confessions* XIII.xi (11) are explored exhaustively. *De Trinitate* underscores the continuing importance of the soul's contemplative nature in the later thought of Augustine. It is not a folly of youth or a Platonic vestige. It is, in fact, a core component of his understanding of Christianity. And how could it not be? He made the interior path to transcendence the centerpiece of his theological autobiography. It is the irrefragable axiom of his anti-materialism and anti-skepticism, the spiritual fulcrum of his conversion narrative. It opened the soul to a higher plane of being and to the hope of attaining it. And it exposed the presence of Wisdom to the soul, as a loving source of grace and as a beloved creator. *De Trinitate* examines more fully the image of God in the soul, explains their deep inter-connection based on a subtle isomorphism, and yet also secures their theistic separation through the concept of creation. It is the theoretic completion of the vision at Ostia, almost a field theory of contemplation. While analysis of the details of *De Trinitate* is a subject too extensive for our present inquiry, the fact that Augustine saw fit to explore the nature of the triune God in relation to contemplation tells us much about his estimation of its continuing significance to his theology as a whole.

If we step back from these later texts, we can now return to the *Confessions* with the conviction that its account of the visionary ascension of the human soul is not merely a rhetorical one, designed perhaps to explain its author's perplexing spiritual itinerary or to authenticate his conversion, but then subsequently jettisoned. It is, in fact, a well-formed theory to which he returned when he had occasion thereafter to discuss the subject in a considered fashion. We might, in consequence, now reflect on Augustine's achievement in formulating this account of contemplation in the *Confessions*.

Contemplation is the practice of Christian transcendence, catalyzing or confirming the act of confession, bearing fruits in the life of the Christian, and disclosing the hidden nature of spiritual reality. These elements may be summarized as follows:

1   The truth of transcendence, of a realm outside space, time, and change, known indubitably by the soul through interior reflection.
2   The shallowness of the soul, its lack of metaphysical depth, its complete embodiment within the world of space and time.
3   The soul's consequent inability to achieve a sustained transcendence, to raise itself out of the lower world.
4   The necessity of divine assistance to effect the soul's transcendence and to draw the soul above its embodied station.
5   The momentary, limited, and extraordinary nature of this excursion.
6   The difference between contemplative transcendence and salvation.
7   The omnipresence of divine consciousness and God's manifest regard for the soul.
8   The soul's conferred capacity to enter into the heavenly consciousness of the saints, a mediated consciousness of God, and an intimation of the final state of the soul.
9   A state of unmediated contact with an aspect of God, the divine Wisdom, but not union with God as a whole or absorption into God.
10   The ecclesial and communal context for the continued practice of contemplation.

These are the principle features element of the theology of contemplation iterated in the *Confessions*.

As we saw in the Introduction, several related interpretive tendencies have stood in the way of understanding Christian contemplation in the *Confessions*. First is the assumption that its ascension narratives constitute descriptions of mystical experiences. Second is the related view that they are efforts at ecstatic experience based specifically on the archetype of the *Enneads*. The reading offered here is an effort to move beyond these twin approaches and to sketch out an alternative. Having now had the opportunity to work through the text, we might look more closely at each of these approaches, and think them through.

If one reads the ascension narratives of the *Confessions* as instances of mystical experience, one is committed to that hermeneutical category as a given fact of human experience. As was noted earlier, *The Varieties of Religious Experience* by William James, first published in 1902, is the classic example of this approach (James 1985). He characterized an experience as mystical if it was ineffable, noetic, transient, and passive. These are taken by James to be a stipulated set of common characteristics across religious traditions. It must be said that James's study remains one of the finest and acute treatments of the subject and is partly responsible for the vernacular concept of mysticism. James's "common core" theory of mystical experience was modified by later theorists who were hard pressed to give a single account for the wide range of putatively mystical experiences across the world's religions. This led to several influential studies that identified several different types of mystical experience, the best of which is *Mysticism: Sacred And Profane* by the Oxford professor of comparative religion R. C. Zaehner (1957). In Zaehner's taxonomy, there are three types of mystical experience: nature mysticism, monistic consciousness, and theistic experience (Zaehner 1957: 28–29). Nature mysticism is the state of feeling united with the natural world, of being subsumed into nature or the world as a whole. Monistic mysticism is the consciousness of non-difference; the experience that the phenomenal world and the self have no independent reality, but are just modes of the Absolute. All is experienced as One. Finally there is theistic mysticism, in which the soul is united with God in love, a union that does not include absorption, but is instead based on the closure of two separate beings. In Zaehner's model, Christian mystical experience is theistic. Recent examples of this research program include studies by William Wainwright (1981), William Alston (1991) and Nelson Pike (1992). They offer the most sophisticated contemporary analyses based on this universalistic, phenomenological approach.

Several features emerging from this characterization of mystical experience are especially problematic for reading the *Confessions*. These include:

1   the distinction between experience and interpretation;
2   the phenomenological character of mystical experience;
3   the individualistic basis of mystical experience; and
4   the epistemic foundations of mystical experience.

Before we consider these issues, one observation is in order. It may be that this approach to the study of religious experience is productive, yielding plausible hypotheses about observable behavior. That is not an issue that can be addressed here. But we would do well to remember that, when one reads a text like the *Confessions*, one is not examining observations reports from a clinical setting. Even the sequences describing contemplation in the *Confessions* are, as we have seen, a confection of culturally dense concepts and autobiographical descriptions. In reading the *Confessions* one is thus engaged in a quite different exercise than analyzing contemporaneous reports of religious experience. This variation in the nature and context of inquiry raises the problems for the Augustinian reader.

Experience and interpretation

The notion of mystical experience rests on the assumption that the experience itself can be described in a fashion that is substantially removed from its subsequent interpretation. Regardless of the methodological adequacy of this move, it is in practice implausible when reading a text like the *Confessions*. We have no adequate means to recover the data set, as it were, of the experiences at Milan or Ostia from the texts before us, saturated as they are with complex concepts and culturally imbedded description. Nor can we isolate the experience itself from the reflective context that immediately accompanies it. Nor can we accurately identify the features of the experience that may have been conditioned by Augustine's prior beliefs and intentions. Even if we suspect that his Pauline and Platonic reading made up the interpretations incorporated into the episode or episodes of Book Seven, how can we draw a line between what is and is not interpretation? But to be committed to the claim that Augustine experienced a mystical state, defined according to the phenomenological criteria of James or Zaehner, for example, one would need to make that determination.

The ascension narratives of the *Confessions* are, in fact, portions of a fairly seamless effort at self-examination and cannot be easily separated into description and interpretation, into observation reports and theology. What we find in the texts of the *Confessions* is, in one sense, entirely interpretive, for the whole text is theological. Even the ascension narratives themselves are theologically rich descriptions. In the *Confessions*, it is theology all the way down, as it were, for there is no level of "pure description" that can be identified on the basis of some hermeneutical key. Conversely, even the more theologically ramified aspects of the text, for example the account of the *caelum caeli* from Book Twelve, are rooted in Augustine's account of his spiritual life and emerge from reflection on that experience in light of the scriptures. Augustine's ongoing meditations on the Ostian vision in the final books of the *Confessions*, and thereafter in later works, constitute part of the afterlife of the initial episode, and are, in a sense, part of its continuation. Our experiences are, after all, not just temporally discreet events, but are part of what we are, and continue to evolve in their meaning. Interpretive memory contributes to what constitutes experience. Augustine knew this only too well, as his discussion of the subject in Book Ten indicates.

Augustine's account of Christian contemplation should be said, then, as having two distinct, though related, phases. It begins with the episodes of transcendence described in the *Confessions* and related as well in later texts.

These accounts certify and describe the transcendent realm, charting the "amazing depth" of the soul. But these texts then open the way into interpretive reflection that follows upon these episodes, providing a fuller representation of what was exposed about the nature of transcendence. Both of these phases follow from the episodes themselves and seem to be a natural process of making sense of them. In the case of the *Confessions*, this experience of memorial interpretation went on for a decade but is truncated in the text, where its fruits are sometimes represented as being tightly woven into the initial events. For all these reasons, the ascension narratives of the *Confessions* do not yield the requisite analysis for asserting that they are instances of mystical experience. They resist the dichotomy of experiential description and theological interpretation. We are left with what we find, a complex record of human experience not easily reduced to a specific model of consciousness.

The phenomenological character of mystical experience

According to James, a mystical experience is a phenomenon that an individual undergoes, one which includes a set of sensations or feelings (James 1985: 302–303). The self experiences a consciousness that is ineffable, that defies characterization in words. It cannot be imparted to anyone else, but must be directly experienced by the individual. In this respect, James maintains that mystical states resemble states of feeling more than states of intellect. They are also radically personal. Yet he holds as well that the subject feels as if truth has been encountered: "Although so similar to states of feeling, mystical states seem to those who experience them to be also states of knowledge." They seem to the subject to be revelations or illuminations. Moreover mystical states are transient, lasting at most an hour or two, and the quality of the experience can only be inadequately reproduced in memory. Finally, mystical states produce a strong sense that the mystic has been grasped by a higher power. All of these features may be taken to be the necessary conditions of mystical experience, defining its recurrence across the religions of the world.

The problem for the Jamesian reader of Augustine is the persuasiveness of this phenomenological category. Since there are competing sets of proposed common core features for the phenomenon of mysticism, it is difficult to have much confidence in any particular model. Yet to assert – for example – that the vision at Ostia is an instance of mysticism requires certainty regarding the interpretive model employed, and thus the conviction that the phenomenon in question really is a recognized feature of human experience. But with so many models to choose from, there is ample reason for doubt. And beyond this concern there is the deeper worry. The description presented by James brings out quite clearly that identifying a mystical experience is, in the end, identifying a psychological state. It is, in Jamesian terms, to uncover the subjective features of the mystic's consciousness. So, if one were to assert that the vision at Ostia is

140

SNATCHED UP TO PARADISE

a mystical experience, one would be making a claim about the psychological condition of Augustine or Monica based on the textual record. It is their feelings that we have discovered, their sense that the experience was cognitive, their consciousness of its brevity, their sensation of powerlessness, their awareness of its indescribability. But nothing more is involved, only feelings. It is a taxonomical assertion about a form of human experience. And that is exactly the point of misease. For the visionary texts of the *Confessions* are far deeper observations than the surface psychology of this type of analysis. The noetic features in the texts are claims about the nature of the soul and the reality of God. They are not just feelings of cognition, they are assertions of truth. Ineffability is attached to the experience as such, but it is understood against the deeper logic of the infinite nature of what is experienced. This depth factor is particularly evident, as we have seen, in Augustine's assertions of brevity and passivity. These claims are not just phenomenological descriptors; they are parts of an immediate recognition of the nature of the soul. That recognition should not be seen as a retrospective inference from the brevity or passivity of the experience but part of its actual content. The Jamesian phenomenological analysis misses that point, committed as it is to the recovery of feelings and sensations alone.

The individualistic basis of mystical experience

The phenomenological model denominates mystical experience in terms of individuals. It proceeds on the assumption that there are a set of feelings or states of consciousness which occur to an individual and which can be described by the individual alone through the use of observation language. The problem with this approach is that it cuts the mystic off from the surrounding religious culture, offering an atomistic view of human experience. It also ignores the social and cultural components of any conceptualization employed to describe the experience. In the case of Augustine, of course, the vision at Ostia is represented as being endemically social, involving two people as its subjects. It begins and ends in conversation. Both Monica and her son participate in the ascension and both are equal in visionary awareness. It would be a stretch to describe the vision at Ostia as two parallel mystical experiences, given the level of mutuality articulated in the passage. So the atomism of the psychological model is another point of friction with the Augustinian text.

The epistemic foundations of mystical experience

No element in the phenomenological notion of mystical experience is more vexing for reading the *Confessions* than the representation of its truth claims. Mystical experience is usually understood by phenomenologists as an attenuated form of ordinary sense experience. It thus makes a posteriori claims that need to be adjudicated empirically. That is then the burden of those who hope to support the veridical nature of such experiences. A particularly good example is the case William Alston has made arguing "that mystical experience can be construed as perception in the same generic sense of the term as sense perception" (Alston 1991: 66). An exception to this empiricist approach to the truth of mystical experience is James, who preferred to support the truth of mysticism in terms of its behavioral "fruits," in keeping with his pragmatist epistemology.

As we have seen, Augustine's accounts of contemplation are completely removed from this epistemic context. The ascension narratives in the *Confessions* and the account of intellectual vision in *De Genesi ad litteram* are especially clear in presenting contemplation as an a priori mode of knowing. It is distinct from the context of sense perception and rests on interior reflection alone. In his study of mystical experience, Nelson Pike recognizes this critical fact and dissociates Augustine from the perceptual and empirical model that he himself develops. As he notes:

> In chaps. VII–XI of *A Literal Commentary on Genesis*, Augustine used the phrase "intellectual vision" to refer to a kind of mental state in which the mystic (visionary) *sees* in the sense of "understands." On Augustine's account, intellectual visions were cognitive events, instances of grasping *truths*.
>
> (Pike 1992: 63, fn 21)

Pike goes on to distinguish between mystical experiences, like those of St Teresa of Avila, in which the notion of "seeing" is a perception verb, from that of Augustine, where the "seeing" involved is a cognition verb. Again, the modern notion of mystical experience fails to fit what Augustine is discussing in the texts.

If we return to the list of characteristics ascribed above to contemplation in Augustine, we can see why the notion of mystical experience does Augustine's conception so little justice. For Augustine only begins in his ascension texts, as it were, with a small experiential footprint, but then moves off to an extended meditation that expands the conceptual field of the initial episode. And that too seems part of the larger experience, part of its continuing and evolving meaning in the life of the contemplative soul. The modern concept of mystical experience foreshortens this process. It reduces the scope to a single episode, and it emphasizes the nature of the experience itself rather than its content. Moreover the truth value of mystical experience is assessed by analogy with ordinary sense experience, whether along empiricist or pragmatist lines. This is in sharp contrast to Augustine's understanding of intuitive vision as a non-empirical, interior mode of knowing whose truth is indubitable and whose epistemic status is a priori. With its tight focus on the psychological condition of the mystic, the contemporary conception of mystical experience also neglects most of the content that Augustine drew from the visionary ascensions depicted in the *Confessions*. It construes the mystical episode to be about the state of an atomistic individual only, whereas for Augustine vision led to a deepened sense of the larger community of souls into whose transcendent state the soul had been admitted and whose contemplation of Wisdom the soul had joined.

Contemplation was the experience of the recovery of a transcendent community, and was not, in the end, about the self. This too the phenomenological reading of the *Confessions* excises by its method and design. It mistakes the passivity of the contemplative soul for a psychological characteristic of the visionary, rather than treating it as a remark about the moral recognition of the soul's condition. Moreover it displaces what might be called the existential insight involved in contemplation, the experience of contingency and the human limitations for moral change. This sort of insight is not apposite to the phenomenological model of mysticism. Thus the brevity of contemplation – so rich in what it immediately discloses to the Augustinian soul about itself – becomes simply a characteristic of the visionary's state of consciousness.

This will not do as an assessment of contemplation in the *Confessions*. It is too thin, too foreshortening, too reductive. In a sense it trades the larger record of experience and self-appraisal depicted in the *Confessions* for the limited horizon of personal sense experience. And yet, despite all these caveats, this approach is not wholly misguided. Besides giving spiritual contemplation continued if diminished life in the hostile environment of the last century, it also gets at one important aspect of Augustine's texts. For Augustine did, in fact, give an autobiographical account of his experiences and that invites analysis of those episodes themselves as experiences. But any serious effort to understand these texts cannot stop there. That is because, as we have seen, Augustine's reflection on contemplation falls into two stages. The first phase is the soul's initial interior movement and its discovery of the levels of reality and knowledge that it can traverse. The knowledge that the soul achieves is not based on sense perception, although it will later give the soul the ability to perceive God in the things that are made by him. The soul's interior knowing is an intuitive grasp of the intelligibles, and then of the divine Wisdom. The soul has an indubitable knowledge of the intelligibles that it understands with the mind's capacity for abstract cognition. Yet there is a shift in Augustine's depictions at this point in the ascension narratives, as the soul comes to "touch" divine Wisdom. This is a type of closure that seems to shift the modal character of intellectual vision, from an intuition of first principles and their necessary definitions to a form of direct acquaintance. Yet it too is represented as indubitable, coming as it does at the apex of the soul's ascension into the transcendent realm. In Augustine's depiction this first ascension phase of contemplation is limited in duration, largely uninvited, and not reliably catalyzed by any specific discipline or practice. For Augustine contemplative vision is brief, veridical, and rare.

That is because its value largely depends upon the second phase of contemplation, as the soul returns to itself and reflects upon what it has discerned. Here the larger meaning of contemplation emerges. For the process of opening up the significance of ascension is, for Augustine, its real purpose. That is why the final books of the *Confessions* are so important and integral to the ascension narratives. It is when the contemplative soul searches "the stomach of its mind," its memory, that it comes to understand the larger context of what it has seen intellectually. It comes to realize why its touch of divine Wisdom could not endure. And it knows too how shallow it is, how fragile is its hold on virtue, how it does not belong in essence to the transcendent. Then it can discern the inchoate longing within itself that had driven it to this moment of vision, and what love had been calling it. Then the conditions for the accomplishment of its initial visionary ascension are fully discerned, and a new representation of reality disclosed. Perhaps most importantly, the soul then discovers that it is a creature which has become immediately aware of the author of its being and the sole source of its salvation. In this it has been brought through vision to confession. That, in the end, is the real value of contemplation. This second phase of contemplation dovetails then with the quotidian tasks of Christian life. It returns the soul to the routine religious practices of life in a transient world, chastened by its understanding of its fallen state but ennobled by the surety of its knowledge. It returns it to the path of salvation, for the limitations of contemplation have been disclosed to it, and it is without presumption. The worth of those dramatic episodes of visionary disclosure is only secured by confession of the soul's trust in God. They only matter because they can lead the fallen soul to renew its relationship of love with God. For Augustine that is the paradox of contemplation.

The mysticism of Augustine is thus two-fold, involving both episodic and reflective aspects. The contemporary model of mystical experience captures only some episodic aspects, but neglects much else and leaves the reader to surmise that most of what Augustine wrote is extraneous. It is the exile of theology that is perhaps the most misguided aspect of this approach to reading the *Confessions*. Interpretation is what the phenomenological student of mystical experience most wants to remove, in the interest of discovering what was actually experienced by the mystic. Theology is thus the enemy of accuracy, the later imposition of the dead hand of orthodoxy and tradition on the fresh experience of the visionary. It is what middle-aged bishops do to the visions of their youth. This is perhaps a popular and satisfying story, part of the on-going appeal of the idea of mysticism as the quintessence of personal spirituality. Yet whatever may be said of this trajectory in contemporary religious culture, it is not well-suited to reading the *Confessions*. Dispensing with its full account of contemplation in the interest of focusing only on its episodic aspects is an act of distortion. To understand why any of this mattered to Augustine, indeed to comprehend what meaning these visions had, one must place the theology of the accounts at the center of one's efforts. That methodological judgment has been the lodestone of our reading.

A final word on Plotinian ecstasy is in order. Just as the tendency to discover mystical experiences in the *Confessions* has had a foreshortening effect upon its understanding, so too has the effort to see the ascension narratives as attempts at Plotinian ecstasy – whether successful or abortive – has been misguided. In some measure this approach to the *Confessions* has been informed by the emphasis on mystical experience throughout the past century. The two approaches are closely conjoined. This reading is, first of all, committed to an episodic concept of mystical ecstasy. It then focuses on isolating moments of mystical ecstasy in the *Enneads* and seeks to transfer this analysis to the *Confessions*. But as we have seen, the *Enneads* are similar to the *Confessions* in embedding accounts of contemplation in a theological framework from which they cannot be extracted without losing their meaning. But if it is a mistake to press the discussions of the soul's contemplative ascension in the *Enneads* into a limited ecstatic model, one compounds it by forcing that reading on to the *Confessions*. And because this reading of both authors focuses only on selected contemplative texts, it neglects the profound differences in their theologies of contemplation, in their conceptions of the soul, and in their representations of the divine. Moreover Augustine's texts nowhere iterate an effort to achieve Plotinian ecstasy. Nor do they indicate that the achievement of ecstatic states is a goal sought by the soul. What Augustine derives from the *libri Platonicorum* is one primary insight: transcendence. The foundationalist epistemology and hierarchical metaphysics that accompany this understanding become permanent in his thinking. But not Platonic theology – that is not part of the story of the *Confessions*. In Augustine there is no solitary flight of the alone to the alone.

The mysticism of Saint Augustine should be understood, therefore, in reference to the whole of his Christian theology of contemplation. Both the threshold experiences of transcendence and the experience of their deepening into theology are desiderative for any comprehensive understanding of contemplation in the *Confessions*. To be sure, Augustine is himself responsible for initiating autobiographical theology. With it came his episodic accounts of visionary ascension, and his iteration of the limitations of contemplation. Readings over the past century have too often taken those episodes as the primary sources for understanding contemplation, whether from methodological intention or simply because they catch the reader's attention by the vividness and force of their narration.

The reading of the *Confessions* offered here is meant to avoid this delimitation of scope, and to move beyond the effort to identify mystical experiences in the interest of recovering Augustine's full account of contemplation in the *Confessions*.

CONCLUSION

On a fine day in April 1336, Petrarch, the Italian Humanist, set out to climb Mount Ventoux in Provence. Having reached its summit, he produced his *vade mecum*, a pocket copy of the *Confessions*, to help interpret this experience of natural beauty surrounding him. In imitation of Augustine in the garden at Milan, he opened the "small but charming" volume at random and read the first words that came to his eyes. As it happened, he hit upon this passage from X.viii (15):

> People are moved to wonder by mountain peaks, by vast waves of the sea, by broad waterfalls on rivers, by the all-embracing extent of the ocean, by the revolutions of the stars. But in themselves they are uninterested.

He immediately concluded that attention to the beauty of nature is misplaced and that nothing is really worthy in comparison with the soul. And so he resolved to attend to the inner self, and no longer to neglect the natural nobility of the soul.

The *Confessions* has long been a template of spiritual experience in the Latin West. Above all it has been an archetype for the inward journey of the soul to God. As the Christian tradition developed, Augustine's theology of contemplation became authoritative in the Catholic articulation of the relation between the soul and God. But by the late medieval period the *via antiqua* of Augustine, with its realist metaphysics and foundationalist epistemology, had fallen from favor, superseded by the philosophy of St Thomas and by the *via moderna* of the Nominalists. This left the notion of contemplation free standing, as it were, cut off from its earlier philosophical foundations. Yet personal visions of the transcendent became ever more important especially in early modern Catholicism, even if they no longer had the same epistemic valence. The searing vision of Blaise Pascal on the night of November 23, 1654 is a good example. He recorded a confidential testament describing an immediate encounter with the God of Abraham, Isaac, and David. There he states that his soul came into direct and indubitable contact with God. But Pascal was no realist in his metaphysics, so that his ascension narrative is not an account based on knowledge of the larger structure of transcendent reality, as in Augustine, but only a personal proof that offers warrants for his own belief in the God of scripture and tradition. We are well on the way to modern episodic notion of mystical experience. In the nineteenth and twentieth centuries, as the notion of mystical experience became part of the religious vernacular, earlier theological accounts of contemplation were secularized in ways that are well-exhibited in the theory of William James. Mystical experience became an unusual but nonetheless highly prized phenomenon, conferring upon its subject the sensation of transcendence and the feeling of certainty. While superficially this conception seems close to the ascension narratives of the *Confessions*, it had – as we have seen – drifted far from their theological significance and intent.

While the dramatic ascension narratives of the *Confessions* subsequently captured the religious imagination of the West, they were by no means the most significant aspects of contemplation to Augustine. The paradox of contemplation to Augustine was that such dramatic episodes occurred only for some people and only as an initiation to the transcendent realm and to God's presence. But they were not a necessary prerequisite for what really mattered, which was bringing the soul into a permanent association with God. That is something these ascensions could not promise. Nor were they sufficient to ensure salvation, since the contemplative soul remained embodied and thus still liable to lose its spiritual way again. These grand spiritual moments were thus fraught with ambiguity, even if they were welcome in demonstrating with personal certainty the existence of a higher realm. What really mattered to the Augustinian soul was the larger vista of meaning that these episodes disclosed: the nature of God, the importance of grace, the reality of a mediator, the hope of resurrection. These define the true meaning of those moments of understanding which the soul would later unpack in its interior meditations. And it is here that the soul would uncover the true source and means of its salvation, and find the strength to pursue it. Contemplation catalyzed Christian confession; that was its ultimate significance. But it is just this that exclusive attention to the ascension episodes neglects.

Yet the episodic conception of mysticism is in part Augustine's invention. He did, after all, write a spiritual autobiography that emphasized, for reasons that we have explored, the momentary nature of human transcendence. Moreover he is responsible for separating the knowledge secured in contemplation from salvation, thus helping to articulate the exact boundaries of the soul in orthodox Christianity. Salvific enlightenment would never thereafter be the goal for the Catholic contemplative, whose hope would rest instead on Christ as mediator and savior. In describing mysticism as only an episode of transcendence Augustine also advanced the self-articulation of the Catholic cause to which he had so importunately converted in that garden in Milan. He helped it find a voice in the late antique debate about the efficacy of contemplation and to proscribe alternative estimations of the depth and power of the human soul. He might in that sense be said to have invented mysticism by his autobiographical descriptions of episodes of transcendence.

In doing so Augustine also contributed to a great peripety in Western culture, its apparently sudden shift in late antiquity to monotheism. What Augustine and the Platonists had in common was a commitment to a unique first principle at the root of all existence. What they differed on was the interpretation of that central credendum. They shared in the belief that an ultimate foundation of reality exists separate from the physical and temporal cosmos. But they gave rival reports on the meaning of the soul's ascension to the transcendent. Contemplation was at the center of this shift to monotheism, promising to reveal the final source of reality and to restore the soul's association with it.

Thus was that "vast musical brocade" woven by those convinced by the practice of contemplation that we never die, but have a transcendent destiny. In this book we have observed the weavers at their ancient task, and have perhaps too discerned the sources of their certainty. To paraphrase Augustine's final line in the *Confessions*: that is how the ancient tradition of contemplation should be received, how it is to be found, and how the door might be opened.

BIBLIOGRAPHY

Editions

Saint Augustine

(1894) *De Genesi ad litteram libri duodecim*, J. Zycha (ed.), Corpus scriptorum ecclesiaticorum latinorum, vol. 28, Vienna: F. Tempsky.

(1895-1923) *Epistulae*, A. Goldbacher (ed.), Corpus scriptorum ecclesiaticorum latinorum, vols 34, 44, 57-8. Vienna: F. Tempsky.

(1968) *De Trinitate*, W. J. Mountain (ed.), Corpus Christianorum Series Latina, vols 50 and 50A, Turnholt: Brepols.

(1970) *Contra academicos*, W. M. Green (ed.), Corpus Christianorum Series Latina, vol. 29, Turnholt: Brepols.

(1970) *De beata vita*, W. M. Green (ed.), Corpus Christianorum Series Latina, vol. 29, Turnholt: Brepols.

(1970) *De magister*, K. D. Daur (ed.), Corpus Christianorum Series Latina, vol. 29, Turnholt: Brepols.

(1970) *De ordine*, W. M. Green (ed.), Corpus Christianorum Series Latina, vol. 29, Turnholt: Brepols.

(1971) *Retractionum libri II*, Almut Mutzenbecher (ed.), Corpus Christianorum Series Latina, vol. 57, Turnholt: Brepols.

(1986) *Soliloquia*, Wolfgang Hörmann (ed.), Corpus Scriptorum Ecclesiaticorum Latinorum, vol 89, Vienna: Hoelder-Pichler-Tempsky.

(1990) *Enarrationes in Psalmos*, D. E. Dekkers O. S. B. and J. Fraipont (eds), Corpus Christianorum Series Latina, vols 38 and 39, Turnholt: Brepols.

(1992) *Confessionum libri tredecim*, J. J. O'Donnell (ed.), vol.1, Oxford; New York: Clarendon Press.

Plotinus

(1964–82) *Plotini Opera*, P. Henry and H. R. Schwyzer (eds), vols 1–3. Oxford: Clarendon Press.

Porphyry

(1964) *Vita Plotini*, P. Henry and H. R. Schwyzer (eds), vol. 1, Oxford: Clarendon Press.
(1975) *Porphyrii Sententiae ad intelligibilia ducentes*, E. Lamberz (ed.), Leipzig: Teubner.
(1982) *Porphyre: Vie de Pythagore, Lettre à Marcella*. E. des Places (ed.), Paris: Les Belles Lettres.

Modern scholarship

(1954) *Augustinus Magister*, Paris: Études Augustiniennes.
Alfaric, P. (1918) *L'évolution intellectuelle de saint Augustin*, Paris: E. Nourry.
Alston, W. P. (1991) *Perceiving God: The Epistemology of Religious Experience*, Ithaca, NY: Cornell University Press.
Armstrong, A. H. (tr.) (1966–1988) *Plotinus I–VII*, Cambridge, MA: Harvard University Press.
Armstrong, A. H. (ed.) (1967) *The Cambridge History of Later Greek and Early Medieval Philosophy*, Cambridge, England: Cambridge University Press.
Armstrong, A. H. (1967) *The Architecture of the Intelligible Universe in the Philosophy of Plotinus: An Analytical and Historical Study*, Amsterdam: A. M. Hakkert.
Armstrong, A. H. (1979) *Plotinian and Christian Studies*, London: Variorum Reprints.
Armstrong, A. H. (ed.) (1986) *Classical Mediterranean Spirituality: Egyptian, Greek, Roman*, New York: Crossroads Press.
Armstrong, A. H. (1990) *Hellenic and Christian Studies*, London: Variorum Reprints.
Athanassiadi, P. and Frede, M. (1999) *Pagan Monotheism in Late Antiquity*, Oxford and New York: Clarendon Press.
Atkinson, M. and Plotinus (1983) *Plotinus, Ennead* vol. 1: *On the Three Principal Hypostases: a Commentary with Translation*, Oxford and New York: Oxford University Press.
Bloom, H. (2002) *Genius: A Mosaic of One Hundred Exemplary Creative Minds*, New York: Warner Books.
Blumenthal, H. J. (1971) *Plotinus's Psychology: His Doctrines of the Embodied Soul*, The Hague: Martinus Nijhoff.
Blumenthal, H. J. and Lloyd, A. C. (eds) (1982) *Soul and the Structure of Being in Late Neoplatonism*, Liverpool, England: Liverpool University Press.
Bochet, I. (1982) *Saint Augustin et le désir de Dieu*, Paris: Etudes augustiniennes.
Bonner, G. (1986 [1963]) *St Augustine of Hippo: Life and Controversies*, Norwich: Canterbury Press.
Bonner, G., Dodaro, R. and Lawless, G. (2000) *Augustine and his Critics: Essays in Honour of Gerald Bonner*, London; New York: Routledge.
Bourke, V. J. (1945) *Augustine's Quest of Wisdom*, Milwaukee, WI: The Bruce Publishing Co.
Bourke, V. J. (1953) *The Confessions of St. Augustine*, New York: Fathers of the Church.
Bourke, V. J. (1964) *Augustine's View of Reality*, Villanova, PA: Villanova University Press.
Boyer, C. (1920) *Christianisme et néoplatinisme dans la formation de saint Augustine*, Paris: G. Beauchesne.
Bréhier, É (1928) *La philosophie de Plotin*, Paris: Boivin & Cie.

Bréhier, É (1958) *The philosophy of Plotinus*, trans. by J. Thomas, Chicago, IL: University of Chicago Press.

Brisson, L., Goulet-Cazé, M. O., Goulet, R. and O'Brien, D (1982) *Porphyre: La vie de Plotin*, Paris: J. Vrin.

Brown, P. (2000 [1967]) *Augustine of Hippo: A Biography*, Berkeley, CA: University of California Press.

Burkert, W. (1985) *Greek Religion*, Cambridge, MA: Harvard University Press.

Burkert, W. (1987) *Ancient Mystery Cults*, Cambridge, MA: Harvard University Press.

Burnaby, J. (1960) *Amor dei; a study of the religion of St. Augustine*, London: Hodder & Stoughton.

Burt, D. X. (1996) *Augustine's World: An Introduction to his Speculative Philosophy*, Lanham, MD: University Press of America.

Bussanich, J. (1988) *The One and its Relation to Intellect in Plotinus*, Leiden; New York: E.J. Brill.

Butler, E. C. (1922) *Western Mysticism*, London: Constable & Co.

Cantor, N. F. (1991) *Inventing the Middle Ages: The Lives, Works, and Ideas of the Great Medievalists of the 20th Century*, New York: William Morrow.

Cary, P. (2000) *Augustine's Invention of the Inner Self: The Legacy of a Christian Platonist*, Oxford; New York: Oxford University Press.

Chadwick, H. (1986) *Augustine*, Oxford; New York: Oxford University Press.

Chadwick, H. (tr.) (1991) *Saint Augustine: Confessions*, Oxford; New York: Oxford University Press.

Clark, G. (1993) *Augustine, the Confessions*, Cambridge; New York: Cambridge University Press.

Clark, M (1959) *Augustine Philosopher of Freedom*, New York: Desclee.

Clark, M (1994) *Augustine*, London: Geoffrey Chapman.

Courcelle, P. (1950) *Recherches sur les Confessions de Saint Augustin*, Paris: E de Boccard.

Courcelle, P. (1963) *Les Confessions de Saint Augustin dans la tradition littéraire: Antécédents et posterité*, Paris: Augustiniennes.

Courcelle, P. (1968) *Recherches sur les Confessions de Saint Augustin*, Paris: E. de Boccard.

Courcelle, P. (1969) *Late Latin Writers and their Greek Sources*, Cambridge, MA: Harvard University Press.

Deck, J. N. (1967) *Nature, Contemplation and the One*, Toronto, IL: University of Toronto Press.

De Gandillac, M. (1966) *La sagesse de Plotin*, Paris, Vrin.

Des Places, É (1981) *Études Platoniciennes*, Leiden: Brill.

Dihle, A. (1982) *The Theory of Will in Classical Antiquity*, Berkeley, CA: University of California Press.

Dillon, J. M. (1977) *The Middle Platonists: 80 B.C. to A.D. 220*, Ithaca, NY: Cornell University Press.

Dillon, J. M. and Morrow, G. (eds) (1987) *Proclus' Commentary on Plato's Parmenides*, Princeton, NJ: Princeton University Press.

Dillon, J. M. (1993) *The Handbook of Platonism*, Oxford; New York: Clarendon Press.

Dodds, E. R. (ed.) (1963) *Proclus: The Elements of Theology*, Oxford: Clarendon Press.

Dodds, E. R. (1965) *Pagan and Christian in an Age of Anxiety: Some Aspects of Religious Experience from Marcus Aurelius to Constantine*, Cambridge, England: Cambridge University Press.

Du Roy, O. (1966) *L'Intelligence de la foi en la Trinité selon saint Augustin, genèse de sa théologie trinitaire jusqu'en 391*, Paris: Études augustiniennes.

Dubal, Y. M. (ed.) (1974) *Ambroise de Milan*, Paris: Études augustiniennes.

Evans, G. R. (1982) *Augustine on Evil*, Cambridge; New York: Cambridge University Press.

Ferrari, L. (1984) *The Conversions of St. Augustine*, Villanova, PA: Villanova University Press.

Festugière, A. J. (1967) *Contemplation et vie contemplative selon Platon*, Paris: J. Vrin.

Gersh, S. (1973) *Kinesis Akinetos: A Study of Spiritual Motion in the Philosophy of Proclus*, Leiden: Brill.

Gersh, S. (1978) *From Iamblichus to Eriugena: An Investigation of the Prehistory and Evolution of the Pseudo-Dionysian Tradition*, Leiden: Brill.

Gersh, S. (1986) *Middle Platonism and Neoplatonism: The Latin Tradition*, Notre Dame, IN: University of Notre Dame Press.

Grant, R. M. (1986) *Gods and the One God*, Philadelphia, PA: Westminster Press.

Hadot, P. (1963) *Plotin ou la simplicité du regard*, Paris: Plon.

Hadot, P. (1968) *Porphyre et Victorinus*, Paris, Études augustiniennes.

Hadot, P. (1981) *Exercices spirituals et philosophie antique*, Paris: Études augustiniennes.

Hadot, P. (1995) *Philosophy as a Way of Life: Spiritual Exercises from Socrates to Foucault*, Malden, MA: Blackwell.

Hadot, P. (2002) *What is Ancient Philosophy?*, Cambridge, MA: Belknap Press, Harvard University Press.

Harris, R. B. (ed.) (1976) *The Significance of Neoplatonism*, Albany, NY: State University of New York Press.

Harris, R. B. (ed.) (1982) *The Structure of Being: A Neoplatonic Approach*, Norfolk, VA: International Society for Neoplatonic Studies.

Harrison, C. (1992) *Beauty and Revelation in the Thought of Saint Augustine*, Oxford; New York: Clarendon Press; Oxford University Press.

Henry, P. (1934) *Plotin et l'Occident. Firmicus Maternus, Marius Victorinus, Saint Augustin et Macrobe*, Louvain: "Spicilegium Sacrum Lovaniense" Bureaux.

Henry, P. (1938) *La vision d'Ostie*, Paris, J. Vrin.

Henry, P. (1948–1961) *Études plotiniennes*, Paris: Desclée de Brouwer.

Henry, P. (1981) *The Path to Transcendence: From Philosophy to Mysticism in Saint Augustine*, Pittsburgh, PA: Pickwick Press.

Inge, W. R. (1899) *Christian Mysticism*, New York: C. Scribner's Sons.

James, W. (1985) *The Varieties of Religious Experience*, Cambridge, MA: Harvard University Press.

Jantzen, G. (1995) *Power, Gender, and Christian Mysticism*, Cambridge; New York: Cambridge University Press.

Katz, S. T. (1978) *Mysticism and Philosophical Analysis*, New York: Oxford University Press.

Katz, S. T. (1983) *Mysticism and Religious Traditions*, Oxford; New York: Oxford University Press.

Katz, S. T. (1992) *Mysticism and Language*, New York: Oxford University Press.

Kenney, J. P. (1986) "Monotheistic and polytheistic elements in classical Mediterranean spirituality," in *Classical Mediterranean Spirituality*, (ed.) A. H. Armstrong, pp. 269–292, New York: Crossroads Press.

Kenney, J. P. (1990) "Theism and divine production in ancient realist theology," in

God and Creation, (ed.) David Burrell and Bernard McGinn, pp. 57–80, Notre Dame, IN: University of Notre Dame Press.

Kenney, J. P. (1991) *Mystical Monotheism: A Study in Ancient Platonic Theology*, Hanover, NH and London: Brown University Press; University Press of New England.

Kenney, J. P. (1992a) "The Platonism of the Tripartite Tractate," in *Neoplatonism and Gnosticism*, (ed.) R. T. Wallis and Jay Bregman, pp. 187–206, Albany, NY: State University of New York Press.

Kenney, J. P. (1992b) "Proschresis revisited: an essay in Numenian theology," in *Origeniana quinta*, (ed.) R. J. Daly, pp. 217–230, Leuven: Peeters Press.

Kenney, J. P. (1993a) "The critical value of negative theology," *Harvard Theological Review*, 86, pp. 439–453.

Kenney, J. P. (1993b) "The presence of truth in the confessions," *Studia Patristica*, 27, pp. 329–336, Leuven: Peeters Press.

Kenney, J. P. (1997) "Mysticism and contemplation in the *Enneads*," *American Catholic Philosophical Quarterly*, 71(3), pp. 315–337.

Kenney, J. P. (1997) "St. Augustine and the invention of mysticism," *Studia Patristica*, 33, pp. 125–130, Leuven: Peeters Press.

Kenney, J. P. (1999) "The Greek tradition in early Christian philosophy," in *The Columbia History of Western Philosophy*, (ed.) Richard Popkin, New York: Columbia University Press.

Kenney, J. P. (2000) "Ancient apophatic theology," in *Gnosticism and Later Platonism: Themes, Figures, Texts*, (ed.) R. Majercik and J. D. Turner, pp. 259–275, Atlanta, GA: Society of Biblical Literature.

Kenney, J. P. (2001) "St. Augustine and the limits of contemplation," *Studia Patristica*, 38, pp. 199–218, Leuven: Peeters Press.

Kirk, G. S. and Raven, J. E. (1957) *The Presocratic Philosophers: A Critical History with a Selection of Texts*, London: Cambridge University Press.

Kirwan, C. (1991) *Augustine*, London; New York: Routledge.

Larkin, P. (2003) *Collected Poems*, New York: Farrar, Straus, Giroux.

Lloyd, A. C. (1990) *The Anatomy of Neoplatonism*, Oxford and New York: Clarendon Press; Oxford University Press.

Louth, A. (1981) *The Origins of the Christian Mystical Tradition from Plato to Denys*, Oxford and New York: Clarendon Press; Oxford University Press.

MacMullen, R. (1981) *Paganism in the Roman Empire*, New Haven, CT: Yale University Press.

Madec, G. (1974) *Saint Ambroise et la philosophie*, Paris: Études augustiniennes.

Mandouze, A. (1968) *Saint Augustin: L'aventure de la raison et la grâce*, Paris, Études augustiniennes.

Marrou, H. I. (1938–1949) *Saint Augustin et la fin de la culture antique*, Paris: E. de Boccard.

Marrou, H. I. (1956) *A History of Education in Antiquity*, New York: Sheed and Ward.

Matthews, G. B. (1999) *The Augustinian Tradition*, Berkeley, CA: University of California Press.

McGinn, B. (1991) *The Presence of God: A History of Western Christian Mysticism*, New York: Crossroads Press.

Merlan, P. (1960) *From Platonism to Neoplatonism*, The Hague: Martinus Nijhoff.

Merlan, P. (1963) *Monopsychism, Mysticism, Metaconsciousness*, The Hague: Martinus Nijhoff.

Miles, M. R. (1992) *Desire and Delight: A New Reading of Augustine's Confessions*, New York: Crossroads Press.

Moreau, J. (1970) *Plotin ou la gloire de la philosophie antique*, Paris, J. Vrin.

Mourant, J. (1969) *Augustine on Immortality*, Villanova, PA: Augustinian Institute, Villanova University.

Mortley, R. (1986) *From Word to Silence*, vols 1 and 2, Bonn: Hanstein.

Nash, R. H. (1969) *The Light of the Mind; St. Augustine's Theory of Knowledge*, Lexington, KY: University Press of Kentucky.

O'Connell, R. J. (1968) *St. Augustine's Early Theory of Man, A.D. 386–391*, Cambridge, MA: Belknap Press of Harvard University Press.

O'Connell, R. J. (1969) *St. Augustine's Confessions; The Odyssey of Soul*, Cambridge, MA: Belknap Press of Harvard University Press.

O'Connell, R. J. (1978) *Art and the Christian Intelligence in St. Augustine*, Cambridge, MA: Harvard University Press.

O'Connell, R. J. (1987) *The Origin of the Soul in St. Augustine's later works*, New York: Fordham University Press.

O'Connell, R. J. (1996) *Images of Conversion in St. Augustine's Confessions*, New York: Fordham University Press.

O'Daly, G. J. P. (1973) *Plotinus' Philosophy of the Self*, New York: Barnes & Noble Books.

O'Daly, G. J. P. (1987) *Augustine's Philosophy of Mind*, London: Duckworth.

O'Daly, G. J. P. (2001) *Platonism Pagan and Christian: Studies in Plotinus and Augustine*, Aldershot; Burlington, VT: Ashgate.

O'Donnell, J. J. (1985) *Augustine*, Boston, MA: Twayne Publishers.

O'Donnell, J. J. (1992) *The Confessions of Augustine*, Oxford: Clarendon Press; Oxford and New York: Oxford University Press.

O'Donovan, O. (1980) *The Problem of Self-love in St. Augustine*, New Haven, CT: Yale University Press.

O'Meara, J. J. (1951) *Against the Academics*, Westminster, MD: Newman Press.

O'Meara, J. J. (1954) *The Young Augustine: The Growth of St. Augustine's Mind up to his Conversion*, London, New York: Longmans Green.

O'Meara, J. J. (1980) *The Young Augustine: An Introduction to the Confessions of St. Augustine*, London; New York: Longman.

O'Meara, D. J. (1982) *Neoplatonism and Christian Thought*, Albany, NY: State University of New York Press.

O'Meara, D. J. (1993) *Plotinus: An Introduction to the Enneads*, Oxford; New York: Clarendon Press; Oxford University Press.

Osborn, E. F. (1993) *The Emergence of Christian Theology*, Cambridge, England; New York: Cambridge University Press.

Pater, W. (1980) *The Renaissance*, Berkeley, CA: University of California Press.

Pike, N. (1992) *Mystic Union: An Essay in the Phenomenology of Mysticism*, Ithaca, NY: Cornell University Press.

Portalié, E. (1975) *A Guide to the Thought of Saint Augustine*, Westport, CT: Greenwood Press.

Proclus, Morrow, G. R. and Dillon, J. M. (1987) *Proclus' Commentary on Plato's Parmenides*, Princeton, NJ: Princeton University Press.

Rappe, S. (2000) *Reading Neoplatonism: Non-discursive Thinking in the Texts of Plotinus, Proclus, and Damascius*, Cambridge; New York: Cambridge University Press.

Rist, J. M. (1967) *Plotinus: The Road to Reality*, Cambridge; New York: Cambridge University Press.

Rist, J. M. (1994) *Augustine: Ancient Thought Baptized*, Cambridge; New York: Cambridge University Press.

Sells, M. A. (1994) *Mystical Languages of Unsaying*, Chicago, IL: University of Chicago Press.

Shaw, G. (1995) *Theurgy and the Soul: The Neoplatonism of Iamblichus*, University Park, PA: Pennsylvania State University Press.

Smith, A. (1974) *Porphyry's Place in the Neoplatonic Tradition: A Study in Post-Plotinian Neoplatonism*, The Hague: Martinus Nijhoff.

Sorabji, R. (1983) *Time, Creation, and the Continuum: Theories in Antiquity and the Early Middle Ages*, Ithaca, NY: Cornell University Press.

Stace, W. T. (1960) *Mysticism and Philosophy*, Philadelphia, PA: Lippincott.

Stead, C. (1994) *Philosophy in Christian Antiquity*, Cambridge; New York: Cambridge University Press.

Stump, E. and Kretzmann, N. (2001) *The Cambridge Companion to Augustine*, Cambridge; New York: Cambridge University Press.

Taylor, C. (1989) *Sources of the Self: The Making of the Modern Identity*, Cambridge, MA: Harvard University Press.

Taylor, C. (2002) *Varieties of Religion Today: William James Revisited*, Cambridge, MA: Harvard University Press.

Taylor, J. (1982) *The Literal Meaning of Genesis*, 2 vols. New York: Newman Press.

TeSelle, E. (1970) *Augustine, the Theologian*, New York: Herder and Herder.

Teske, R. J. (1996) *Paradoxes of Time in Saint Augustine*, Milwaukee, WI: Marquette University Press.

Trouillard, J. (1955) *La procession Plotinienne*, Paris: Presses Universitaires de France.

Trouillard, J. (1955) *La purification Plotinienne*, Paris: Presses Universitaires de France.

Turner, D. (1995) *The Darkness of God: Negativity in Christian Mysticism*, Cambridge; New York: Cambridge University Press.

Underhill, E. (1930) *Mysticism: A Study in the Nature and Development of Man's Spiritual Consciousness*, New York: E. P. Dutton.

Van Fleteren, F. (ed.) (1994) *Augustine: Mystic and Mystagogue*, New York: Peter Lang.

Wainwright, W. J. (1981) *Mysticism: A Study of its Nature, Cognitive Value, and Moral Implications*, Madison, WI: University of Wisconsin Press.

Wallis, R. T. (1972) *Neo-Platonism*, New York: Scribner's.

Wetzel, J. (1992) *Augustine and the Limits of Virtue*, Cambridge; New York: Cambridge University Press.

Whittaker, J. (1984) *Studies in Platonism and Patristic Thought*, London: Variorum Reprints.

Wolfson, H. A. (1956) *Philosophy of the Church Fathers*, vol. 1: *Faith, Trinity, Incarnation*, Cambridge, MA: Harvard University Press.

Wolfson, H. A. (1965) *Religious Philosophy: A Group of Essays*, New York: Atheneum.

Zaehner, R. C. (1961 [1957]) *Mysticism, Sacred and Profane*, Oxford: Oxford University Press.

INDEX